Malcolm Mann
Steve Taylore-Knowles

Laser B1

Student's Book

MACMILLAN

Contents

Contents

Contents

Do the Laser Quiz

Try to do this quiz as quickly as you can. Follow the instructions for each question.

1 **What's the name of Lisa's brother in the story on page 23?**

____

Now take the 2nd letter of your answer and write it in the 5th box at the bottom of page 7.

2 **What is there a list of on page 172?**

____

Now take the 4th letter of the word beginning with 'p' and write it in the 11th box at the bottom of page 7.

3 **What's the last word of the article on page 45?**

____

Now take the final letter of this word and write it in the 8th box at the bottom of page 7.

4 **What's the title of the leaflet on page 98?**

____

Now write the 1st letter of the 3rd word in the 14th box at the bottom of page 7.

5 **Who wrote the report on page 149?**

____

Now take the 5th letter of the surname and write it in the 13th box at the bottom of page 7.

6 **These start on page 152. What are they?**

____

Now take the 6th letter of the 3rd word and write it in the 2nd box at the bottom of page 7.

7 **What's the title of Unit 14?**

____

Now take the 2nd letter of the first word and write it in CAPITALS in the 1st box at the bottom of page 7.

8 **What are the people called in picture e on page 91?**

____

Now take the 1st letter of your answer and write it in the 12th box at the bottom of page 7.

9 **Which author of this book has a surname with four letters?**

____

Now take the last letter of his 1st name and write it in the 6th box at the bottom of the page.

13 **Now take the 12th letter of the English alphabet and write it in the 3rd box at the bottom of the page.**

10 **Now look at the letter you wrote in the 2nd box at the bottom of the page and write the same letter in the 7th box.**

14 **Which author of this book has three names?**

____

Now take the 4th letter of his 2nd name and write it in CAPITALS in the 10th box at the bottom of the page.

11 **What's the name of the girl the email on page 64 was sent to?**

____

Now take the 5th letter of her name and write it in the 4th box at the bottom of the page.

15 **What starts on page 175?**

____

Now take the 5th letter of the 2nd word and write it in CAPITALS in the 15th box at the bottom of the page.

12 **Look at pages 134 and 135. What's the name of the inventor in the article?**

____

Now take the 4th letter of his second name and write it in the 9th box at the bottom of the page.

16 **Which unit of the book is called *Welcome Back!*? Write the number of the unit in the 16th box at the bottom of the page.**

Laser Quiz

1	2	3	4	5	6	7		8	9		10	11	12	13	14	15	16

1

Welcome Back!

Get warmed up!

Discuss the following. Work in pairs or in groups.

- What are your three most favourite subjects at school? Why?
- Are there any subjects you don't enjoy? What don't you like about them?

Reading 1.01

1 Look at the blog and choose the correct answers.

1 Where can you read a blog like this?
 A in a newspaper
 B on the internet

2 Whose blog is it?
 A Nicole's
 B Adem's

3 Who wrote the comments on the blog?
 A people who have read the blog
 B the writer's English teachers

2 Read the blog and decide if the statements are true (T) or false (F).

1 Nicole wants to blog about her summer holiday. T/F
2 Nicole's first language is Spanish. T/F
3 Adem doesn't think he is good at learning grammar. T/F
4 Alessandra watches films while she does her homework. T/F
5 Lupita has friends in another country. T/F

3 Match the ideas with the people who mention them. Some ideas match with more than one person.

1 use an English dictionary __
2 listen to music in English __
3 go to another country __ , __
4 watch films in English __ , __
5 write a blog in English __ , __
6 read a lot in English __ , __
7 use new vocabulary __
8 read things on the internet __ , __
9 work in a quiet place __

a Nicole
b Adem
c Alessandra
d Lupita

HOMEWORK!

Do the Reading exercise on page 4 of your Workbook.

www.kidblog.co.uk/nicole-blog

Hi, everyone! I'm Nicole, and I live in Paris, France. Next week is the start of the new year, and here's my new blog! I'm looking forward to telling you all about my life at school, at home and with my friends! I had a fantastic summer, but now it's time to get back to work. This is a big year for me, and I want to do very well.

I'm very fond of learning languages, and I speak French (of course!), German, a little Spanish and English. I need to practise my English, and that's why I'm writing this blog. My teacher says that reading and writing as much as you can in English is a great way to learn more. I try to read a book in English every week, and I use a dictionary to help me with any words I don't know. And I read articles on the internet in English about my favourite bands and film stars!

What about you? I love reading your comments, so tell us about learning English and share your tips for learning!

It's My Life!

About me | Photos | Other blogs I like

Hi, Nicole! Great blog! I'm Adem from Ankara, the capital of Turkey! Like you, I'm studying English and I read as much as I can, especially blogs like yours! I'm good at learning vocabulary, but I need to work on my grammar – sorry if I make any mistakes! My tip for learning new words is to use them soon after learning them. When you use them yourself, they stick in your mind!

Welcome to my blog, Adem, and thanks for the tip. Don't worry about mistakes – we all make them and learn from them!

Hello from Rome! I'm Alessandra. Here in Italy, we work very hard at school and have to do a lot of homework. Personally, I think the secret to learning a language is hard work! When you do your homework, make sure you're in a quiet room and you can concentrate. Don't try to listen to music or watch TV at the same time! In your free time, why not watch films in English? Turn the subtitles on or off – both can help you learn!

Hi, Alessandra, and welcome to my blog! Great ideas! I agree that watching films is a good idea. I turn the subtitles off, then turn them on when I'm not able to understand a scene. And don't forget that songs in English also help!

Lupita from Mexico City here! I love your blog! I'm beginning to think that I should do the same thing. I learn English in a private language school, and our teachers organise a trip to an English-speaking country every year. It's a fantastic way to practise, and you make lots of new friends! After the trip, we stay in touch through email – another great chance to practise!

Thanks, Lupita! I'd love to go to an English-speaking country and I'm sure it helps a lot.

DICTIONARY CORNER

Complete each sentence using a word from the blog. Use the words in bold to help you.

1 Chris is not very **g**__________ **at** being quiet in class.
2 Can you **h**__________ **me with** this exercise, please?
3 I'm not really **a**__________ **to** write a long letter in English yet.
4 **Andrea's** not very **f**__________ **of** read**ing** books in English.
5 Are you **looking f**__________ **to** learning lots of new things this year?
6 **I'm b**__________ to think that English isn't that difficult, after all!

Have your say!

- Which ideas from the blog for learning English do you like?
- Do you have other ideas for learning and practising?

HOMEWORK!

Do exercises 1, 2 and 3 on page 5 of your Workbook.

Grammar 1

Present simple and present continuous

Look at *Grammar database 1* pages 175–176 before you do the exercises.

1 Choose the correct form of the verb.

1 Our English lessons **usually last / are usually lasting** about an hour.
2 This week, **we revise / we're revising** what we did last year.
3 **They work out / They're working out** the school timetable at the moment.
4 Good teachers **never shout / are never shouting** at their students.
5 My dad **always tells / is always telling** me to work harder at school. It's so annoying!
6 The end of term **gets / is getting** closer and closer!
7 Alison **does work / work** hard, actually.

2 Put the verbs in brackets into the correct form, present simple or present continuous. Be careful with the position of the adverbs.

1 Diana ______________________ (**sometimes forget**) to do all her homework.
2 I ______________________ (**try**) to do this exercise at the moment.
3 The students ______________________ (**just start**) to get to know each other.
4 Our teacher ______________________ (**always tell**) us a joke at the beginning of the lesson.
5 Our English tests ______________________ (**get**) harder and harder!
6 Learning new vocabulary ______________________ (**often take**) a lot of hard work.

3 Write questions using the notes. Look at the blog on pages 8–9 again and find the answers to the questions.

1 what / Nicole / read / every week
Q: ______________________
A: ______________________

2 what / Nicole / write / practise English
Q: ______________________
A: ______________________

3 where / Adem / study / English
Q: ______________________
A: ______________________

4 why / Adem / use new words
Q: ______________________
A: ______________________

HOMEWORK!
Do exercises 1, 2, 3, 4 and 5 on pages 5 and 6 of your Workbook.

Listening

1 Match the icons to the subjects.

a art ___
b history ___
c geography ___
d science ___
e computer studies ___
f PE (physical education) ___
g music ___
h maths ___

2 1.02 Listen to part of a radio show. For each speaker, write the country they are from and the school subject they enjoy the most.

1 Ganika
From: ________
Favourite subject: ________

2 Eugen
From: ________
Favourite subject: ________

3 Valeriya
From: ________
Favourite subject: ________

4 Dirk
From: ________
Favourite subject: ________

3 1.02 Listen again and complete each sentence with a word or short phrase.

1 What does Ganika say about maths?
It's ________.

2 What does Eugen say about history?
It's ________.

3 What does Valeriya say about French?
It's ________.

4 What does Dirk say about English?
It's ________.

HOMEWORK!
Do the Listening exercise on page 9 of your Workbook.

DICTIONARY CORNER

1 Match the words 1–7 with their definitions a–g.

1	subject	**a**	a series of lessons in a subject
2	lesson	**b**	a period of rest between lessons at school
3	course	**c**	the studying of something again, often before an exam, etc
4	break	**d**	something you learn at school, such as maths
5	timetable	**e**	a document written by a teacher about a student's progress
6	report	**f**	a short period of time in which you study a subject
7	revision	**g**	a schedule/programme of lessons, courses, etc

2 Complete the advertisement with the correct form of the words from exercise 1.

Study German in Germany at The Munich School of German

- one- and two-week summer ________ for all ages
- ________ classes for students about to take exams
- fun, varied ________ : ________ every morning, trips and sports every afternoon
- 10-minute ________ every hour in the morning
- ________ on student's progress given at end

The Munich School of German – bringing the ________ of German to life!

HOMEWORK!
Do exercises 1 and 2 on page 7 of your Workbook.

G Grammar 2

Stative verbs

Look at *Grammar database 2* page 176 before you do the exercises.

1 **Tick (✔) the correct sentences. Put a cross (✘) next to those that are incorrect.**

1 I'm having a headache at the moment. ______
2 Fiona is really liking her new German teacher. ______
3 I want you to do exercise 3 on page 36 now. ______
4 Nina is not being here today. ______
5 Jim, you're being silly! ______
6 What are you thinking about? ______
7 It is seeming it's the end of the lesson. ______

2 **Complete the school report. Put the verbs into the present simple or the present continuous.**

Name: Darren Williams
Year: 9
Subject: Geography

I (1)____________ (**be**) very pleased that Darren (2)____________ (**seem**) to be enjoying geography much more this term and I (3)____________ (**think**) that, on the whole, he has worked hard in class. He says that he (4)____________ (**like**) the book we (5)____________ (**do**) in class at the moment. This (6)____________ (**be**) positive. However, I (7)____________ (emphatic: **want**) him to spend a lot more time on his homework from now on. He (8)____________ (**believe**) he (9)____________ (**not need**) to spend very long working on his own at home and that is not true. Without serious study, I (10)____________ (**doubt**) he'll do very well in the exam at the end of the year. I (11)____________ (**know**) he (12)____________ (**think**) about becoming a musician when he's older, and I (13)____________ (**wish**) him every success, but he has to understand that, without any academic qualifications, he may have serious problems in later life.

Soundstation

1 🎧 **1.03 Listen. Can you hear the difference between the words in each pair?**

pill / peel
ship / sheep
grin / green
lid / lead
filling / feeling
chick / cheek

2 🎧 **1.04 Listen to these sentences and circle the words you hear.**

1 Where's the **pill** / **peel**?
2 Look at that **ship** / **sheep**!
3 That's a nice **grin** / **green**.
4 Where did you put the **lid** / **lead**?
5 What a fantastic **filling** / **feeling**!
6 Look at her **chicks** / **cheeks**!

HOMEWORK!

Do exercises 1, 2, 3, 4 and 5 on pages 7 and 8 of your Workbook.

Speaking

1 1.05 **Listen to an interview with a teenage girl and answer the questions.**

1 Does she give one-word answers? **yes / no**
2 Does she always speak in full sentences? **yes / no**
3 Does she use 'Well' and 'Oh' to start some of her answers? **yes / no**

2 **Answer the questions about yourself. Make short notes.**

1 What time do you get up on school days?
2 How do you usually get to school?
3 What's your favourite subject? Why?
4 What do you usually do at the weekends?
5 How often do you have English lessons?
6 Are you reading any books at the moment?
7 What do you want to do when you leave school?

	you	your partner
1		
2		
3		
4		
5		
6		
7		

3 **In pairs, ask and answer the questions in exercise 2 and make notes of your partner's answers. Then report back to the class.**

Phrase Bank! P

Well, I usually get up at …
My favourite subject's probably/definitely …
We have English lessons three times/twice/etc a week.
I haven't really decided yet what I want to do when I leave school, but maybe I'll …

See *Speaking database* on page 174.

Use your English!

Read the article and choose the correct answer A, B, C or D to complete it.

	A	B	C	D
1	reports	lessons	courses	breaks
2	watching	looking	seeing	viewing
3	subject	timetable	revision	course
4	with	for	to	at
5	for	of	on	with
6	on	to	at	with
7	report	timetable	revision	subject
8	hate	hating	hates	are hating
9	to do	to doing	do	doing
10	report	break	revision	lesson

How to Survive School!

You know the feeling! You've already had four (1) ___ today and now it's two o'clock on a Wednesday afternoon, and you're really not (2) ___ forward to the next one. It's the (3) ___ you hate. Perhaps it's maths, which you've never been very good (4) ___ . Or perhaps it's French, and you're really not fond (5) ___ languages. Whatever it is, here are a few simple tips that might make your life a little easier!

- Don't suffer in silence! Tell your teachers how you feel and they'll find ways to help you (6) ___ any problems.
- Look at your (7) ___ to see which days of the week might make you feel depressed. If the subject you (8) ___ is on Wednesday, plan a trip to the cinema on Wednesday evening to cheer yourself up!
- If you are beginning (9) ___ badly in a subject, think about doing some (10) ___ . It'll be hard work, but you might like the subject a little more if you can understand the lessons!

Good luck!

Writing

Paragraphing

1 **Look at the different parts of the letter. Put them in the right order.**

1 ____ 4 ____ 6 ____
2 ____ 5 ____ 7 ____
3 ____

A
Penny

B
It's strange having to wear a school uniform. It's the first time I've ever worn one. We have to wear a blue skirt and a white blouse. If it's cold we also have a blue sweater. I guess I'll get used to it. At least I don't have to decide what to wear in the morning!

C
Dear Donna,

D
Anyway, I'd better go now. Mum wants me to help with the housework before I do my homework. Take care, Donna, and stay in touch!

E
Lots of love,

F
Thanks for your letter. It was great to hear from you! I'm really glad your dog's much better now.

G
Well, today was my first day at my new school. It's called Parkingham Comprehensive School and there are over a thousand students here. It's very big! Actually, it seems a nice place. The kids in my class are very friendly. I've made one friend so far – a girl called Alison, who I sit next to in French. She's really cool and she helped me find my way around.

2 **Match each part of the letter with its purpose.**

Part	Purpose
1 ____	**a** to continue with your news
2 ____	**b** to mention their last letter and something in it
3 ____	**c** to give a reason for ending the letter
4 ____	**d** to greet the person you're writing to
5 ____	**e** to express love
6 ____	**f** to give your main news

3 **Match to make correct statements about paragraphs.**

1 Each paragraph in a letter __
2 You should never write a letter __
3 When you start a new subject, you __
4 The first sentence of a paragraph often __
5 The rest of a paragraph often __

a tells us what it's about.
b gives us more details and examples.
c as one long paragraph.
d should start a new paragraph.
e should have a clear purpose.

HOMEWORK!
Do exercises 1, 2 and 3 on page 9 of your Workbook.

Get ready to write

Informal letter

1 Read the letter and answer the questions.

1 Who wrote the letter?
2 Who is he writing to?
3 Underline all the short forms (eg *haven't*, *doesn't*) in the letter.
4 Underline one example of an incomplete sentence.
5 Circle one example of informal punctuation.
6 Find informal words and phrases in the letter that mean the same as these more formal words and phrases:
  a How are you?
  b Thank you very much
  c we have
  d a lot of
7 What two expressions did the writer use before signing his name?
8 How many main paragraphs are there?

Dear Adam,

Hi! How's it going? Thanks a lot for your postcard. Sounds like you had a great time in Switzerland. Well, we went back to school today for the first day of the winter term. Boring! I can't believe how quickly the summer holidays went. Actually, it wasn't that bad. There are a couple of new guys in my class this year and they both seem really nice. One of them is really good at football. I'm going to try to get him on the team!

Talking of football, we've got our first match next week. We're training hard at the moment, and I think we've got a good chance of winning. Wish us luck! Anyway, I'd better go now. I've got loads of homework to do tonight (unfortunately!).

Write soon!

All the best,

Gary

2 Read the writing task and make notes to answer the questions below.

> **Today was your first day back at school after the summer holidays. Write a letter to your pen friend about the day, mentioning any other news you have as well.**

1 What's the name of your pen friend?
2 What will you mention about your pen friend's letter in the first main paragraph?
3 How was your first day back at school?
4 What news do you have about your first day?
5 What other news do you have?
6 Why do you have to stop writing?
7 What expression(s) will you write above your name?
8 What name will you write at the end?

3 Make a plan in *Composition Planner 1* on page 152.

HOMEWORK!

You are now ready to write the first draft of your letter. Write between 120 and 150 words. When your teacher has commented on your letter, write the final version.

2

The Weird and the Unexplained

Get warmed up!

Discuss the following.
Work in pairs or in groups.

- Do you believe in ghosts?
- How would you feel if you saw a ghost? (eg *I'd be scared, I'd be excited*, etc)
- What would you do if you saw a ghost? (eg *I'd scream, I'd run out of the room*, etc)

Reading 1.06

1 **Read the article quickly and match each of the stories 1–4 with a picture a–d.**

2 **Read the article again and choose the best heading for each of the stories 1–4.**

1 **a** Was it the Moon?
b A visitor from another planet?
c A plane or a helicopter?

2 **a** A frightening experience
b An enjoyable experience
c An ordinary experience

3 **a** A plane full of ghosts
b Unknown ghosts
c Many witnesses

4 **a** Who decided to stay?
b When did they return?
c Where did they go?

IT'S A STRANGE WORLD!

This week in It's a strange world! our fearless reporter Fiona Tyler investigates four cases of weird and unexplained true stories from North America.

1 Did former President of the USA Jimmy Carter see a UFO (Unidentified Flying Object)? He says he did. It all happened back in 1969, when Carter was Governor of Georgia. He was waiting outside with ten other people for an evening meeting to begin when suddenly a very bright object appeared in the sky above them. Carter says it was glowing red and green and was circular in shape. As the people were standing there amazed, it moved closer to them, then moved further away, came back again, and suddenly disappeared. Carter officially reported his UFO sighting to the US government. Some disbelievers say, however, that all he actually saw was the planet Venus. What do you think?

2 Talking of seeing strange things in America, you don't get much stranger than this! In 1988, seventeen-year-old Christopher Davis was changing a tyre on his car on a road in South Carolina when he saw something very large running towards him across a field. He jumped into his car and locked the door but the creature grabbed the door and tried to open it. Christopher later described the creature as being very tall, with red eyes and green skin. He said it was like a cross between a lizard and a man. Unable to open the door, the creature jumped onto the roof of the car. Christopher started the engine and drove off as quickly as he could. Thankfully, the Lizard Man soon fell off. Christopher was shaking with fear when he got home and there were deep scratches on the roof of the car. Bizarre!

3 **Match each of the stories 1–4 with a sentence a–e. There is one extra sentence which you will not need.**

a They appeared to friends and colleagues.
b His whole community vanished.
c A famous person witnessed this incident.
d They disappeared in front of hundreds of people.
e What he saw terrified him.

HOMEWORK!
Do the Reading exercise on page 10 of your Workbook.

DICTIONARY CORNER

Complete each sentence using a word from the article.

1 That's **o**____________________. I'm sure my pen was here a minute ago.
2 It was really **w**____________________. I was just about to phone Jill when she phoned me.
3 How **b**____________________! I wonder what happened to all those people.
4 The UFO flew around for about five minutes and then suddenly **v**____________________.
5 The magician just **a**____________________ out of nowhere. I don't know where he came from.
6 I wouldn't be **s**____________________ if I saw a ghost. I'd be excited!
7 It was the most frightening **e**____________________ I've ever had.
8 The **i**____________________ occurred at half past three in the morning.

3 Pilot Bob Loft was flying Eastern Airlines Flight 401 when it crashed in Florida in 1972. Loft, Flight Engineer Don Repo and ninety-nine others died in the crash. Not long after the accident, on more than 20 occasions, crew members and passengers on other Eastern Airlines flights claimed to have seen the ghosts of Loft and Repo. On one occasion, just before take-off, the captain and two flight attendants saw and spoke to Loft. They said he suddenly vanished before their eyes. The experience left them so scared they cancelled the flight. On another occasion, Repo appeared on board a plane in front of three crew members, one of whom had been a friend of Repo's. Repo warned them to 'Watch out for fire'. He then suddenly disappeared. Later during the flight, a fire did break out but luckily the crew managed to land the plane safely.

4 And while we're on the subject of people suddenly disappearing, how about this odd incident? In November 1930, a hunter from an Inuit village in northern Canada – the Inuit are also sometimes called Eskimos – said goodbye to his friends and family and went off for two weeks' hunting in the mountains. When he returned home, he discovered that the entire population of his village, over 2,000 people, had completely disappeared. Cooking pots were simmering gently on the stoves in the small huts they lived in, but there were no people left at all. And there were no tracks or footprints in the snow leading away from the village. A massive search found no trace of the tribe and no-one knows what happened to them. Now isn't that strange?

Have your say!

Do you think President Carter saw a UFO, the Moon, the planet Venus or something else? Why?

I think President Carter (probably) saw … because …

HOMEWORK!
Do exercises 1, 2 and 3 on page 11 of your Workbook.

Grammar 1

Past simple and past continuous

Look at *Grammar database 3* pages 177–178 before you do the exercises.

1 Look at the article on pages 16 and 17 and underline all the sentences which have both a verb in the past simple and a verb in the past continuous. Then find one example of the emphatic past simple.

2 Write the question and negative form of these sentences.

1 Naomi saw a UFO last week.
2 Bob Loft was flying the plane.
3 The people were standing there amazed.
4 The ghosts suddenly disappeared.
5 It was the planet Venus.
6 He was driving his car when he saw the creature.

3 Put the verbs in brackets into the correct form, past simple or past continuous, to complete the story.

Last year, my grandmother (1) ________ (**have**) a very weird experience. One evening, she (2) ________ (**sit**) alone at home in Glasgow watching TV. Suddenly, she (3) ________ (**hear**) a strange noise outside, so she (4) ________ (**go**) to see what it (5) ________ (**be**). When she (6) ________ (**open**) the door, she (7) ________ (**see**) a lovely large grey cat. It (8) ________ (**wear**) a collar that (9) ________ (**have**) its name and a mobile phone number on it: 'Cassie – 6784547322'. The cat (10) ________ (**run**) into the living room and (11) ________ (**sit down**).

The cat (12) ________ (**look**) hungry, so Grandma (13) ________ (**decide**) to give it some food. While Cassie (14) ________ (**eat**), Grandma (15) ________ (**call**) the number.

'Hello,' she (16) ________ (**say**). 'I've got a cat here called Cassie. Is it yours?'

'Yes!' a man's voice (17) ________ (**reply**). 'Cassie (18) ________ (**run away**) three weeks ago. Where are you?'

My grandmother (19) ________ (**tell**) the man where she lived.

'I don't believe it!' said the man. 'We lived in that house eight years ago. Cassie (20) ________ (**love**) that house!'

'Where do you live now?' asked my grandmother.

'About 600 kilometres away – in Plymouth!'

Listening

1 Look at the pictures. What are the different places?

A

B

C

D

E

HOMEWORK!

Do exercises 1, 2, 3 and 4 on pages 11 and 12 of your Workbook.

2 🎧 **1.07 You are going to listen to four friends talking about strange experiences they have had. As you listen, match each speaker with one of the pictures on page 18. There is one extra picture you will not need.**

Speaker 1: ______
Speaker 2: ______
Speaker 3: ______
Speaker 4: ______

3 🎧 **1.07 Listen again and circle the correct answer to complete each sentence.**

1 One explanation for Speaker 1's incident is that ____________________.
 a he went to the wrong place
 b time completely stopped
 c he went back in time

2 Speaker 2's uncle ____________________ when he described the fire.
 a was out with his wife
 b thought he was someone else
 c was finding out about history

3 In Speaker 3's story, ____________________.
 a Nick Rice secretly pushed the clock
 b no-one touched the clock
 c the clock broke because they looked at it

4 Speaker 4's father was ____________________.
 a lucky
 b careful
 c clever

HOMEWORK!
Do the Listening exercise on page 15 of your Workbook.

DICTIONARY CORNER

1 Choose the correct words.

1 be wide **asleep / awake**
2 be fast **asleep / awake**
3 have a high **fever / temperature**
4 a narrow **escape / freedom**
5 be far **away / distant**
6 for a long **hour / time**
7 take a short **way / cut**
8 in slow **movement / motion**
9 in a deep **noise / voice**
10 be in big **trouble / problem**

2 Complete the story using nine of the phrases above. You may need to change the verb forms.

School days

I wasn't feeling well yesterday and, because I (1) ____________, my mum said I had to go to bed. After about five minutes, I (2) ____________ and I had a really strange dream. In my dream, I was walking to school. I was really late, so I decided to (3) ____________ through the woods. I walked through the woods (4) ____________ but the school still seemed to (5) ____________ in the distance. I decided to run but I realised I couldn't run very quickly. It was like I was running (6) ____________ – like in a movie. I began to panic. Then I heard my teacher, Mr Hickson, say (7) ____________, 'If you don't get to school in the next three minutes, you'll (8) ____________.' I was terrified.

Suddenly, I saw my school up ahead. I ran as quickly as I could – through the doorway, up the stairs and into Mr Hickson's classroom. He was counting backwards from three minutes. 'Five seconds … four … three … two,' he said. I made it to my seat just in time. It had been (9) ____________, and all the other kids in the class clapped. I guess my dream means something, but I've got no idea what. Any ideas?

HOMEWORK!
Do the Dictionary Corner exercise on page 13 of your Workbook.

Grammar 2

used to and *would*

Look at *Grammar database 4* page 178 before you do the exercises.

1 **Tick (✔) the correct sentences. Put a cross (✘) next to those that are incorrect.**

1 Carl used to believe in ghosts but he doesn't anymore. ______

2 I would love reading about mysteries when I was younger. ______

3 Did you use to thought there were monsters under your bed? ______

4 Would you go to sleep with the light on when you were very young? ______

5 Miranda never used to buy books about UFOs. ______

2 **Complete each second sentence using the word given so that it means the same as the sentence before it. Use no more than five words.**

1 My grandma always said there was an explanation for everything. **used**
My grandma always ____________________ there was an explanation for everything.

2 I never believed in UFOs until I saw one. **believe**
I ____________________ in UFOs until I saw one.

3 Uncle Bob did great card tricks whenever he came to visit. **would**
Uncle Bob ____________________ great card tricks whenever he came to visit.

4 Kate's sure she saw ghosts regularly when she was a small child. **to**
Kate's sure she ____________________ ghosts regularly when she was a small child.

Speaking

1 1.08 **Listen to two students describing pictures A and B below. Tick (✔) the phrases they use.**

Phrase Bank!

Student 1	Student 2
I can see …	I'm not really sure …
This is a picture of …	I don't really understand …
I don't think …	It must be …
I think it isn't …	It could be …
	It's difficult to tell
	It seems to be …
	Perhaps it's a …

2 **Make notes about these pictures.**

eg *picture C. a UFO in the sky*

3 **Describe the pictures using your notes and the phrases you ticked.**

4 **Turn to page 168. In pairs, do the role-play activity unit 2.**

See *Speaking Database* on page 174.

HOMEWORK!

Do exercises 1, 2, 3, 4, 5 and 6 on pages 13 and 14 of your Workbook.

Soundstation

1 **Look back at unit 1, Soundstation on page 12. Can you remember the difference in pronunciation within each pair?**

2 **Play the Soundstation Game. Your teacher will explain the rules to you.**

What an incredible …! ______________________

bin / bean	grin / green	ship / sheep	chick / cheek
hill / heel	sill / seal	din / dean	lid / lead
will / wheel	filling / feeling	lip / leap	fist / feast
mill / meal			

Use your English!

Read the report and rearrange the letters to complete each gap.

THE PHILADELPHIA EXPERIMENT

Case number: 2178
Case name: The Philadelphia Experiment
Date incident occurred: July–October 1943
Location: Philadelphia, USA

Incident report: US naval scientists (1) **ddi** __________ an experiment to make a ship, the *USS Eldridge*, invisible. While the scientists were (2) **taghnwic** __________ what was happening from another ship, a green fog covered the *Eldridge*. As the fog (3) **sidprdpaaee** __________, it became clear that the *Eldridge* had disappeared too. The scientists (4) **erwe** __________ extremely pleased. After 15 minutes, they (5) **ptdosep** __________ the experiment, and the *Eldridge* reappeared. Unfortunately, the men on the *Eldridge* all (6) **letf** __________ ill, and didn't (7) **nwko** __________ what had happened to them. A few months later, they did the experiment again, but this time they only (8) **aewdtn** __________ the ship to become invisible to radar – not to the human eye. The experiment (9) **netw** __________ wrong, and the ship completely disappeared again. At the same time, people hundreds of kilometres away in Virginia saw the *Eldridge* appear in front of them for a few minutes. It then (10) **aihdvsen** __________, and reappeared in Philadelphia. This time, the sailors on the *Eldridge* were extremely ill, and some of them died.

Denial: The US Navy denies the experiment (11) **otko** __________ place.

Conclusion: Did the *Eldridge* actually (12) **asdiprpea** __________, and was it teleported to Virginia? We'll probably never know for sure.

Weirdness rating: ★ ★ ★ ★ ★

Writing

Descriptive language

1 **We can use the words below to make a story descriptive. Write them in the correct box.**

amazing	claim	explain	great	promise	stare	tiny
answer	disastrous	fantastic	horrible	reply	state	watch
ask	dreadful	gaze	huge	rubbish	suggest	whisper
awful	enormous	glance	marvellous	scream	terrible	wonder
brilliant	excellent	glimpse	notice	shout	terrific	wonderful

1 say

2 look, see

3 very good

4 very bad

5 very big

6 very small

2 **Choose the correct word. Be careful! More than one word may be correct in each sentence.**

1 'I'm locked in the bathroom!' **shouted / asked / screamed** Aden.
2 Melissa **stared / gazed / glanced** at the strange animal.
3 I saw a(n) **great / enormous / wonderful** film last night!
4 That was a(n) **awful / terrible / horrible** story.
5 That building is **huge / enormous / tiny** – it's got more than 100 floors!

3 **Write a word from exercise 1 in the correct form in each gap to complete the sentences. More than one word may fit in each gap.**

1 I ______________ a documentary about ghosts on TV last night. It was ______________ !
2 Simon ______________ at the newspaper and suddenly saw his own photograph on the front page.
3 I heard a(n) ______________ noise coming from inside the old factory.
4 'What's that? Do you think it's a UFO?' ______________ Tracy.
5 The alien had ______________ eyes and ______________ ears.
6 'Help!' ______________ Eliot. 'Please help me!'
7 I had a(n) ______________ dream last night.

HOMEWORK!
Do exercises 1, 2, 3 and 4 on pages 14 and 15 of your Workbook.

Get ready to write

Short story

1 Read the story and answer the questions.

THE DREAM

One night, 13-year-old Lisa Levington had a strange dream. In the dream, her brother Rob, who was travelling round the world at the time, came to see her. 'Hi Lisa,' he said. 'I've got a message for you to give to Mum and Dad.'

Rob explained that he had been in a serious accident in Brazil and was unconscious in hospital. He asked Lisa to tell their parents not to worry. 'I'll be all right,' he promised.

As Lisa was telling her parents about the dream, the phone rang. It was Rob's best friend, Colin. 'I'm afraid I've got some terrible news,' said Colin. 'Rob's been in an accident.'

For six days they waited for news. Mr and Mrs Levington were so upset, but Lisa kept reminding them about her dream. That evening, Colin called. 'Great news!' he said. 'Rob's awake. The doctor says he's going to be fine.'
'I knew it!' shouted Lisa with joy, and she always believed in her dreams from that day on.

1 What is the main tense used to tell the story?
2 Underline a verb in the past continuous.
3 Which verbs, apart from 'said', are used to show that someone spoke?
4 Which tense is used in the second paragraph to show that the accident happened before Rob spoke to Lisa?
5 Is the direct speech formal or informal?
6 Is the rest of the story formal or informal?
7 How many main paragraphs are there?
8 How many people use direct speech in the final paragraph?
9 Which word does Colin use to mean 'very good'?
10 Does Lisa's direct speech in the final paragraph start on a new line?

2 Read the writing task and make notes to answer the questions below.

> You have decided to enter a short story competition. The rules of the competition state that your story must *end* with the words *'… and he always believed in his dreams from that day on.'*
>
> Write your **story** for the competition.

1 Who is 'he'?
2 What happened in his dream?
3 Did he tell anyone about his dream? Who?
4 How did his dream come true?
5 How did he react?
6 How must your story end?

3 Make a plan in *Composition Planner 2* on page 153.

HOMEWORK!

You are now ready to write the first draft of your story. Write between 120 and 150 words. When your teacher has commented on your story, write the final version.

Revision
Units 1–2

1 Patterns

Choose the correct word or phrase to complete each sentence.

1 I'm not very fond **to do** / **of doing** tests.
2 Jessica's really looking forward **to go** / **to going** back to school.
3 My dad helped me **with** / **for** this composition.
4 Pedro's not very good **at** / **in** learning new vocabulary.
5 All the students are able **of writing** / **to write** letters to their pen friends.
6 Are you beginning **to understand** / **understanding** the difference between past simple and past continuous?

2 Phrases

Match to make phrases.

1	be fast	____	**a**	escape
2	be wide	____	**b**	temperature
3	a high	____	**c**	motion
4	a narrow	____	**d**	voice
5	a short	____	**e**	asleep
6	in slow	____	**f**	trouble
7	in a deep	____	**g**	awake
8	be in big	____	**h**	cut

3 Education vocabulary

Write a word from the box in each gap to complete the sentences.

break • course • lesson • report • revision • subject • timetable

1 Please remember to do your homework before the next ____________ .
2 I hope Mrs Lockwood says I'm working hard when she writes her end-of-term ____________ .
3 What's your favourite ____________ at school?
4 We've got a history test next week, so I've got to do lots of ____________ this weekend.
5 We have a five-minute ____________ between every lesson.
6 Look at the ____________ to find out when and where all your lessons are.
7 I'm thinking of doing a two-week English ____________ in London next summer.

4 Present simple and present continuous

Tick (✔) the correct sentences. Underline the mistake in the incorrect sentences and write the correct word(s).

1 My sister is wanting me to help her with her homework. ____________
2 They're taking a test at the moment. ____________
3 Tony often forget to bring his books to class. ____________
4 I'm getting better and better at speaking English. ____________
5 Sarah isn't really liking her geography teacher. ____________
6 What do you think about at the moment? ____________
7 Where lives Dana Banach? ____________

5 Past simple and past continuous

Put the verbs in brackets into the correct form, past simple or past continuous.

1 The Lizard Man quickly ____________ (**jump**) onto the roof and ____________ (**try**) to get into the car.
2 Last year, we ____________ (**write**) a composition in English once a week.
3 I ____________ (**watch**) TV when I ____________ (**fall**) asleep.
4 ____________ (**you/be**) excited when you ____________ (**hear**) the news?
5 Sean ____________ (**not drive**) too fast when he ____________ (**have**) the accident.

6 *used to* and *would*

Find the extra word in each sentence and write it on the line.

1 I was used to believe that a monster lived under my bed! ____________
2 Sindy would always to sleep with the light on. ____________
3 Harry did never used to enjoy mystery stories. ____________
4 Were you being scared of spiders when you were very young? ____________
5 My grandfather would taught me how to do card tricks. ____________
6 Did Alicia were use to believe in UFOs? ____________

7 Revision of tenses

Put the verbs in brackets into the correct form, present simple, present continuous, past simple or past continuous, to complete the paragraph.

UFOs

We (1) ____________ (**do**) a project on mysteries at school at the moment, and some of the stories (2) ____________ (**be**) extremely weird. For example, a few years ago over a hundred children (3) ____________ (**play**) in the playground at their school in France when a UFO suddenly (4) ____________ (**appear**) in the sky above them. Their teachers (5) ____________ (**see**) it too. It (6) ____________ (**be**) big and round and (7) ____________ (**have**) lots of lights and windows. After about 10 minutes, it suddenly (8) ____________ (**fly**) away. Generally, I (9) ____________ (**not believe**) in things like UFOs, but I (10) ____________ (*emphatic:* **think**) it's difficult to explain incidents like that.

3

The Law's the Law

Get warmed up!

Discuss the following. Work in pairs or in groups.

- Think of as many crimes as you can.
- Why do some people commit crimes?
- Is crime a serious problem where you live?

Reading 1.09

1 Read the paragraphs quickly and answer these questions.

1 When is it illegal to eat mince pies in Britain?
2 Where are you not allowed to tie your giraffe to a streetlight?
3 What must dolls have in France?

2 Read the article again and put the paragraphs in the correct order. Use the words and phrases in bold to help you.

Paragraph 1 __A__
Paragraph 2 ____
Paragraph 3 ____
Paragraph 4 ____
Paragraph 5 ____

IT'S THE LAW

A We all know that murder, burglary and shoplifting are illegal. (1) ______ We probably all think that, faced with a particular situation, we could make a good guess whether it's legal or not. But in fact there are **some extremely weird** laws around.

B While we're on the subject of **America**, the Americans seem to be particularly keen on passing strange animal laws. In Atlanta, it's illegal to tie a giraffe to a streetlight. In Wilbur, Washington, you're committing a crime if you 'ride an ugly horse' and in Barber, North Carolina, it's against the law for cats and dogs to fight! (2) ______ In Nevada, it's illegal to ride a camel on the highway. So, if you're planning to go camel riding in Nevada, do be careful. You don't want to end up in prison!

C It's **not just in Britain** that these kind of laws exist. (3) ______ In France, for instance, shops are not allowed to sell dolls that don't have a human face. (4) ______ In Quebec, Canada, there's a law that says margarine must be a different colour to butter. In Salt Lake City, Utah, in the USA, it's illegal to carry a ukelele (a musical instrument) on the street unless it's wrapped up. In **Alabama, USA**, it's a crime to carry a comb in your pocket.

3 **The sentences below have been removed from the article. Write the letters a–f in gaps 1–6. Use the words in bold to help you.**

a **Many countries** have some **equally bizarre** examples.

b **And** that boiled eggs must not be broken at the sharp end?

c We all know that we're not allowed to go around hijacking planes, kidnapping people or committing acts of terrorism.

d **They** don't even know **it's** officially illegal.

e **Cats** in International Falls, Minnesota, are not allowed to chase dogs up telegraph poles.

f **So** it's officially illegal for them to sell **dolls** of aliens like E.T.

HOMEWORK!

Do the Reading exercise on page 17 of your Workbook.

D But before you think that everyone **in Britain** must be mad, we ought to point out that no-one is ever arrested for breaking **these laws**. Well, not these days, anyway. Millions of people eat mince pies on Christmas Day and don't get into trouble. (5) _____ Laws like these were passed hundreds of years ago and the thing about laws is that they remain laws until someone changes them. The **British** government's got much more important things to do than change an old law about wearing socks.

E Did you know, **for example**, that **in Britain** it's illegal for a woman to eat chocolates on public transport? And that it's against the law to eat mince pies on Christmas Day? And that you're not allowed to stand within 100 metres of the King or Queen if you're not wearing socks? (6) _____ **They're all laws.**

DICTIONARY CORNER

1 **Complete each sentence using a word or phrase from the article.**

1 I didn't know I was **c**_____________ a **c**_____________ when I tied my giraffe to the street lamp!

2 In Maryland, it's **a**_____________ the **l**_____________ to keep chickens in your hotel room.

3 I was **a**_____________ for riding a camel. The policeman handcuffed me and took me to the police station.

4 In Turkey during the 16th and 17th centuries, it was **i**_____________ to drink coffee. The punishment was death!

5 Are cats and dogs ever punished for **b**_____________ the law?

6 'You're **u**_____________ **a**_____________! You have the right to remain silent. Anything you say can and will be used in a court of law.'

2 **Look at the list of words connected with *crime* and *law* below. For each word on the left, write the name of the person on the right.**

Crimes	People
murder	*murderer*
burglary	
theft/stealing	
robbery	
shoplifting	
smuggling	
Other words	
law	
crime	
prison	
police	*policeman/*

Have your say!

Choose one of the strange laws from the article and say why you think they made that law.

Perhaps margarine and butter have to be a different colour in Quebec because people got confused and bought the wrong one.

HOMEWORK!

Do exercises 1, 2, 3 and 4 on page 18 of your Workbook.

G Grammar 1

Countable and uncountable nouns

Look at *Grammar database 5* pages 178–179 before you do the exercises.

1 Put the nouns into the correct rows in the table.

advice • cake • chicken • chocolate • crime • food • furniture
glass • hair • information • job • knowledge • law • luggage
money • news • person • sheep • suitcase • time • work

always countable	
always uncountable	
countable and uncountable	

2 Choose the correct word to complete each sentence.

1 My advice **was** / **were** to see a lawyer.
2 **Is** / **Are** there any news about that burglary?
3 It's difficult for ex-prisoners to find **works** / **work**.
4 The police don't have **many** / **much** information yet.
5 A large **amount** / **number** of money was stolen in the robbery.
6 **Few** / **Little** criminals are never brought to justice.

3 Find the mistake in each sentence and write the word or phrase correctly.

1 How many money was in your wallet? ______
2 They thought there was a bomb in my luggages! ______
3 A lots of mobile phones are stolen each year. ______
4 Let me give you an advice. ______
5 He was arrested for smuggling bars of chocolates. ______
6 Crime are a serious problem in most cities. ______

4 Write a word or phrase from the box in each gap.

little • piece • few
a little • number • a few

1 I've only got ______ months until I can get out of prison.
2 When I got here, I had ______ money in my pocket, but now it's gone!
3 The police have ______ information to help them solve the crime.
4 There are a ______ of reasons for thinking that John did it.
5 I'm sure that ______ people enjoy being in prison.
6 I had a ______ of cake on my plate and someone's eaten it!

HOMEWORK!

Do exercises 1, 2, 3, 4 and 5 on pages 18 and 19 of your Workbook.

Listing

1 What are the different places in the pictures?

2 1.10 You are going to listen to five people talking about a crime. As you listen, match each speaker with a picture above.

Speaker 1: ___ Speaker 2: ___ Speaker 3: ___
Speaker 4: ___ Speaker 5: ___

3 1.10 Listen again and decide whether the statements are true (T) or false (F).

1 Speaker 1 says Jackson stole a lot of money.
2 Speaker 2 immediately knew Jackson was a burglar.
3 Speaker 3 says Jackson didn't admit to his crimes.
4 Speaker 4 thought Jackson might be innocent.
5 Speaker 5 is probably a prison guard.

HOMEWORK!
Do the Listening exercise on page 22 of your Workbook.

DICTIONARY CORNER

Complete each sentence using the correct form of the phrasal verbs. Look at the *Phrasal verb database* on page 172 to help you. You will need to use one of the phrasal verbs twice.

get off • go off • let off
make off • take off • turn off

1 We ______________ the TV because we heard a strange noise outside.
2 The thieves ______________ with over a million pounds worth of diamonds.
3 Luckily, no-one was injured when the bomb ______________ .
4 They ______________ my dad ______________ with a warning when they caught him speeding.
5 The burglar stupidly ______________ his mask and everyone saw his face.
6 The plane ______________ late because of a security alert at the airport.
7 They arrested him for smuggling as soon as he ______________ the plane.

HOMEWORK!
Do exercises 1 and 2 on page 20 of your Workbook.

Soundstation

1 1.11 Listen and circle the word in bold that each speaker stresses.

1 It **seems** to **me** that prisons don't really work.
2 As far as **I'm concerned**, everyone who breaks the law should be punished.
3 In **my opinion**, no country should have the death penalty.
4 If **you** ask **me**, most people would never break the law.

2 Now say the sentences. Make sure you stress the correct words.

G Grammar 2

Articles

Look at *Grammar database 6* pages 179 – 180 before you do the exercises.

Complete the gaps with the articles *a*, *an* or *the*. If no article is necessary, put a dash (–).

CRAZY CRIMINALS!

There are lots of stories about how stupid criminals can be! They may be true, or they may just be myths, but there's no doubt they're funny!

- In (1) ________ shop in (2) ________ Baltimore, USA, (3) ________ robber pulled out his gun and put (4) ________ bag over his head to disguise his face. (5) ________ man demanded all (6) ________ money from (7) ________ till – and then realised that he had forgotten to put eyeholes in (8) ________ bag! He was soon arrested by a security man.
- When (9) ________ police officers stopped (10) ________ man in Peekskill, New York, in his car, (11) ________ man knew he was in trouble. He was wanted for (12) ________ earlier crime. When (13) ________ police officers asked for his name, he thought quickly and gave them his brother's name. Unfortunately, his brother was also wanted, so they arrested him!
- Police in Derbyshire, England, came up with (14) ________ unusual idea to catch criminals. Every time they went to (15) ________ homes of the men they were looking for, there was no-one there, so they decided to send (16) ________ letters to the men. (17) ________ letters said that each man had won (18) ________ free crate of beer! When the men turned up to collect (19) ________ beer, they got arrested! Even after that, some of them wanted to know where (20) ________ free beer was!

HOMEWORK!

Do exercises 1, 2, 3, 4, 5 and 6 on pages 20 and 21 of your Workbook.

Use your English!

Complete each second sentence so that it means the same as the sentence before it. Use no more than three words.

1 The thief escaped on a motorbike.
The thief made ________________________ on a motorbike.

2 I won't punish you this time.
I'll let ________________________ this time.

3 I didn't know it was illegal to sing out of tune!
I didn't know it was against ________________________ to sing out of tune!

4 She broke the law when she lied in court.
She committed ________________________ when she lied in court.

5 Not many people know what it's really like in prison.
Not a ________________________ people know what it's really like in prison.

6 The bomb exploded at 6.30 this morning.
The bomb went ________________________ at 6.30 this morning.

7 There weren't many people in the bank at the time of the robbery.
There were only ________________________ people in the bank at the time of the robbery.

Speaking

- No bullying
- No graffiti on school property
- No cheating in tests or exams
- No hats
- No earrings
- No mobile phones
- No fizzy drinks and sweets
- No swearing
- No running in the corridors
- No chewing gum in class
- No being late to class
- No smoking

Phrase Bank!

Expressing opinion

As far as I'm concerned, …
I don't think that …
It seems to me that …
In my opinion, …
I think that …
Personally, …
If you ask me, …
I really feel that …

Introducing reasons

… because …
… as …
… since …

Introducing results

… so
Because of this, …

1 Look at the school rules above and discuss the questions. Use the words and phrases on the left to help you.

1 Which rules do you think are 'good' and which are 'bad'? Why?

2 What would be 'good' and 'bad' punishments for students who break these rules? You can use the list of possible punishments to help you.

3 Can you think of any other rules the school should introduce?

Possible punishments or measures:

- a warning
- not letting them in the classroom
- making them stand outside the classroom
- giving them a black mark on a punishment board
- giving them a bad report
- giving them extra homework
- telling their parents
- confiscation (taking something from them for a short time)
- detention (making them stay after school)
- exclusion (making them stay away from school for a certain period of time, perhaps permanently)

2 Turn to page 168. In pairs, do the role-play activity unit 3.

See *Speaking database* on page 174.

Writing

Essay: useful words and phrases

1 Match each group of words and phrases 1–9 that you would find in an essay with one of the purposes a–i.

1 ☐
Firstly, …
To begin with, …

2 ☐
In addition, …
Moreover, …
Second(ly), …

3 ☐
Finally, …
Lastly, …

4 ☐
On the one hand, …
On the other hand, …

5 ☐
As a result, …
Because of this, …

6 ☐
Although …
… but …
However, …

7 ☐
For example, …
… such as …

8 ☐
I believe (that) … In my opinion, …

9 ☐
In conclusion, …
In summary, …

a giving examples
b expressing the result of an action
c introducing a conclusion
d expressing an opinion
e introducing a further point in a list of points
f presenting two contrasting (different) views
g introducing the final point in a list of points
h expressing contrast (a different view)
i introducing the first point in a list of points

2 Look at this picture and answer the questions.

1 Do you see police officers in schools like this in your country?
2 Why do schools in some countries have police officers?
3 Do you think it's a good idea?

3 Write a word or phrase from exercise 1 in each gap to complete the essay.

In some countries, schools have police officers present all the time to prevent crime. (1) ________, this is unnecessary in my country and would be a bad idea. (2) ________, crime at school is a bigger problem in other countries. In America, (3) ________, there are many problems with drugs and knives and other weapons in schools. (4) ________, these things are very rare in schools here. (5) ________, schools in other countries face problems such as theft. (6) ________ this sometimes happens in my country too, (7) ________ it is a very small problem.

There may be some advantages to having the police in schools, but there are many disadvantages. (8) ________, some students might feel a little safer, but (9) ________ the majority of students would feel uncomfortable. Students in my country are not used to seeing the police at school. (10) ________, school would not be a relaxing place to learn.

(11) ________, I would say that police officers are not necessary in our schools and would actually have a negative effect.

HOMEWORK!
Do exercises 1, 2 and 3 on page 22 of your Workbook.

Get ready to write

Essay

1 Read the essay and answer the questions.

1 Underline all the essay words and phrases used.
2 What is the purpose of the first paragraph?
3 What is the purpose of the second paragraph?
4 What is the purpose of the third paragraph?
5 What is the purpose of the final paragraph?
6 Does the writer use any short forms (*don't*, *hasn't*, etc)?
7 Is the language of the essay formal or informal?
8 How many advantages of prisons are mentioned?
9 How many disadvantages are mentioned?
10 Which punishments are mentioned apart from imprisonment?

There is no doubt that prisons keep us safe from dangerous criminals such as murderers. However, prisons do not completely solve the problem of crime.

On the one hand, prisons have many advantages. Firstly, they protect us from people who might harm us. Secondly, they punish people who have committed crimes. In addition, they teach people that 'crime doesn't pay'. As a result, when criminals come out of prison, they usually do not break the law again.

On the other hand, some prisoners learn in prison how to commit worse crimes. When they leave, they break the law again. Moreover, some people who commit crimes are mentally ill and doctors can help them much more than prisons can.

In conclusion, I believe that prisons are necessary for criminals who are a danger to society, unless they need medical help. It may be better for society if less dangerous criminals receive different punishments, such as community service or a fine.

2 Read the writing task and make notes to answer the question below.

> You have been doing a class project on crime. Your teacher has asked you to write an essay about the following statement:
>
> - Any student caught stealing at school should be immediately and permanently excluded.
>
> You should state whether you agree or disagree with the statement. Write your essay.

1 What does the statement mean?
2 Should we allow stealing at school?
3 Should a student be permanently excluded for repeatedly stealing money from other students? Why?/Why not?
4 Should a student be permanently excluded for stealing a pen from the school office? Why?/Why not?
5 So should the punishment depend on the circumstances?
6 Can you think of any problems with permanent exclusion as a punishment?
7 What other punishments could be given instead?
8 Why are they more suitable?
9 Can you sum up your opinion in one sentence?

3 Make a plan in *Composition Planner 3* on page 154.

HOMEWORK!

You are now ready to write the first draft of your essay. Write between 120 and 150 words. When your teacher has commented on your essay, write the final version.

4

Meet the Stars

Get warmed up!

Discuss the following. Work in pairs or in groups.

- Think of a famous person and explain what he/she is famous for.
- Would you like to be famous? Why?/Why not?
- Who's your favourite celebrity? Why?

Reading 1.12

1 **Who are the people in the photos? Find their names in the blog post and comments.**

2 **Read the blog post and comments again and decide if the statements are true (T), false (F) or doesn't say (DS).**

1 Laura has met a lot of famous people. ___
2 Mike's favourite picture is his photo of Ben Stiller. ___
3 Clare sent Lady Gaga an email. ___
4 Antonio got Angelina Jolie's autograph. ___
5 Sophie belongs to a fan club. ___

3 **Write the name of a person (Laura, Mike, Clare, Antonio or Sophie) to answer each question.**

Who …

1 sometimes sees famous actors outside a cinema?
____
2 went to the USA on holiday last year?
____
3 has a parent who works in the media?
____
4 communicates with other fans of a celebrity?
____
5 is waiting to hear from a pop star?
____
6 has seen a celebrity in real life?
______________, ______________

HOMEWORK!
Do the Reading exercise on page 23 of your Workbook.

www.my-blog.com/angela's_blog

ANGELA'S BLOG

Hi! I'm Angela. I'm 13 years old and I live in Taunton.
Welcome to my blog!

21st May

Have any of you ever met a famous person? Have you ever written to a celebrity? Have you maybe got a film star's or pop star's autograph? Tell me your celebrity stories!

Hi, Angela! I've been reading your blog for a year now and I always enjoy it! To answer your question, I've never met a celebrity, but my dad has. He's been working as a journalist for about 15 years and he's interviewed lots of famous people, including Leonardo DiCaprio, Penélope Cruz and Scarlett Johansson! That's cool, isn't it?
I want to work in the media too when I'm older – then I can meet some famous people too!
Laura P

I've been living in Los Angeles since I was 10 (I'm 14 now) so whenever a new movie comes out I stand outside the premiere and try to take photos of the celebrities! I've got some great photos of Megan Fox, Ben Stiller, Isla Fisher and Johnny Depp. I haven't ever asked a film star for their autograph though – I'm too shy!
Mike

Great blog, Angela! I've been a huge fan of Lady Gaga for about two years now. About a month ago, I found the address of her record label online, and sent her a letter, asking for a signed photo. I haven't had a reply yet. I'll let you know if I get one!
Clare Dawson

The only famous person I've ever seen in real life is Angelina Jolie. Last summer, we went on holiday to New York. While we were shopping in a big department store, my mum suddenly said, 'Look! That's Angelina Jolie!' And it was! She was shopping with several other people. Someone went up to her and asked for her autograph. She smiled, said 'Sure!' and signed her name on a piece of paper. She seemed really nice!
Antonio

My favourite actor is Robert Downey Jr. I've always wanted to meet him but I've never had the chance. I get very excited if there's an interview with him in a newspaper or magazine! I'm also a member of an online unofficial fan club, so I get to chat to lots of other fans. Some of them have met him! Maybe I'll meet him too one day. I hope so!
Sophie

DICTIONARY CORNER

Complete each sentence using a word from the blog post and comments.

1 If a famous person gives you their ________________, they sign their name somewhere.
2 A ________________ is a person who writes for newspapers and magazines, etc.
3 Newspapers, magazines, TV, radio and film are all examples of the ________________.
4 When a film ________________ out, you can go and see it at the cinema.
5 The first time they show a film at the cinema is known as the ________________.
6 Famous people, particularly pop stars, actors and TV presenters are sometimes known as ________________.
7 If you really like a musician/actor/etc, you're a ________________.
8 There's an interesting ________________ with Katy Perry in this week's *Gossip!* magazine.

Have your say!

Did you enjoy reading the blog and comments? Why?/Why not?
What comment would you write on the blog?

HOMEWORK!
Do exercises 1 and 2 on page 24 of your Workbook.

G Grammar 1

Present perfect simple and present perfect continuous

Look at *Grammar database 7* pages 180–181 before you do the exercises.

1 **Look at the blog post and comments on pages 34 and 35 and answer the questions.**

1 Find one example of the present perfect simple starting with *I*.
2 Find one example of the present perfect simple starting with *He* or *She*.
3 Find one example of the present perfect simple in the question form.
4 Find one example of the present perfect simple in the negative form.
5 Find three examples of the present perfect continuous.

2 **Choose the correct word or phrase.**

1 Laura's dad **has interviewed / has been interviewing / interviewed** three celebrities so far this week.
2 **I'm writing / I've written / I've been writing** this short story for two hours now and I still can't get the ending right.
3 She's been a journalist **from / since / for** 2011.
4 I haven't read Jay Z's autobiography **yet / still / already**.
5 Have you ever **gone / been / going** to a TV studio?
6 Adam **just has downloaded / has just downloaded / has downloaded just** the new *Black Eyed Peas'* album.
7 I **still / yet / already** don't understand the difference between present perfect simple and present perfect continuous!

3 **Put the verbs in brackets into the correct form, present perfect simple or past simple. Use short forms where possible.**

4 **Which actor is speaking in exercise 3: A, B or C?**

Who Am I?

I was born in 1974 and (1) ________ (**grow up**) in Hollywood, California. Although (2) ________ (**I/work**) as an actor since the age of five, (3) ________ (**I/only/be**) a major Hollywood star since the late 1990s. My first movie, *Critters 3*, (4) ________ (**come out**) in 1991 and, since then, (5) ________ (**I/star**) in a large number of hit movies, including *Romeo + Juliet*, *The Beach*, *Gangs of New York*, *Catch Me If You Can*, *Blood Diamond*, *Inception*, and, of course, *Titanic*. (6) ________ (**I/win**) many awards throughout my career, although (7) ________ (**they/not/give**) me an Oscar® so far! My name begins with 'L'. (8) ________ (**you/work out**) who I am yet?

A

B

C

HOMEWORK!
Do exercises 1, 2, 3 and 4 on pages 24 and 25 of your Workbook.

DICTIONARY CORNER

1 **Write the negative form of these adjectives in the correct column.**

~~able~~ • certain • comfortable • employed
happy • helpful • honest • legal • patient
popular • possible • tidy

un-	dis-	il-	im-
unable	______	______	______
______	______	______	______
______	______	______	______
______	______	______	______
______	______	______	______

2 **Complete the sentences with five of the negative adjectives from exercise 1.**

1 It was always almost ______ to get an interview with Michael Jackson.
2 I was ______ for six months before I finally got a part in a play.
3 Don't be so ______ ! The film will be out soon.
4 Pretending to be a journalist in order to meet famous people is a very ______ thing to do!
5 Is it ______ to take photos of celebrities without permission?

HOMEWORK!

Do exercises 1 and 2 on page 26 of your Workbook.

Listening

1 Look at the lyrics of the song opposite. Can you think of any words that fit in the gaps?

2 **1.13** Listen to the song and complete the lyrics by writing one word in each gap.

HOMEWORK!

Do the Listening exercise on page 28 of your Workbook.

I'm your number one fan

You've never had a hit record
You've never been on (1) ______
I've never seen your face in a (2) ______
Or a Hollywood (3) ______
You don't have any money
And you don't dress like a (4) ______
No-one's visited your web page
You don't even have a (5) ______

But I'm your number one fan!
And I'll do whatever I can
To show you you're the (6) ______
Much better than the rest
To show you that I (7) ______
And that I'll always be there
Yes, I'm your number one fan!

No-one's ever asked your (8) ______
About the issues of the day
No-one (9) ______ has ever called
To see if you're OK
You've never signed an (10) ______
And you probably never will
And there'll never be a (11) ______
To tell us that you're ill

Grammar 2

Comparatives and superlatives

Look at *Grammar database 8* page 182 before you do the exercises.

		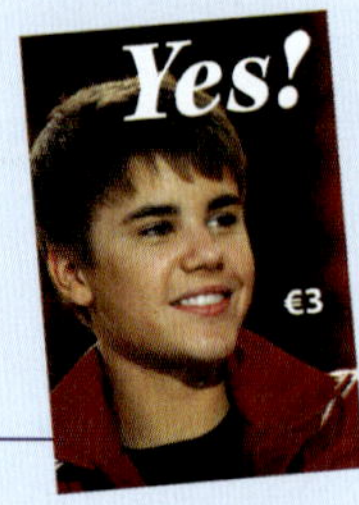	
Cost	€ 3.20	€3	€3.50
Size	100 pages	95 pages	75 pages
Popular	✔✔✔	✔✔✔✔✔	✔
Comes out	once a month	once a week	once a month

1 **Look at the information above about three magazines and complete the sentences using the words given. You may need to change the form of the words.**

1	*Now!* is ____________ magazine.	**expensive**
2	*Yes!* is ____________ *Hi!*	**cheap**
3	*Hi!* is ____________ *Yes!*	**cheap**
4	*Hi!* is ____________ magazine.	**big**
5	*Yes!* is ____________ *Hi!* but ____________ *Now!*	**small, big**
6	*Yes!* is ____________ magazine	**popular**
7	*Now!* is ____________ .	**popular**
8	*Hi!* is ____________ *Yes!*	**popular**
9	*Yes!* comes out ____________ *Hi!* and *Now!*	**often**
10	*Hi!* comes out ____________ *Now!*	**often**

HOMEWORK!

Do exercises 1, 2, 3, 4 and 5 on pages 26 and 27 of your Workbook.

Soundstation

1 **1.14** **Listen to these sentences. Do the parts highlighted have the same vowel sound?**

He's a pop star.

It's the best magazine.

I love these books.

2 **1.15** **Now listen to these sentences. Underline all the vowel sounds that are the same as those underlined in the example.**

She's a journalist.

1 Have you ever met a famous person?
2 The magazine costs about a pound.
3 I felt uncomfortable interviewing Madonna.
4 He's a well-known writer.
5 Could you pass me the newspaper?
6 This video is better than that one.

3 **Now say the sentences. Be careful with the unstressed vowels.**

Speaking

1 1.16 Listen to three students answering questions. What questions do you think they were asked? What words and phrases do they use to give examples?

	Question	Words and phrase(s) used to give examples
Student 1	What ______________ do you like?	
Student 2	What kind of ______________ do you like?	
Student 3	What kind of ______________ do you like?	

2 Ask and answer these questions. Give examples.

What kind of …

TV programmes
films
magazines
books
music
websites
celebrities

… do you like?

3 Interview a friend. Use the questions below.

- Would you like to be famous? Why? / Why not?
- Have you ever seen or met a famous person in real life?
- Which famous person would you like to meet most? Why?
- What have you been reading recently?
- Is it important to read a newspaper regularly? Why? / Why not?
- Is TV just for entertainment, or does it educate us too?
- How often do you use the internet? What kind of things do you use it for?

See *Speaking database* on page 174.

4 Turn to page 168. In pairs, do the role-play activity unit 4.

Use your English!

Use the words given in capitals to form a word that fits in the space in the same line.

Celebrities

Would you like to be (1) ______________? Do you think you would enjoy — FAME
being a rich and successful (2) ______________? Although it sounds — CELEBRATE
attractive, a lot of stars are more (3) ______________ than you would think. — HAPPY
Some feel (4) ______________ being in the public eye all the time. They're — COMFORT
often (5) ______________ even to go to the supermarket without being — ABLE
followed by the press. Many of them complain it's (6) ______________ — POSSIBLE
to have a private life. Others are terrified of becoming (7) ______________ — POPULAR
They're (8) ______________ about their future and worry that they'll lose — CERTAIN
their fame and career, and end up (9) ______________. It may be hard work — EMPLOY
getting to the top, but it's even (10) ______________ to stay there! — HARD

Writing

Interpreting notes

1 Read this extract from an email from your friend. Match each question in the email with an answer on the notepad.

write reply send

From: Ben <Ben@benfamily.com>
To: Neil <neilovery@dmail.com>
Subject: School project

We're doing a project at school on stars and their fans, and I remembered you're a big fan of Ryan Reynolds. (1) Can I ask you some questions? ___

(2) Why do you like him so much? ___

(3) How long have you been a fan? ___

(4) Which of his films have you seen? ___

(5) Which is your favourite and why? ___

a about 2 years
b He's so funny!
c 'Definitely, Maybe': clever and funny at the same time
d all of them
e Yes!

2 Which of these sentences are suitable for your reply, and which are not? Choose a or b.

1 **a** I'd be very happy to answer your questions about Ryan Reynolds!
b Yes, you can ask me some questions.

2 **a** Why do you like him? He's so funny!
b I like him because he's so funny! He always makes me laugh.

3 **a** I have been a fan about two years.
b I've been a fan for about two years.

4 **a** I've actually seen all of his films. My favourite, of course, is *Definitely, Maybe*. I like it so much because it's clever and funny at the same time.
b All of them. *Definitely, Maybe*: clever and funny at the same time.

HOMEWORK!
Do exercises 1, 2, 3 and 4 on page 28 of your Workbook.

Get ready to write

Informal email

1 Read the email and answer the questions.

1 Is the email formal or informal?
2 Does Neil include all the points from the notes?
3 Does he add some information that is not in the notes?
4 How many paragraphs are there in the email?

write reply send

From: Neil <neilovery@dmail.com>
To: Ben <Ben@benfamily.com>
Subject: School project!

Dear Ben,

Thanks a lot for your email. It was great to hear from you. I'm glad you like the CD I sent you.

Your project on stars and their fans sounds interesting. I'd be very happy to answer your questions about Ryan Reynolds!

So, what can I tell you? I've been a fan for about two years now. I like him because he's so funny! He always makes me laugh. And he's a really good actor too. I've actually seen all of his films (and I've got them all on DVD too!). My favourite, of course, is 'Definitely, Maybe'. I like it so much because it's clever and funny at the same time. Have you seen it?

Anyway, let me know if you have any other questions, and I'd love to see the finished project. I'd better go now as I've got lots of homework to do.

Take care, and write back soon.

All the best,

Neil

2 Read the writing task and make a plan in *Composition Planner 4* on page 155.

A friend of yours has sent you an email asking for help with a school project. Read the extract from your friend's email and the notes you have made. Then write an email to your friend answering the questions.

write reply send

We're doing a project at school on pop stars and their fans, and I remembered you're a big fan of Carla Martinez.

voice, songs, video → Why do you like her so much?
over a year → How long have you been a fan?
'Life is love' – great to dance to! → Which of her songs is your favourite and why?
no – next year, I hope! → Have you ever seen her in concert?

HOMEWORK!

You are now ready to write the first draft of your email. Write between 120 and 150 words. When your teacher has commented on your email, write the final version.

Revision
Units 3–4

1 Crime and law vocabulary

Rearrange the letters to find the people. The first letter of each word is given in bold.

	M**C**LRIAIN	CRIMINAL
1	GURR**B**LA	______
2	H**T**IFE	______
3	M**S**GUEGRL	______
4	O**P**ILECOWNAM	______
5	RNOSEIR**P**	______
6	RRED**M**REU	______
7	B**R**BORE	______
8	YW**L**RAE	______

2 Phrasal verbs

Complete each second sentence using the word given so that it means the same as the sentence before it. Use no more than three words.

1 The car bomb exploded at eight o'clock this morning. **off**
The car bomb ______ at eight o'clock this morning.
2 The bank robbers escaped as quickly as they could. **off**
The bank robbers ______ as quickly as they could.
3 The teacher only gave me a warning this time. **off**
The teacher ______ with a warning this time.
4 I didn't know who he was until he removed his sunglasses. **off**
I didn't know who he was until he ______ his sunglasses.
5 Check you have all your things before you leave the plane. **off**
Check you have all your things before you ______ the plane.

3 Countable and uncountable nouns and articles

Choose the correct word or phrase to complete each sentence.

1 She's done **lot** / **lots** of interviews with famous people.
2 There isn't **many** / **much** milk left in the fridge.
3 **How many** / **How much** money have you got on you?
4 Not **many** / **much** people know what it's like in prison.
5 There are only **a few** / **a little** copies of that magazine left.
6 Was **the** / **an** information I gave you useful?
7 All your advice **was** / **were** really helpful. Thanks!
8 I'll see you in about **a** / **an** hour.
9 Do you know who invented **the** / **a** telephone?
10 People like reading about **the** / – famous people.

4 Present perfect simple and continuous

Read the text and choose the correct answer A, B or C to complete it.

The Working Life of a Journalist

(1) ______ as a journalist for the last five years, but (2) ______ freelance for two years. Before that, (3) ______ for a newspaper. (4) ______ into a new office here in Manchester,which I'm really happy with. (5) ______ all morning to arrange an interview with the famous 100 m runner, Carlos Santiago. Unfortunately, so far, his secretary (6) ______ that he'll be available next week. I'll keep trying this afternoon. In the past week, (7) ______ four interviews, and four stories which I wrote last week (8) ______ in newspapers and magazines.What are my ambitions? Well, (9) ______ an award for my work, so I'd like that to happen. I (10) ______ an interview on TV. That would be great too!

	A	B	C
1	**A** I am working	**B** I've been working	**C** I worked
2	**A** I've only been	**B** I'm only	**C** I've only been being
3	**A** I've worked	**B** I've been working	**C** I worked
4	**A** I just move	**B** I've just moved	**C** I was just moving
5	**A** I try	**B** I've been trying	**C** I'm trying
6	**A** didn't confirm	**B** hasn't been confirming	**C** hasn't confirmed
7	**A** 'm doing	**B** I've done	**C** I've been doing
8	**A** have appeared	**B** have been appearing	**C** appear
9	**A** I've never won	**B** I've never been winning	**C** I'm never winning
10	**A** also never did	**B** have also never done	**C** have also never been doing

5 Comparatives and superlatives

Look at the information and complete each sentence using a comparative or superlative form.

Name	Nasty Nick	Bad Ben	Dangerous Dan
Age	67	56	84
No. of crimes	227	31	179
Money in the bank	€100	€1000	€340

1 Bad Ben is *younger than* Nasty Nick. (age)
2 Nasty Nick is ______ Bad Ben. (age)
3 Dangerous Dan is ______ of the three criminals. (age)
4 Nasty Nick has committed ______ crimes. (number of crimes)
5 Nasty Nick has committed ______ crimes ______ Dangerous Dan. (number of crimes)
6 Dangerous Dan has ______ money in the bank ______ Bad Ben. (money in bank)
7 Bad Ben has made ______ money from his life of crime. (money in bank)
8 Nasty Nick has made ______ amount of money. (money in bank)

6 Negative adjectives

Complete the sentences using the negative form of these adjectives.

able • employed • honest • legal
popular • tidy

1 If the law says you're not allowed to eat chocolate, then eating chocolate is ______.
2 If something is ______, then people don't like it.
3 If you don't tell the truth, you are ______.
4 If you can't do something, you are ______ to do it.
5 If your bedroom's a mess, it is very ______.
6 If you haven't got a job and you're trying to find one, you're ______.

5

The Space Race

Get warmed up!

Discuss the following. Work in pairs or in groups.

- How many words connected with space do you know in English?
- Would you like to travel to another planet? Why?/Why not?
- Do you think people will have holidays on other planets in the future?

Reading 1.17

1 Read the article quickly and match the information on the left with what it refers to on the right.

1 2002 NT7
2 July 2002
3 February 2019
4 February 2060
5 2.2 years

a how often the asteroid goes round the Sun
b the name of an asteroid
c the asteroid was discovered
d the asteroid will come very close again
e the asteroid will probably just miss the Earth

2 Read the article again and circle the correct word or phrase to show what each paragraph is about.

Paragraph 1
Scientists **think / don't think** it will happen.

Paragraph 2
We'll **never / probably** be in danger.

Paragraph 3
We'll / We won't be able to find a solution.

Paragraph 4
We're going to be **like the dinosaurs / prepared**.

Invaders from Outer Space

1

Is a huge asteroid going to hit the Earth in February 2019? Probably not, according to scientists, but it's going to be close. The asteroid, called 2002 NT7, was discovered in July 2002. Since then, astronomers have been working hard to calculate its exact path. They are now fairly confident that it will just miss the Earth in 2019.

2

But will it ever collide with Earth in the future? Scientists are not sure. The next possible collision date is February 2060 and, as the asteroid orbits the Sun every 2.2 years, it's quite likely that it will hit us at some point in the future. If it does, it will almost certainly destroy an area the size of Europe and cause global climate changes.

3

But before you start panicking, we'll have plenty of time to prepare for the collision and prevent it from happening. Unlike in the movies, though, this probably won't be done by destroying it with nuclear weapons. There will be two simpler options. The first will involve landing a small rocket on the asteroid and 'driving' it slightly off course so it misses the Earth. The second option will be to use a 'solar sail', which is a bit like the sail on a ship, to change the asteroid's course.

4

Meteors (asteroids which enter the Earth's atmosphere) have hit the Earth before and caused huge damage. Indeed it's possible that a meteor was responsible for the dinosaurs becoming extinct. These days, however, we have the technology to detect them in time and to take appropriate action. Next time it happens, we'll be ready for it.

3 **Read the article again and decide if the statements are true (T) or false (F).**

1 Scientists are certain that 2002 NT7 will not hit the Earth in 2019. T/F

2 The Earth will next be in danger 2.2 years after February 2019. T/F

3 Scientists will use nuclear weapons to destroy dangerous asteroids. T/F

4 We will probably try to change the position of a dangerous asteroid. T/F

5 We know for sure that a meteor killed all the dinosaurs. T/F

HOMEWORK!

Do the Reading exercise on page 30 of your Workbook.

DICTIONARY CORNER

Complete each sentence using a word from the article. Use the words in bold to help you.

1 We have to **p**____________ asteroids **from** enter**ing** the Earth's atmosphere.

2 Do we **have t**____________ **to** find a way to save the planet?

3 Protecting the Earth will **i**____________ build**ing** more powerful telescopes.

4 Technology **is r**____________ **for** major changes in the way we live our lives.

5 How do astronauts **p**____________ **for** space travel?

6 **Is** it **l**____________ **that** we'll discover life on other planets in the future?

7 NASA isn't **r**____________ **for** a manned mission to Mars yet.

Have your say!

Which of these statements do you agree with? Say why.

- I'm not worried about an asteroid hitting the Earth. It's never going to happen!
- I'm worried about an asteroid hitting the Earth. It could happen any day!

HOMEWORK!

Do exercises 1 and 2 on page 31 of your Workbook.

Grammar 1

will and *be going to*

Look at *Grammar database 9* page 183 before you do the exercises.

1 Write the question and negative form of these sentences. Use short forms where possible.

1 The solar sail will destroy the asteroid.
2 We'll be able to have holidays in space soon.
3 They're going to send a manned spaceship to Mars.
4 Mark is going to be an astronomer.
5 You'll have to wear a spacesuit.

2 Choose the correct form to complete each sentence.

1 **We'll / We're going to** look round the Science Museum on Saturday. I can't wait!
2 Look! The Space Shuttle **will / is going to** take off in a minute.
3 Oh, do you need a hand with your science project? **I'll / I'm going to** help you!
4 **I'll / I'm going to** be a famous astronomer when I grow up.
5 **Shall / Will** we watch *Mars Attacks!* on DVD tonight?

3 Choose the correct reason for your answers to exercise 2.

1 The plan was made **at / before** the moment of speaking.
2 This is a prediction **with no / based on** evidence.
3 This is **an offer / a prediction based on evidence**.
4 The speaker first had the intention **at / before** the moment of speaking.
5 This is a **question about a future fact / suggestion**.

HOMEWORK!

Do exercises 1, 2, 3, 4 and 5 on pages 31 and 32 of your Workbook.

Listening

1 Describe what you think this picture shows. Use the words given to help you. Use a dictionary if necessary.

- astronaut
- Mars
- captain
- mission
- crew
- press conference
- reporters

2 1.18 Listen to this press conference. Match the people to the ideas they mention. You won't use all the ideas.

1 Professor Jenkins ___
2 Captain Larsen ___
3 Astronaut Davies ___
4 Astronaut Borkowski ___

a boredom on the trip
b the dangers of the trip
c the cost of the mission
d missing people at home
e the aims of the mission
f finding life on Mars

3 1.18 Listen again and write a word or short phrase in each gap.

1 Professor Jenkins says that living things need ________ .
2 Captain Larsen says their daily ________ will help to keep them busy.
3 Astronaut Davies thinks that they will get useful ________ from this trip.
4 Astronaut Davies is looking forward to seeing ________ from Mars.
5 Astronaut Borkowski says the trip will take ________ .
6 Astronaut Borkowski says getting ________ could be dangerous.

HOMEWORK!
Do the Listening exercise on page 35 of your Workbook.

DICTIONARY CORNER

Write a word from the box in each gap to complete the sentences.

develop • discover • invent

1 Do you think we'll ever ________________ life on other planets?
2 They're going to ________________ the software further so it's much faster.
3 I wish they'd ________________ a machine that does your homework for you!

engine • equipment • machine

4 TVs, videos and DVDs are all examples of electrical ________________ .
5 There's a problem with the ________________ , so Dad's going to take the car to the garage.
6 I'll put the washing ________________ on this evening.

battery • electricity

7 There's a tiny ________________ in this calculator.
8 If you don't pay the bill, they'll cut off your ________________ .

investigation • research

9 Who's going to carry out the ________________ into why the satellite crashed?
10 We'll have to do a lot more ________________ before we're sure that the asteroid won't hit us.

HOMEWORK!
Do exercises 1 and 2 on page 33 of your Workbook.

G Grammar 2

Present simple and present continuous to talk about the future

Look at *Grammar database 10* page 184 before you do the exercises.

1 Choose the correct tense to complete each sentence.

1 Tonight, the planet Jupiter **appears / is appearing** in the sky at midnight.
2 I **meet / am meeting** Noah later to see his new telescope.
3 When you **see / are seeing** the rings of Saturn, you'll be amazed.
4 My favourite astronomy show, *Tonight's Sky*, **starts / is starting** at nine o'clock.
5 **Do you go / Are you going** to the astronomy club meeting this week?
6 The International Space Station **passes / is passing** overhead at 10 tonight.

2 Put the verbs in brackets into the correct form, present simple or present continuous.

'Hello, and welcome to *Tonight's Sky*, the astronomy show. This is going to be a fantastic month! First of all, the full moon (1) ________ (**appear**) on the third. It's a great chance to take photos of the Moon, and I (2) ________ (**travel**) to Chesterton Astronomy Club to meet the members there and share some tips on photographing the Moon. Then, on the 12th, the National Astronomy Festival (3) ________ (**begin**). That's the start of a week of events, and we at *Tonight's Sky* (4) ________ (**organise**) our own celebration of this fantastic hobby. We (5) ________ (**have**) a star party on the 14th, when you can come and look through some amazing telescopes. Saturn (6) ________ (**rise**) early that evening, so you might get the chance to see the wonderful rings! Also, on the 16th, I (7) ________ (**speak**) at the festival about some amazing discoveries. That (8) ________ (**start**) at seven, so get there in plenty of time. And now, let's get on with tonight's programme.'

HOMEWORK!

Do exercises 1, 2, 3 and 4 on pages 33 and 34 of your Workbook.

Soundstation

1 1.19 Listen to these words. Can you hear the difference between them?

hat • heart • hut

2 1.20 Now listen to these words. For each pair, circle the word you hear.

1 **cat / cut**
2 **cart / cut**
3 **had / hard**
4 **pan / pun**
5 **fan / fun**
6 **ladder / larder**
7 **bat / but**
8 **dark / duck**

Speaking

1 Imagine you are going on a trip to the Moon for two weeks. Here are some things you can take with you. Discuss which things will be useful on the trip and which won't. Use the words and phrases opposite.

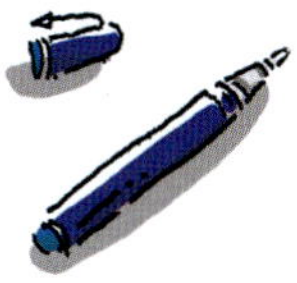

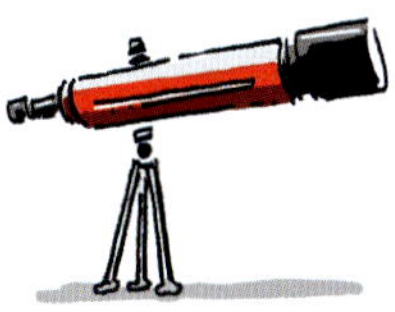
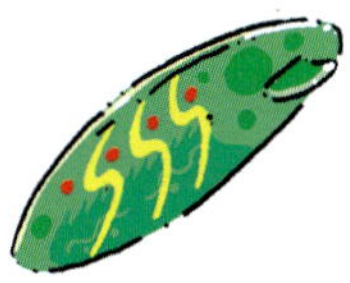

Phrase Bank!

Expressing an opinion

I (don't) think we'll need …
Maybe we should take …
A(n) … is(n't) going to be very useful …
A(n) … will/won't be very useful …
I'm/We're definitely taking …
We'll/We won't be able to use …

Giving reasons and results

… because …	Because of this, …
… as …	… so …
… since …	… 'cause …
… seeing as …	

One/The main reason is (that) …

2 You can take three other things with you. What are you going to take, and why?

3 Turn to page 168. In pairs, do the role-play activity unit 5.

See *Speaking database* on page 174.

Use your English!

Complete the text with one word in each gap.

One day, millions of years (1) ____________ the future, the Sun (2) ____________ going to explode. Unfortunately, we can't prevent this (3) ____________ happening and it means that humans won't (4) ____________ able to live on Earth anymore. Luckily, we (5) ____________ lots of time to prepare (6) ____________ it. It's likely (7) ____________ this preparation will involve working out how to travel very long distances through space, and (8) ____________ another suitable planet to live on. We (9) ____________ need a planet that doesn't go round the Sun but orbits another star instead. The nearest one is a very (10) ____________ way away. With the technology we have today, the journey will (11) ____________ 50,000 years! If we can discover a way to travel much faster – at just below the speed of light – then the journey will (12) ____________ very quick: only six years!

Writing

Using set phrases

1 Read the letter. Do you think it is well written? Why?/Why not?

Dear (1) **Whatever-your-name-is,**

(2) **I'm writing about** your (3) **advert** for pieces of land on the Moon, which I saw in 'Planet Monthly' last Tuesday. (4) **I'm thinking of** buying one. (5) **But** I (6) **want** some more information first.

(7) **Tell me** how much they cost.

(8) **Also,** (9) **I want you to** send me further information (10) **about** transportation to the Moon.

(11) **Can you** also let me know (12) **if I'll** be able to build a swimming pool on the land?

(13) **Please write back!**

(14) **Lots of love,**

(15) **Annabel**

2 Match a word or phrase in bold in the letter with a more formal word or phrase below.

a However, ___
b would like ___
c Secondly, ___
d I am writing with regard to ___
e I look forward to hearing from you. ___
f I would be grateful if you could tell me ___
g whether I will ___
h Sir/Madam, ___
i regarding ___
j Yours faithfully, ___
k I am interested in ___
l Could you ___
m Annabel Davis ___
n advertisement ___
o I wonder if you could ___

3 Rewrite the letter using formal words and phrases.

HOMEWORK!
Do exercises 1, 2 and 3 on page 35 of your Workbook.

GO Get ready to write

Formal letter

1 Read the letter and answer the questions.

1 Is the letter formal or informal?
2 Find words in the letter which have a similar meaning to these words and phrases:
   a a place to stay
   b more
   c rooms and equipment which people can use
   d able to be used
   e say that something is definitely true
   f need
3 Which of these do not take a question mark (?) at the end of the sentence?
   a I would be grateful if …
   b I wonder if you could …
   c Could you …

Dear Sir/Madam,

I am writing with regard to your advertisement for holidays on Mars, which I saw in 'The Daily Gazette' on 24th July. I am very interested in a weekend break to Mars. However, I would like some more information first.

I would be grateful if you could let me know the exact cost of a three-day trip during the summer, including transportation and accommodation, for two adults and two children (aged 12 and 14).

Secondly, I wonder if you could send me further information about the facilities which are available at the Martian Hotel. My daughter would particularly like to know whether there is a nightclub.

Could you also confirm that we will not require either injections or passports?

I look forward to hearing from you.

Yours faithfully,

Steve Knight

2 Read the writing task and make a plan in *Composition Planner 5* on page 156.

You have seen this advertisement and would like further information. Carefully read the advertisement and the notes you have made. Then write a **letter** to the company.

The Space Bus

Would you like to see the Earth from space?

Now you can!!!

- 6-hour and 12-hour trips round the world on the new Space Bus
- reasonable prices
- trips every Saturday and Sunday in summer

The Space Bus the most exciting trip you'll ever take!

For further information, please contact:
The Space Bus Corporation

- 6-hour trip sounds enough
  how much – 1 adult, 2 kids?
- seats available
  Sat. 24th July?
- ad in 'The Daily News', 2nd Feb

HOMEWORK!

You are now ready to write the first draft of your letter. Write between 120 and 150 words. When your teacher has commented on your letter, write the final version.

6

It Takes All Sorts

Get warmed up!

Describe someone in the class without saying who they are. Mention one physical detail and something about their personality. The rest of the class must guess who you are describing. Work as a class.

Reading 1.21

1 **Read the story and tick (✔) the adjectives which describe Zarena.**

bright • rude • hard-working • selfish • jealous
shy • lonely • sociable • popular • strict

ZARENA AND VANTURA

EVERY evening in Tarrigon, the younger gefods met inside the dragon's old cave. There, they chatted and gossiped and had a little fun for an hour or two before nightfall.

Zarena rarely joined them. She didn't like to go to the cave. No, that's not quite true. After a long day collecting food, sometimes all she wanted was to have some company. But Zarena was shy and couldn't make friends easily. When she did go to the cave, she usually stood alone, away from the other gefods, and didn't feel secure enough to join in their conversations.

Zarena found being sociable very difficult. The other gefods mistook her quietness for arrogance. They thought that because she was more intelligent than them, she was looking down on them. They were also jealous because she worked so hard and kept her burrow so clean and tidy. So they teased her or ignored her and made her feel sad. Because of **that**, she didn't like going to the cave.

'Perhaps I am a bit lonely,' she said to herself sometimes, 'but at least I work hard. I wouldn't want to be like Vantura even though she's much more popular than me.' (Vantura bullied Zarena more than the other gefods.) 'She's nasty and selfish and rude and unkind. **1** ______ And I bet most of her friends only pretend to like her. They're just scared of her. I'm sure none of them trust her.' Zarena was strict with herself: 'Never change who you are just to become more popular,' she told herself.

One day, Zarena was out searching for food. **2** ______ She stopped. 'What was that?' she whispered to herself. Then she heard it again. Very carefully and quietly, Zarena went to investigate.

Zarena soon discovered what was making the noise. It was Vantura, who was in serious trouble. There was an old rusty tin can stuck on her head. **3** ______ The noise Zarena had heard was a combination of Vantura shouting 'Help!' and her banging the can against the ground in an attempt to remove **it** from her head.

Zarena didn't know what to do. 'Vantura doesn't know I'm here, so I could just leave quietly,' she thought to herself. 'No, maybe I don't like Vantura, but I still have to help her.'

Zarena went over to Vantura. 'Vantura, it's me – Zarena. Don't worry. I'll help you. Just keep still.' **4** ______ 'Oh dear,' said Zarena. 'It's on very tight. I can't pull it off. But don't worry, Vantura, I won't leave you. There must be a way to help you.'

Zarena thought carefully. 'What should I do?' she said to herself. Then she had an idea. 'Vantura,' said Zarena, 'I'm going to try to cut the can with my teeth. **5** ______' Zarena managed to get a piece of the top end of the can between her teeth. It tasted horrible, but she started to chew. Fifteen minutes later, Vantura was free.

They both lay breathless on the grass. Vantura was bleeding from where the can had cut her face. Zarena was bleeding from where the can had cut her mouth. 'Thank you,' said Vantura eventually. 'I'll never forget **this**.'

What do you think happened next? Did Vantura tell all the gefods about how Zarena saved her, and they all loved Zarena from that day on? Not quite. Vantura didn't tell anyone because she didn't want to look ridiculous. Zarena didn't tell anyone because she didn't want to show off. **6** ______ Dorgo Quando witnessed the whole thing, and quickly told **everyone**. But no-one ever mentioned it to Vantura.

Vantura never bullied Zarena again. And when Zarena did go to the cave – and perhaps she went a little more often than before – the other gefods started to treat her with respect (although they never mentioned the incident to her either) and she slowly started to gain the confidence she needed to talk to them. **It** was a start.

HOMEWORK!

Do the Reading exercise on page 36 of your Workbook.

2 Look at the words in bold in the story. What do they refer to?

1 that *(paragraph 3)*
  a Zarena keeping her burrow clean
  b the situation at the cave

2 it *(paragraph 6)*
  a the tin can
  b the ground

3 this *(paragraph 10)*
  a Zarena helping her
  b her cut face

4 everyone *(paragraph 11)*
  a Vantura, Zarena and the other gefods
  b all the gefods except Vantura and Zarena

5 It *(paragraph 12)*
  a the change in the situation
  b the fact that Zarena helped Vantura

ZARENA

VANTURA

3 Complete the gaps 1–6 in the story with the correct sentence A–F. Write the letter of the correct sentence in the gap.

A Zarena tried to pull the can off Vantura's head, but it wouldn't move.
B It's the only way to get you out.
C I'm glad I'm not like that, even if she has got more friends than me.
D She was running through some high grass when she heard a noise.
E The gefods all soon knew, however.
F She couldn't get it off, and was starting to panic.

DICTIONARY CORNER

Complete each sentence using a word or phrase from the story. You may need to change the word.

Positive characteristics

1 If someone is **k**__________, they are caring, gentle and helpful.
2 If you **t**__________ someone, you believe they won't lie to you or hurt you.
3 If someone has the **c**__________ to do something, they believe in their ability to do it well.
4 If you feel **s**__________ about something, you feel safe and happy about it.
5 If you **r**__________ someone, you have a good opinion of them.

Negative characteristics

1 If you **g**__________ about people, you talk about them when they are not there.
2 If you are **a**__________, you feel you are better and more important than other people.
3 If you **t**__________ someone, you say things to hurt, embarrass or annoy them.
4 If you **b**__________ someone, you use your power to hurt or frighten them.
5 If someone **s**__________ **o**__________, they try too hard to impress other people.
6 If someone is being **r**__________, they are behaving in a silly and stupid way.

Have your say!

Did you enjoy reading the story? Why?/ Why not?
Can you think of other possible endings to the story?

HOMEWORK!

Do exercises 1 and 2 on page 37 of your Workbook.

G Grammar 1

Modals 1 (ability, obligation, advice, permission)

Look at *Grammar database 11* pages 184–185 before you do the exercises.

1 Read the text below and choose the correct words or phrases.

My best friend Andy (1) **may** / **can** dance really well. In fact, his mum says he started dancing before he (2) **could** / **can** even walk! He's so good, I think he (3) **should** / **ought** become a professional when he's older. I wish I (4) **could** / **can** dance as well as Andy, but unfortunately I (5) **can't** / **mustn't**.

Andy's in a ballroom dancing team and takes part in amateur competitions, so he (6) **has to** / **should** practise a lot. Next year, when he and his dancing partner Michelle are 16, he'll (7) **be able to** / **can** enter the British Adult Ballroom Dancing Championships. They're going to be held in London. My mum says that if Andy gets into the final, I (8) **will** / **can** go and support him. I (9) **mustn't** / **can't** wait! She also says, though, that I (10) **don't have to** / **mustn't** be disappointed if he doesn't get into the final, as it's very difficult. She's right, of course. I'm just going to (11) **must** / **have to** hope for the best, I suppose.

2 Write a word or phrase from the box in each gap to complete the sentences.

can • could • doesn't have to • had to • must • should

1 Andy ______________ miss two competitions when he sprained his ankle last year.
2 I think he ______________ buy a new costume if he gets into the final.
3 He ______________ pay for the ticket to London as his dancing club will pay.
4 Andy ______________ also dance really well to pop music.
5 You ______________ be very dedicated if you have a hobby like ballroom dancing.
6 Michelle ______________ dance really well when she was a baby too.

3 Each of the words or phrases in bold is incorrect. Rewrite them correctly.

Andy: Sorry I'm late, Michelle. I (1) **must** to talk to my history teacher about my homework. __________

Michelle: No problem! But we (2) **got** to practise three dance routines! __________

Andy: I think we should (3) **to start** with the easiest one, don't you? __________

Michelle: The waltz? OK. (4) **You can** put the CD on? __________

Andy: Sure! … Oh, I can't (5) **finding** it. Do you know where it is? __________

Michelle: I ought (6) **charge** you every time I help you find a CD! It's in your bag. You took it home yesterday. __________

Andy: Ah, you're right! Let's get dancing!

HOMEWORK!

Do exercises 1, 2, 3 and 4 on pages 37 and 38 of your Workbook.

Listening

1 **When we speak, we say things differently depending on our mood. Choose one of the moods below and say this sentence: *I can't believe it!* in that mood. Everyone else must guess which mood you chose.**

annoyed • furious • depressed • surprised
upset • excited • scared • shocked • nervous

2 **You are going to hear people talking in five different situations. Before you listen, look at the questions and make sure you understand all the words.**

3 **1.22 Listen and choose the correct answer A, B or C.**

1 You hear someone talking about their exam results. How do they feel?
   A annoyed
   B furious
   C depressed
2 You hear two people talking about going on a roller-coaster at a funfair. How does the boy feel?
   A surprised
   B upset
   C excited
3 You hear a mother talking to her son. How does she feel?
   A scared
   B shocked
   C nervous
4 You hear someone talking about their holiday plans. Where are they going to go?
   A Australia
   B America
   C Germany
5 You hear two friends talking. What is one friend trying to persuade the other to do?
   A make a phone call
   B choose a present
   C pick up a friend from a party

HOMEWORK!
Do the Listening exercise on page 41 of your Workbook.

DICTIONARY CORNER

Write the phrases in the correct row. Some of them can go in more than one row.

a bath • care of someone • ~~a decision~~
a dream • an effort • fun of someone
a fuss • a good/nice time • a holiday
an idea • a mistake • part in something
pity on someone • someone a favour
someone good • the housework
time to do something • our best
up your mind • your homework

make ...

a decision

do ...

have ...

take ...

a decision

HOMEWORK!
Do exercises 1 and 2 on page 39 of your Workbook.

G Grammar 2

Modals 2 (possibility, probability, certainty)

Look at *Grammar database 12* pages 185–186 before you do the exercises.

1 Read the sentences. For each sentence decide what the speaker is saying.

> You must be really strong!

1 **I'm sure / It's likely / It's possible** that you're really strong.

> Tammy might enter the competition.

2 **I'm sure / It's likely / It's possible** that Tammy will enter the competition.

> We should win on Saturday.

3 **I'm sure / It's likely / It's possible** that we'll win on Saturday.

2 Look at the picture and write five sentences using the modals below.

must *She must be very fit.*
must ______
may ______
might ______
could ______
can't ______

3 Think of three people you know. Where do you think they are or what do you think they are doing right now? Write short sentences using *should* or *ought to.*

My dad should be at home right now.

1 ______
2 ______
3 ______

HOMEWORK!
Do exercises 1, 2, 3, 4 and 5 on pages 39 and 40 of your Workbook.

Speaking

1 1.23 Listen to a student comparing the first two pictures. Circle the words or phrases they use.

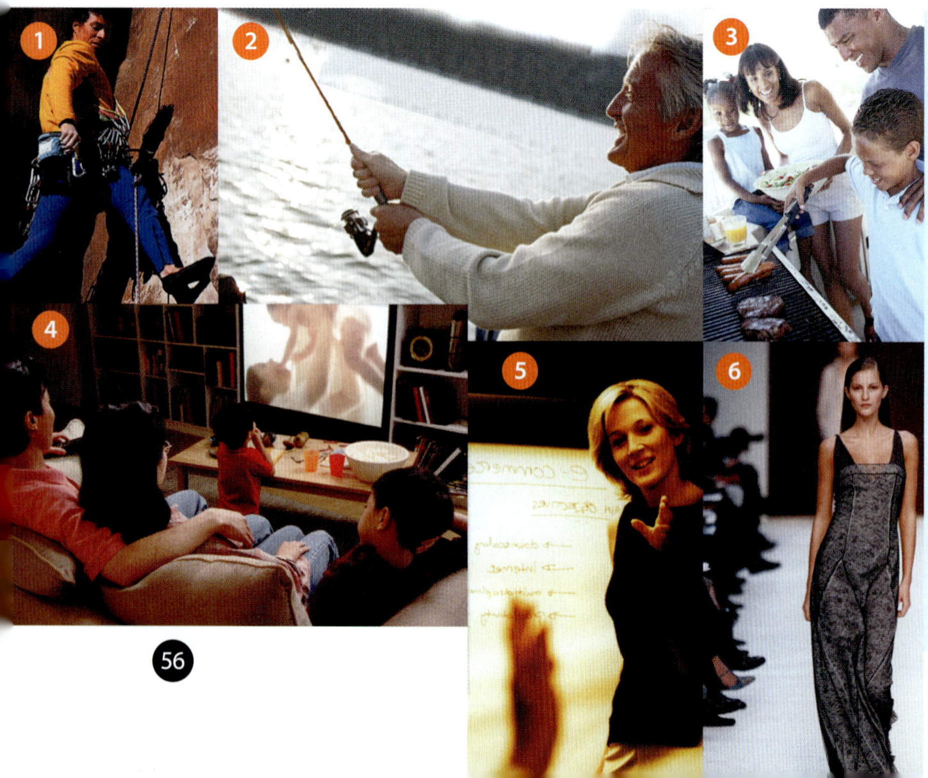

Phrase Bank! P

1 … **at first / to begin with** …
2 … they're both pictures **of / with** …
3 The first picture **is a / is a photo of a** man
4 … **much older than / as old as** the man in the first picture …
5 **They're both / Each of them is** outside …
6 … **they are different because / one main difference is** …
7 … very active to go rock climbing, **whereas / however** fishing is a much more relaxing hobby.

2 Make notes about pictures 3 & 4 and 5 & 6.

pictures	main similarities	main differences
1 & 2	people doing sports	young/old
3 & 4		
5 & 6		

3 Compare pictures 3 & 4 and 5 & 6 using your notes and the phrases you circled in exercise 1.

4 Turn to page 168. In pairs, do the role-play activity unit 6.

See *Speaking database* on page 174.

Soundstation

1 Look back at unit 5, Soundstation on page 48. Can you remember the difference in pronunciation between *hat*, *heart* and *hut*?

2 Play the Soundstation Game. Your teacher will explain the rules to you.

hat / hut	shack / shark	garter / gutter
cat / cart	calf / cuff	batter / butter
bark / buck	rag / rug	ladder / larder
pan / pun	chat / chart	starter / stutter

That ____________ was very nice/ interesting/big/strange, etc.

Use your English!

Complete the advertisement with one word in each gap.

VOLUNTEER FOR THE OVERTON YOUTH THEATRE FESTIVAL!

If you can't (1) ________ up your mind what to do this summer, why not try something different? You don't (2) ________ to spend your holidays lying on the beach for two weeks doing nothing. Holidays (3) ________ be challenging and fun, shouldn't they?

Come and work as a volunteer at the Overton Youth Theatre Festival. You'll meet loads of interesting people, (4) ________ a great time and do something creative. You'll enjoy taking (5) ________ in this important cultural event, and you'll feel a great sense of achievement at the end of it.

You do the work (eight hours a day, Saturday to Friday) and we'll take care (6) ________ the rest: accommodation, all meals and leisure time activities. So (7) ________ yourself a favour and (8) ________ a different kind of holiday at the Overton Youth Theatre Festival. It'll (9) ________ you good!

No experience of theatre necessary, but you should be hard-working, willing to learn and able to work in a team.

Please note: you (10) ________ be over 16 years old to apply.

Writing

Layout and text structure

1 Read the report and decide if the statements are true (T) or false (F).

To: All the students using Laser B1
From: Malcolm Mann (one of the authors of Laser B1)
Subject: How to write a report

Introduction
The aim of this report is to demonstrate how to write a report in English. Although it is not difficult, there are a number of things you have to remember. These are described below.

To:/From:/Subject:
Reports usually start with *To:* and then the name of the person who will read the report. On the next line, we write *From:* and then the name of the person writing the report. Below that, we write *Subject:* followed by what the report is about. Below that, if necessary, we write *Date:* and the date the report was written. For example, 'Date: 24th July'.

Headings
Each paragraph of a report has a heading. It briefly describes what the paragraph is about. The first heading is usually 'Introduction' and the final heading is usually either 'Conclusion' or 'Recommendation'.

Length of paragraphs
Some paragraphs can be quite short.

Formality
Reports are generally formal.

Set phrases
There are several set phrases we can use in a report:
1. The aim of this report is to ...
2. As requested, I have looked at/examined/visited, etc ...
3. My findings are presented below. We can also use discursive words and phrases such as *Firstly, Furthermore, However*, etc.

Lists
As you can see from the previous paragraph, we can include lists in reports if they are the clearest way to present information.

Conclusion
If you follow the information presented above, you will find writing a report easy. Good luck!

1 Reports are generally informal. T/F
2 Every main paragraph of a report has a heading. T/F
3 Paragraphs must be at least four sentences long. T/F
4 You should always begin with *Dear Sir/Madam,*. T/F
5 The point of a report is to present information clearly. T/F

2 Your teacher will read out a report. Write it down with the correct layout.

HOMEWORK!
Do exercises 1, 2, 3 and 4 on page 41 of your Workbook.

Get ready to write

Report

1 Read the report and answer the questions.

1 Who wrote the report?
2 Who is going to read the report?
3 Find words or phrases in the report that have a similar meaning to these words and phrases:
 a find out
 b if
 c generally
 d at the moment
 e make smaller
 f think about

To: Jane Peters
From: Alison Webster
Subject: Merdington Youth Club

Introduction

As requested, I have interviewed members of the Merdington Youth Club to discover whether they are satisfied with the facilities. My findings are presented below.

The building

All twenty-eight members of the club felt that the building should be redecorated. Several of the older members said that they would be willing to help with the redecoration if the local council provided paint and brushes.

Club activities

On the whole, members were pleased with the range of club activities. However, many of the older teenagers would prefer the club to stay open later on Friday evenings. It currently closes at 9pm. They suggest that there is a disco from 9pm to 11pm for club members aged 16–18.

Conclusion

Merdington Youth Club is a popular and well-run club. I would recommend, however, that the building is redecorated. This could be done by the members to reduce the cost. We should also consider providing a Friday evening disco for older teenagers.

2 Read the writing task and make notes to answer the questions below.

You work for Tapperton Council. Your manager has asked you to interview members of the Tapperton Sports Club to find out what they think about the facilities the club offers. Write your **report** for your manager.

1 What facilities does the club offer? (choose two or three main ones)
________________________________.

2 Are the members happy with them? How could they be improved?
________________________________.

3 What recommendations are you going to make?
________________________________.

HOMEWORK!

You are now ready to write the first draft of your report. Write between 120 and 150 words. When your teacher has commented on your report, write the final version.

3 Make a plan in *Composition Planner 6* on page 157.

Revision
Units 5–6

1 Expressing future time

Five of these sentences are correct. The other five are incorrect. Tick (✔) the correct sentences. If it is incorrect, rewrite the word or phrase in bold correctly on the line.

1 **I'm being** a scientist when I'm older. ____________
2 I'll phone you when **I will have** some news. ____________
3 If the asteroid hits, **we'll be** in big trouble. ____________
4 I know! **I'll get** Jason a telescope for his birthday. ____________
5 Look out! **We will** crash! ____________
6 The train **arrives** at midnight. ____________
7 **Will** you help me carry these boxes? ____________
8 **Will** I help you carry these boxes? ____________
9 If you **will come** to the party, you'll make some friends. ____________
10 **We're going to go** in a few minutes. ____________

2 Modals 1

Choose the correct word or phrase to complete each sentence.

1 **Could / Should** I have some more lemonade, please?
2 Dan **could / can** play the piano well. Let's ask him to join our band.
3 Dan **could / can** play the piano when he was two years old.
4 I'd hate to **must / have to** go and live on another planet.
5 In the future, we **can / will** be able to travel all round the universe.
6 My advice is that you **should / may** see a doctor.

3 Modals 2

Complete each second sentence using an appropriate modal (*may, could, can't*, etc) and any other necessary words so that it means the same as the sentence before it.

1 I'm sure that's Dave at the door.
That ____________ Dave at the door.
2 I'm sure that Diane isn't jealous of Linda.
Diane ____________ jealous of Linda.
3 It's very likely that NASA will announce a mission to Mars soon.
NASA ____________ a mission to Mars soon.
4 It's very likely that the asteroid won't do any damage.
The asteroid ____________ any damage.
5 It's possible that people will panic.
People ____________ panic.
6 It's possible that an astronaut is walking on the Moon right now.
An astronaut ____________ on the Moon right now.

4 Patterns

Complete the sentences using the correct form of the verbs *make*, *do*, *have* or *take*.

1 My dad ______________ most of the housework because my mum works very long hours.
2 I've got to ______________ care of my niece while her parents are away this weekend.
3 Simon has ______________ a real effort this term. Well done!
4 I ______________ a very strange dream last night.
5 Could you ______________ me a favour?
6 I wish you would ______________ up your mind!
7 I think you've ______________ a mistake.
8 Are you going to ______________ part in the school play?

5 Adjectives

Match a word from the box with each sentence.

jealous • kind • lonely • popular • rude • selfish • shy • strict

1 'My sister never lets me play her CDs.' ______________
2 'Everyone likes Adam.' ______________
3 'Jessica helped me such a lot when I broke my leg.' ______________
4 'I wish I had as much money as Dean does.' ______________
5 'Mrs Walker never lets us talk in class.' ______________
6 'Since we moved here, I haven't made any friends.' ______________
7 'You should never speak to your teacher like that.' ______________
8 'Sean feels very uncomfortable talking to strangers.' ______________

6 Grammar and vocabulary revision

Choose the correct answer A, B, C or D to complete the text.

TIME MACHINES

(1) _______ you imagine what would happen if we (2) _______ that time travel was possible? People would be able to go back and change the past. And that, of course, would affect the present. So, is it likely that someone will (3) _______ a machine for travelling through time? The answer is no, (4) _______ to most scientists. The main problem is that time travel (5) _______ breaking the laws of physics. Of course, we (6) _______ have misunderstood these laws, but a lot of (7) _______ has been carried (8) _______ in the past hundred years or so to work out exactly what 'time' is. We now believe that, although time is not constant – it (9) _______ speed up and slow down – we will never (10) _______ go back in time. There is another very good argument why time travel isn't possible. We don't see people coming back from the future to visit us!

	A	B	C	D
1	**A** May	**B** Can	**C** Will	**D** Should
2	**A** investigated	**B** developed	**C** invented	**D** discovered
3	**A** invent	**B** discover	**C** investigate	**D** involve
4	**A** speaking	**B** listening	**C** according	**D** agreeing
5	**A** prevents	**B** contains	**C** includes	**D** involves
6	**A** ought to	**B** should	**C** must	**D** might
7	**A** investigation	**B** research	**C** development	**D** discovering
8	**A** out	**B** off	**C** over	**D** away
9	**A** will have to	**B** mustn't	**C** can	**D** ought to
10	**A** be able to	**B** can	**C** could	**D** should

7

Going Out and Staying In

Get warmed up!

Discuss the following. Work in pairs or in groups.

- How many places can you think of that people go to in their spare time?
- What do you like doing in your free time?
- How often do you go out with friends?
- What kind of places do you usually go to?

Reading 1.24

1 Match each of the texts A–H with a description.

1 a message about a phone call
2 an email
3 a poster in a cinema
4 a note left for a parent
5 instructions in a theatre
6 a notice in a school
7 a warning on a box
8 a notice in a club

2 Read the texts. What does each one say?

Extract A

A Speak to Mr Jackson if you want to see the school play.
B Mr Jackson will contact you if he wants you in the school play.
C If you want to be in the school play, speak to Mr Jackson.

Extract B

A Jacob should make sure he calls his mum before six o'clock.
B Jacob's mum will call him later on her mobile phone.
C Jacob can call her at the office if it's not yet six o'clock.

Extract C

A This film has already been shown at this cinema.
B This film hasn't been shown yet at this cinema.
C This film won't be shown at this cinema for a long time.

Extract D

A Members of the club are not allowed to use the games.
B You can use the games but you should put them back afterwards.
C Ask other club members if you want to find a game.

Extract E

A Someone is coming to the house at four to fix the TV.
B Lisa's mum has to go to the shop before four o'clock.
C Lisa will call her mum at four o'clock to tell her what to do.

A

ACTORS WANTED
The school play, directed by Mr Jackson, will take place on June 15th next year. Anyone interested in acting should contact him during the lunch break.

B

Jacob – your mum rang. She can't meet you at the cinema after all because she has to work late. Call her before six at the office or after six on her mobile.

C

Coming soon!
THE TOURISTS
is a romantic comedy set on a tropical island. You'll love the crazy plot and the even crazier jokes!
Showing Sat-Wed, 7pm, 9pm, 11pm.

D

Please return all games to the place where you got them. This is so that other youth club members will know where to find them. Thank you.

E

Mum – there's something wrong with the TV. I can't turn the set on with the remote control. I've called the shop and they're coming round at four. See you tonight. Lisa

F

From: Charlie
To: Emma
Subject: your party

I should have told you before. Can't come to the party because I've got tickets for a concert. See you at Jenny's on Friday, though!

G

Copying this DVD is not allowed, apart from one personal copy, which must not be sold, lent or given to anybody else.

H

Select date, the show you want to see, and number of tickets. When seating map appears, select available seats (shown in green). Collect chosen tickets from ticket office.

Extract F

A Charlie expects to meet Emma at the concert.
B Charlie expects to meet Emma at her party.
C Charlie expects to meet Emma later in the week.

Extract G

A You are not allowed to make any copies.
B You can make one copy of the DVD for yourself.
C You are allowed to make copies, but only for friends.

Extract H

A Choose your seats before you choose the date of the performance.
B Collect your tickets after deciding what seats you want.
C Choose the show then speak to the ticket office about available seats.

3 Read the texts again and decide which text(s) …

1 tell us when something is going to happen. _____ _____ _____
2 say someone has to change their plans. _____ _____
3 give instructions for using something. _____ _____
4 tells you not to do something. _____
5 describes a problem with equipment. _____
6 talk about contacting other people. _____

HOMEWORK!
Do the Reading exercise on page 43 of your Workbook.

DICTIONARY CORNER

1 Complete each sentence using a word from the extracts.

1 Our school play was **d**__________ by our drama teacher.
2 The novel is **s**__________ in Japan during the Second World War.
3 *Fight Club* is such a complicated film that it's difficult to understand the **p**__________ at times.
4 Why don't you turn off your TV **s**__________ and do something more interesting instead?
5 Toys don't have winners and losers and rules but **g**__________ do.
6 I want to change channels but I can't find the **r**__________ **c**__________ .
7 My friends and I usually go to the **y**__________ **c**__________ on Friday evenings.

2 Fill in the missing letters. Can you find the hidden word?

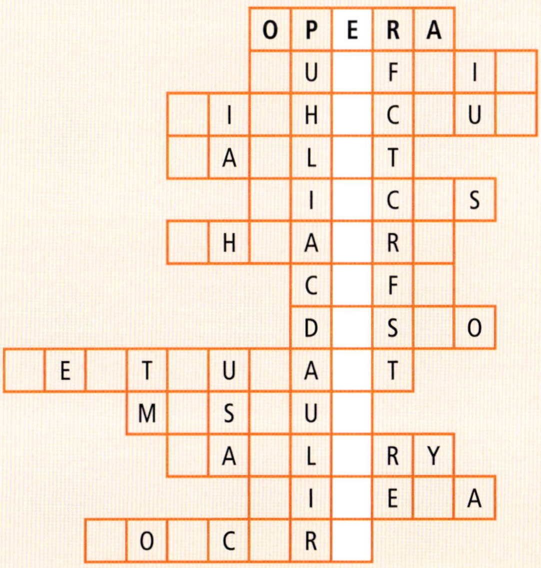

1 A play with classical music and singing.
2 You can go on a roller-coaster here.
3 People can dance and have a drink here.
4 A story told through classical dance.
5 I love the acrobats and clowns.
6 You see plays here.
7 Let's go for a coffee!
8 Let's go dancing!
9 Anyone hungry?
10 We look at exhibits from the past here.
11 You look at paintings here.
12 Shall we go and see a film tonight?
13 Classical or pop?

Have your say!

- Have you ever been to a concert, the theatre or the cinema?
- Describe what you saw and how you felt about it.

HOMEWORK!
Do exercises 1 and 2 on page 44 of your Workbook.

G Grammar 1

Modal perfect

Look at *Grammar database 13* pages 186–187 before you do the exercises.

1 Choose the correct word.

write reply send

To: Francesca <Fran123@freemail.it>
From: Joanne <jps@uknet.uk>

Subject: Hi!!!

I (1) **must** / **should** have been mad to enter the karaoke competition last night. What was I thinking? I really (2) **can't** / **should** have thought about it a bit more carefully. Why did I agree to it when I (3) **could** / **would** have stayed at home and watched a DVD instead? But no! I made a complete fool of myself in front of all my friends. It might (4) **be** / **have been** all right if they'd given me a song I knew. But it was this really weird song I'd never heard before. I (5) **can't** / **mustn't** have got any of the notes right. It was so embarrassing!

2 Complete each second sentence so that it means the same as the sentence before it. Use no more than three words.

1. Why didn't you buy the tickets today?
   You should ____________________ the tickets today.
2. It's possible that Rachel remembered to set the video.
   Rachel might ____________________ to set the video.
3. They obviously forgot what time the concert starts.
   They must ____________________ what time the concert starts.
4. There's no way Dave was a stand-up comedian!
   Dave can't ____________________ a stand-up comedian!
5. There was a chance I'd win the talent contest but I didn't.
   I could ____________________ the talent contest but I didn't.

3 For each situation, write what you say using the prompts.

1. Your friend had a party and didn't tell you. (should/tell/your party)
   'You ______________________________!'
2. You see a friend coming out of the cinema with a box of popcorn. (must/see/a film)
   'He ______________________________.'
3. You see people coming out of a concert looking unhappy. (can't/be/a good concert)
   'It ______________________________.'
4. Your friend has lost her voice after singing for a long time. (must/sing/for hours)
   'She ______________________________!'
5. You want to see a show but there are no tickets left. (ought/buy/tickets/yesterday)
   'We ______________________________.'

HOMEWORK!

Do exercises 1, 2, 3 and 4 on page 45 of your Workbook.

Listening

1 You are going to listen to five people talking about what they like doing in their spare time. First, look at the pictures. What are the people doing?

2 **1.25 Listen to the speakers and match each speaker with one of the activities above.**

Speaker 1: ___ Speaker 4: ___
Speaker 2: ___ Speaker 5: ___
Speaker 3: ___

3 **1.25 Listen again and match a statement with each speaker.**

A The speaker thinks this activity will help them with their job.
B The speaker feels that they'll never be perfect at this activity.
C The speaker likes this activity because it's a break from routine.
D The speaker uses this activity to make other people happy.
E The speaker says this activity is great, however you feel.

Speaker 1: ___ Speaker 4: ___
Speaker 2: ___ Speaker 5: ___
Speaker 3: ___

HOMEWORK!
Do the Listening exercise on page 48 of your Workbook.

DICTIONARY CORNER

Complete each sentence using the correct form of the phrasal verbs. Look at the *Phrasal verb database* on page 172 to help you.

do up • give up • make up • pick up
put up • set up • take up • turn up

1 Could you ____________ me ____________ outside the library at 6.30?
2 We're thinking of ____________ a computer games club at school.
3 I couldn't believe it when Sheena ____________ at the party with her new boyfriend.
4 They're planning to ____________ the old cinema and turn it into a nightclub.
5 I'm going to ____________ stamp-collecting and find a more interesting hobby.
6 You should have ____________ a less expensive hobby, like photography.
7 Ralph's always ____________ unbelievable stories about his friends.
8 Would you mind ____________ me ____________ for the night when I come to town for the pop concert?

HOMEWORK!
Do exercises 1 and 2 on page 46 of your Workbook.

G Grammar 2

-ing form or full infinitive?

Look at *Grammar database 14* page 187 before you do the exercises.

1 **Some of the sentences below contain a mistake. Tick (✔) the correct sentences. If a sentence is incorrect, write the word or phrase correctly.**

1 I'm really looking forward to go ice-skating tomorrow. ______
2 Sean's decided taking up skateboarding. ______
3 I love going to outdoor cinemas in the summer. ______
4 Did you remember buying the tickets for the concert? ______
5 I don't really feel like seeing a film tonight. ______
6 The music was great - we didn't stop to dance all night! ______

2 **Complete the paragraph with the correct form of the verbs.**

Spare Time

Although I enjoy (1) ______ (**visit**) art galleries, I've never been very good at (2) ______ (**draw**) and (3) ______ (**paint**) pictures myself. For a long time I've wanted (4) ______ (**learn**) some of the basic skills. At first, I considered (5) ______ (**study**) on my own at home, but then a friend of mine suggested (6) ______ (**go**) to evening classes and I realised that would be much more fun. So, I've decided (7) ______ (**join**) an evening art class at the local Technical College. I've met the instructor, Mr Philips, and he seems (8) ______ (**be**) really nice. First, we'll practise (9) ______ (**draw**) very simple objects, and then we're going to move on to more difficult things, like people and buildings. I know it's not going to be easy, but I intend (10) ______ (**stick**) at it. I'm not going to give up (11) ______ (**try**). And I hope by the end of the course I'll be able (12) ______ (**see**) a real improvement in my artistic ability.

HOMEWORK!
Do exercises 1, 2, 3 and 4 on pages 46 and 47 of your Workbook.

Soundstation

1 1.26 **Listen to these pairs of words. Can you hear the difference between them?**

hand / had
send / said
finger / figure

2 1.27 **Now listen and circle the words you hear.**

1 Look at that **land** / **lad**!
2 That's **banned** / **bad**.
3 I'm going to go round the **bend** / **bed**.
4 That's a strange **trend** / **tread**.
5 It's a very big **finger** / **figure**.
6 Have you read 'The **Jungle** / **Juggle** Book'?

Speaking

1 **Complete the table with one word from the box in each gap.**

about • his/her • how • idea
if • suggest • that • to

Phrase Bank! P

Phrases for recommending and making suggestions

1 *She/He could/Ought ________ /should* + bare infinitive
2 *I (would) ________* + *-ing* form or noun
3 *What ________* + *-ing* form or noun?
4 *________ about* + *-ing* form or noun?
5 *I'd say that* + *-ing* form or noun *is a good/bad ________ because …*
6 *What ________ she/he* + present simple or past simple?
7 *I'd recommend (________) she/he* + present simple
8 *I'd recommend (________)* + *-ing* form

2 **Write the names of the hobbies.**

1

2
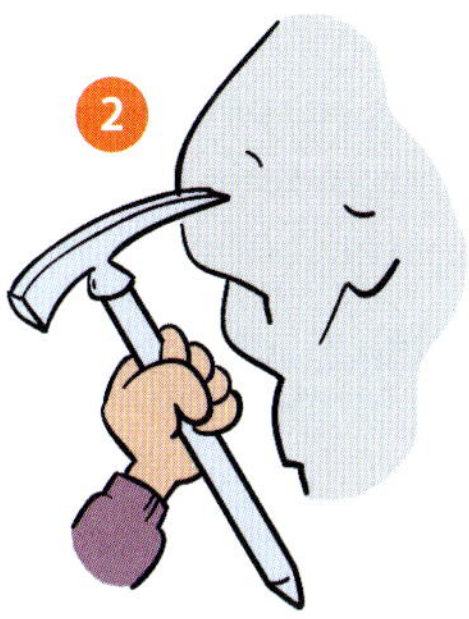
3

4

5

photography
collecting
painting and drawing
rock climbing
horse-riding

3 **Work in pairs. Read the information about Carla and discuss how suitable each hobby in exercise 2 is. Choose the best one to recommend.**

A friend of yours, Carla, aged 14, wants to take up a new hobby. The hobby should:

- be something that gets her out of the house
- involve making new friends and
- not be too expensive.

4 **Write a short note to Carla (35–45 words). In your note, you should:**

- say that you and your friend have thought about possible hobbies for her
- mention one or two hobbies you don't recommend, and say why
- recommend one or two hobbies to Carla.

5 **Turn to page 168. In pairs, do the role-play activity unit 7.**

See *Speaking database* on page 174.

Use your English!

Complete each second sentence using the word given so that it means the same as the sentence before it. Use no more than five words.

1 Have you stopped learning a new card trick every day? **up**
Have you ______________________ learning a new card trick every day?
2 I don't really want to go out this evening. **feel**
I don't really ______________________ out this evening.
3 It's not possible that Sarah saw the film last week. **have**
Sarah ______________________ the film last week.
4 I didn't invite Hanif to the party and I regret that now. **should**
I ______________________ Hanif to the party.
5 I can't wait to see you at the circus tomorrow! **forward**
I'm really ______________________ you at the circus tomorrow!

Writing

Awareness of target reader

1 Match the different types of writing with the people who are going to read them.

1 a letter applying for a job ___
2 an essay about a project you've done in class ___
3 a letter describing a film you've just seen ___
4 an article for an international young people's magazine ___
5 a letter of complaint to a hotel ___
6 a short story for a national magazine ___

a the Hotel Manager
b a friend or relative
c someone interested in reading fiction
d a manager in a company
e a student in another country
f your teacher

2 Read the extracts from the writing tasks and decide:

a who the target reader is for each one
b what style the writing will be in each one.

1 Look at the notes your pen friend has made and write a letter to the Theatre Manager …

Target reader:
a the Theatre Manager
b your pen friend

Style:
a formal
b fairly informal
c very informal

2 Your teacher has asked you to write a story for a national short story competition …

Target reader(s):
a the competition judges
b your teacher

Style:
a descriptive
b academic
c persuasive

3 Write a report for your manager recommending …

Target reader:
a someone whose name you know
b someone whose name you don't know

Style:
a formal
b fairly informal
c very informal

4 Your school magazine has asked you to write an article about students …

Target readers:
a students at your school
b students all round the world

Style:
a very formal, with no short forms (*can't*, *won't*, etc)
b fairly informal, with everyday English and some short forms
c very informal

5 You have been doing a project at school on television. Your teacher has asked you to write an essay on how much television young people in your country watch …

Target reader(s):
a young people in your country
b your teacher

Style:
a very formal, with no short forms (*can't*, *won't*, etc)
b fairly informal, with everyday English and some short forms
c very informal

6 Write a letter to the Theatre Director applying for …

Target reader(s):
a someone you know personally
b someone you have never met

Style:
a formal
b fairly informal
c very informal

HOMEWORK!
Do exercises 1 and 2 on page 48 of your Workbook.

Get ready to write

Article

1 Read the article and answer the questions.

1 Why does the writer start with a question?
 a She wants the reader to answer the question.
 b She thinks it will make the reader interested.

2 Does the writer use any short forms (*won't*, *can't*, etc)?

3 Is the style very formal, fairly informal or very informal?

I went on a quiz show!

Have you ever been on a TV quiz show? I have. I went on *Quizbusters*, and it was the most exciting experience I've ever had.

I arrived at the studio half an hour before the show was due to begin and met the four other contestants. We all admitted how nervous we were. Then Bob Harty, the presenter, came in and told us not to worry.

He said we should just have fun. We recorded the programme in the afternoon. I started off well and answered more questions correctly than the others. To my surprise, I was through to the next round! Things continued to go well and suddenly I was in the final: it was me against a girl called Joanne. We were both so nervous! In the end, Joanne got six questions right, and I only got five, so she was the winner.

Although I didn't win the big prize, I had a fantastic time and I'd love to go on another quiz show in the future.

2 Read the writing task and make notes to answer the questions below.

You have just seen the following announcement in a young people's magazine. Write your article.

Have you ever taken part in a talent contest? If you have, we'd love to hear about your experience. What kind of act did you do? What happened? How did you feel? Did you win? We'll publish the best articles in next month's issue.

1 Where was the talent contest (*school, youth club, on TV*)?

____

2 When (*last year, last week*)?

____

3 What did you do (*sing, dance, tell jokes*)?

____

4 How did you feel (*before, during, after*)?

____

5 Was it a success? (*Did people laugh, clap, etc?*)

____

6 Did you win? (*If yes, what was the prize?*)

____

3 Make a plan in *Composition Planner 7* on page 158.

HOMEWORK!

You are now ready to write the first draft of your article. Write between 120 and 150 words. When your teacher has commented on your article, write the final version.

8

The Problem Page

Get warmed up!

Discuss the following. Work in pairs or in groups. Your teacher will read out some definitions of family relationships.

- What's the English word for each one? For example, your **mother's sister** is your **aunt**.
- Are there any agony aunts in magazines in your country?
- What problems do young people ask for advice about?

Reading 1.28

1 **Read three letters to a problem page in a magazine for teenagers and the responses. Match each letter 1–3 to one of the responses A–C.**

Letter 1 ______ Letter 2 ______ Letter 3 ______

2 **Decide whether these sentences from the problem page are opinion (O) or fact (F).**

1 He's so gorgeous!
2 My elder brother has been going out with his girlfriend for about two years …
3 If we move, I'll lose all my friends from school …
4 Don't say you're worried about his fiancée …
5 These situations often arise …
6 … you have to think very carefully before you do anything.

Ask Miranda!

If you have a problem, our agony aunt **Miranda Miracle** can help you find a solution. Write to Miranda Miracle now. Here are this week's letters and Miranda's advice.

1

Dear Miranda,

I think I'm in love with my best friend's boyfriend! I can't stop thinking about him. He's so gorgeous! I don't know how he feels about me and I don't know what to do. I haven't told anyone about this and it's driving me crazy. If I tell my best friend, she'll hate me forever. Should I tell her boyfriend how I feel?

Please help me!

Alison (aged 15), Manchester

2

Dear Miranda,

My elder brother has been going out with his girlfriend for about two years and in fact they're now engaged. But recently he's started treating her badly. He's rude to her in front of other people and I know he sometimes lies to her. I love my brother but I don't want to see his girlfriend get hurt. She's a really nice person. If I get involved, it'll affect my relationship with my brother, but I can't just stand back and do nothing. What do you think I should do?

Carl (aged 16), London

3

Dear Miranda,

My mum and dad got divorced a few months ago. I live with my mum, but my dad lives nearby and my little brother and I still see him regularly (usually two or three times a week). The problem is that my mum wants us to move to Glasgow to be nearer her family. If we move, I'll lose all my friends from school and my brother and I won't be so near our dad. I'll be so upset if we have to leave Edinburgh. What do you suggest I do?

Stephanie (aged 14), Edinburgh

A

If you said something to your brother, it wouldn't necessarily affect your relationship with him. It depends what you say and how you say it. Don't say you're worried about his fiancée and that he's treating her badly. Say you're worried about him. Ask him if he's happy being engaged. Tell him that sometimes it seems like he doesn't like his girlfriend very much. Try to find out what the cause of his behaviour is. If he says everything's fine, then maybe you'll have to talk to his fiancée and find out how she feels. But talk to your brother first.

B

These situations often arise when parents split up and I want you to remember a few things. First, if you do move house, you won't be very far away from your father and your friends. It's not like you're moving to another country! Maybe you'll be able to stay with your dad every weekend, and then you'll also be able to see your friends. Secondly, don't forget you'll make lots of new friends at your new school, and you'll be nearer your mum's family. Most importantly, I think you should talk to your mum and dad about this. If you discuss it with them, I'm sure they'll understand how you feel and maybe they'll be able to come up with a solution that you're happy with. Good luck!

C

You're in a very difficult situation and I know you must be feeling very confused, but you have to think very carefully before you do anything. What do you want to achieve? If you manage to 'steal' your best friend's boyfriend, you'll end up losing your best friend. And if you tell her boyfriend how you feel and he doesn't feel the same way, you'll still probably lose your best friend. Do you really want that? If I were you, I'd try to forget him. Find a boyfriend of your own. Do you really have to destroy your best friend's happiness and your relationship with her to get a boyfriend? No. There are lots of gorgeous boys out there. Go out and meet one!

3 Read the letters and responses again and choose the correct answer A, B, C or D.

1 Alison thinks that her best friend's boyfriend
- **A** doesn't feel the same way about her.
- **B** is extremely good looking.
- **C** has put her in a difficult situation.
- **D** isn't really in love with her best friend.

2 Miranda believes that
- **A** Carl's brother will admit he's treating his fiancée badly.
- **B** Carl has to do something to solve his brother's problems.
- **C** if Carl discusses the situation with his brother, there will not necessarily be problems.
- **D** Carl will have to have a talk with his brother's fiancée.

3 Miranda thinks that Stephanie should
- **A** not see moving as a disaster.
- **B** argue with her parents.
- **C** stay in Edinburgh.
- **D** move to another country.

HOMEWORK!

Do the Reading exercise on page 49 of your Workbook.

DICTIONARY CORNER

Complete each sentence using a word or phrase from the problem page.

1 Maybe I should write to a(n) ______________________ ______________________ for some advice.

2 Daniel and Gloria have just got ______________________ . They're planning to get married sometime next year.

3 My parents got ______________________ last year. I live with my mum now but I see my dad every weekend.

4 I fell in ______________________ with her the first time I spoke to her.

5 Joe and Jo have just ______________________ up. It's really sad.

6 We've been going ______________________ with each other for almost a year.

7 I actually have a very good ______________________ with my mother-in-law.

Have your say!

Do you agree with Miranda's advice to Alison, Carl and Stephanie? What other advice would you give them?

HOMEWORK!

Do exercises 1 and 2 on page 50 of your Workbook.

G Grammar 1

Zero, first and second conditionals

Look at *Grammar database 15* page 188 before you do the exercises.

1 Match to make sentences.

1 If you have no-one to talk to,
2 If Baz asks me to go out with him,
3 If Liz ever left me,
4 If I were you,

a it would break my heart.
b I'd talk to your teacher about this.
c it's difficult to solve your personal problems.
d I'll say yes!

2 Match each of the sentences in exercise 1 with a description.

a This is an unlikely future situation. ______
b This is a piece of advice. ______
c This is a general truth. ______
d This is a possible or likely future situation. ______

3 Read the letter and choose the correct answer.

Dear Miranda,

I want to get my ears pierced but my parents won't let me. I'd look really cool if I (1) **have** / **had** pierced ears but if I (2) **do** / **will do** it without permission, my parents (3) **will** / **would** be really angry. I don't want to hurt or disobey them, but if they (4) **understand** / **understood** how old-fashioned their views are, they'd let me do it. If I (5) **don't** / **didn't** get my ears pierced, all my friends at school will laugh at me.

If you were me, what (6) **will** / **would** you say to them to make them agree?

Please help!

Jason (aged 13), Basildon

4 Write one word in each gap to complete Miranda's reply to Jason. Be careful! Short forms (eg *won't*) count as one word.

I understand how you feel, Jason, but if I were you, (1) ________ listen to Mum and Dad and do what they say – for now. You're only 13. That's quite young to get your ears pierced. If you wait a year or so before you ask them again, maybe they (2) ________ say yes! You say that everyone at school will laugh at you if you (3) ________ get your ears pierced now, but is that really true? I think your friends will understand (4) ________ you say to them, 'I really want to get my ears pierced when I'm a bit older.'

And – let's be honest – if your friends laugh at you and say you're not cool, they (5) ________ very good friends, are they?

HOMEWORK!
Do exercises 1, 2, 3, 4 and 5 on pages 50 and 51 of your Workbook.

Listening

1 1.29 **You are going to listen to part of a radio programme in which an agony aunt gives advice to callers. As you listen, decide whether these statements are true (T) or false (F).**

1 Jenny's problem is with a member of her family. T/F
2 Jenny and Adrian fight all the time. T/F
3 Miranda says that Jenny is wrong about something. T/F
4 Miranda's advice will solve Jenny's problem but not Adrian's. T/F
5 Jenny is going to make a suggestion to Adrian. T/F

2 **Look at these statements. Was the idea expressed by either Miranda or Jenny? Write Y for Yes and N for No.**

1 Jenny and Adrian are in love with each other.
2 Jenny and Adrian have always had serious disagreements.
3 It would be best if Jenny and Adrian split up.
4 Jenny and Adrian should always make decisions together.
5 Miranda's advice will definitely not work.

3 1.29 **Now listen again and check your answers.**

HOMEWORK!
Do the Listening exercise on page 54 of your Workbook.

DICTIONARY CORNER

Form nouns from the verbs and adjectives below. Write the nouns in the correct column.

Verbs
~~agree~~ • ~~appear~~ • argue • arrange • enjoy • entertain • excite • involve • perform • prefer • pretend • ~~relate~~

Adjectives
~~confident~~ • different • friendly • important • innocent • intelligent • patient • ~~possible~~ • responsible • violent

Nouns

-ship *relationship* ______
______
______

-ment *agreement* ______
______
______

-ance *appearance* ______
______
______

-ence *confidence* ______
______
______

-ity *possibility* ______
______
______

HOMEWORK!
Do exercises 1, 2, 3 and 4 on page 52 of your Workbook.

G Grammar 2

Time clauses

Look at *Grammar database 16* pages 188–189 before you do the exercises.

1 **Write the verbs in the correct form to complete the dialogue.**

Kelly: Hey Alana! I want to ask you something before the teacher (1) ________ (**come**) in. How are you and Adam?

Alana: Well, actually I think I'm going to tell Adam that I don't want to go out with him anymore.

Kelly: What? Wow! He's going to be really upset when you (2) ________ (**tell**) him.

Alana: I know, but I have to do it. And he'll be fine after he (3) ________ (**realise**) it's for the best.

2 **Choose the correct word or phrase to complete the dialogue.**

Kelly: So, why do you want to break up with Adam anyway?

Alana: Because I've fallen in love with Darren!

Kelly: Really?

Alana: Yes, so I've got to tell Adam (1) **until / as soon as / before** I can. It's not fair to wait (2) **when / as soon as / until** he finds out from someone else.

Kelly: So, when are you going to tell him? This evening?

Alana: No, he's coming to my house at eight in the morning, so I'll tell him (3) **while / until / as soon as** we walk to school together. And then (4) **while / until / as soon as** Darren gets to school, I'm going to tell him I can go out with him!

Kelly: You're going to have an interesting day tomorrow. Good luck!

3 **Write a word from the box in each gap to complete the dialogue.**

after • until • while

Kelly: Tell me all your news (1) ________ we walk to class! How did it go? Did you tell Adam? Are you going out with Darren now?

Alana: No. I couldn't do it. I've decided to stay with Adam, after all.

Kelly: What? Why?

Alana: Because he's so sweet! I can't wait (2) ________ I see him at lunchtime!

Kelly: And what about Darren?

Alana: I'll see him (3) ________ I have lunch with Adam. He'll be fine! He'll understand!

HOMEWORK!

Do exercises 1, 2, 3 and 4 on page 53 of your Workboo

Soundstation

Play the Soundstation Game. Your teacher will explain the rules to you.

1 I think it's **banned / bad**.
2 The **land's / lad's** a long way away!
3 What does **'trend' / 'tread'** mean?
4 Can you see the **bend / bed** from here?
5 It's a very strange **finger / figure**.
6 Did you buy 'The **Jungle / Juggle** Book'?

Speaking

1 Read the answers A–G that some students gave in an English exam interview and match them to the examiner's questions 1–9 below. There may be more than one answer for each question.

2 Tick (✔) the answers in exercise 1 you think are successful. Put a cross (✗) next to those that are not so successful. Then explain why.

3 In pairs, ask and answer the following questions.

1 Have you got any brothers and sisters? Do you get on well with them/him/her?

2 Do you come from a large family?

3 What's your best friend like?

4 What do your parents do?

5 How important is friendship to you? Why?

6 How would you describe your personality?

7 Are you closer to your friends or your family?

8 What job do you want to do when you're older?

9 Who would you go to if you had a serious personal problem?

Phrase Bank! P

A Well, my dad's a civil servant and my mum's a doctor.

B My family consists of four members.

C Indeed I do. My siblings are named Daz and Sharon.

D My father is currently employed by the state and my mother practises medicine.

E Yes.

F Yes, I've got a brother and a sister. My brother's called Simon – he's a year older than me – and my sister's called Fiona. She's only seven.

G There are four of us. Me, my sister and my mum and dad.

4 Turn to page 169. In pairs, do the role-play activity unit 8.

See *Speaking database* on page 174.

Use your English!

Use the word given in capitals to form a word that fits in the space in the same line.

Ask Miranda!

Dear Miranda,

I'm really lonely. I've been having lots of (1) ______ and	DISAGREE
(2) ______ with my parents recently and I don't have	ARGUE
anyone to talk to. I don't have any close (3) ______ with anyone	RELATE
my own age as I don't have the (4) ______ to make friends	CONFIDENT
easily. You see, I'm really shy. I know how important (5) ______	FRIEND
is, but what can you do when you don't have any friends?	
Do you have any (6) ______ as to what I could do? I thought	SUGGEST
that one (7) ______ might be to start wearing trendier clothes.	POSSIBLE
Do you think if I change my (8) ______ it will make a big	APPEAR
(9) ______ ? Please help! Everyone thinks I'm happy but I'm	DIFFER
not. And I can't keep up the (10) ______ much longer.	PRETEND

Writing

Making suggestions

1 **Match to make suggestions.**

1	How about	**a**	waiting until you're a bit older.
2	If I were you,	**b**	to wait until you're a bit older.
3	My advice would be	**c**	wait until you're a bit older.
4	Perhaps you should	**d**	waiting until you're a bit older?
5	I'd suggest	**e**	wait until you're a bit older?
6	Why don't you	**f**	I'd wait until you're a bit older.

2 **Rewrite each sentence beginning with the words given to make suggestions.**

1	*suggestion*:	talk to your parents about this	*I'd suggest* ______
2	*suggestion*:	tell Megan the truth	*How about* ______
3	*suggestion*:	get a weekend job and earn some money	*Why don't you* ______
4	*suggestion*:	apologise to Phil	*If I were you,* ______
5	*suggestion*:	stay calm and see what happens	*My advice would be* ______
6	*suggestion*:	explain to them how you feel	*Perhaps you should* ______

3 **Write suggestions for these situations.**

Your best friend wants to go to a pop concert but his/her parents won't let him/her.

Your brother really likes a girl in his class but is too scared to tell her.

Your sister thinks that her best friend might have lied to her.

Your pen friend wants a new computer for his/her birthday, but his/her parents have said they can't afford it.

Your cousin is thinking of leaving school at 16 and getting a job.

A friend of yours, who is 14 years old, really wants to get a tattoo.

HOMEWORK!

Do exercises 1, 2 and 3 on page 54 of your Workbook.

Get ready to write

Letter of advice

1 Read Jessica's letter and answer the questions.

1 Is the letter formal or informal?
2 Is Linda's problem the first thing Jessica mentions?
3 In which paragraph does Jessica express her opinion about the argument?
4 In which paragraph does Jessica make her suggestions?
5 How many suggestions does she make?
6 Underline her suggestions.

Dear Linda,

Thanks for your letter. I'm glad you passed your history test!

I was sorry to hear about the argument you had with your parents about your pocket money. I know you get less than most of your friends but if your parents can't afford to give you any more, I guess there's not much you can do about it (unfortunately!).

If I were you, I'd try not to argue about this. Why don't you get a part-time job, maybe on Saturdays or after school and earn a bit of extra money that way? It can be quite fun delivering newspapers. That's what I do! Or perhaps you should tell everyone that you don't want presents for Christmas or your birthday, but that you'd rather have money. And if you're careful how you spend it, you'll have more during the year for CDs and clothes and all the other things you want to buy.

Anyway, keep smiling whatever happens! I'd better go now as I've got loads of homework to do (as always!).

Write back soon!
Love,
Jessica

2 Read the writing task and answer the questions.

Below is part of a letter you have received from your pen friend. Write a **letter** to your pen friend giving your advice.

I really want to go on holiday with my friends this summer but my parents won't let me. They say I'm too young and that I have to stay with them. But I'm 14 years old and it's so boring at home in the summer! What do you think I should do? Any suggestions???

1 Do you think your pen friend's parents are right or wrong? Why?
2 What should your pen friend do? Write down two or three suggestions.

3 Make a plan in *Composition Planner 8* on page 159.

HOMEWORK!

You are now ready to write the first draft of your letter. Write between 120 and 150 words. When your teacher has commented on your letter, write the final version.

Revision
Unit 7–8

1 Conditionals

Complete the sentences using the correct form of the verbs in brackets. Use short forms where possible.

1 If you get the drinks ______________ (**I/get**) the popcorn!
2 If I was a Hollywood actor, ______________ (**I/live**) in Beverly Hills.
3 If your mother has a brother, you ______________ (**have**) an uncle.
4 I'll be so happy if Liana ______________ (**ask**) me to go out with her.
5 If you ______________ (**write**) a novel, what would it be about?
6 If you ______________ (**not have**) any brothers or sisters, you are an only child.

2 Word formation

Complete the letter using the correct form of the words in brackets.

Dear Toby,

This is just a quick note to thank you for all your hard work directing our play. I don't think we could have done it without your (1) ______________ (involve)! You had a wonderful (2) ______________ (relate) with all the members of the cast and you gave them the (3) ______________ (confident) to give a very professional (4) ______________ (perform). You taught them what (5) ______________ (entertain) really means. In rehearsals, we all appreciated your (6) ______________ (patient) at difficult moments. It really made a (7) ______________ (different)! There's a (8) ______________ (possible) that we'll put on another show later in the year. I hope you'll consider directing that one too.

All the best,

Carla

3 Modal perfect

Complete each second sentence using a modal from the box so that it means the same as the sentence before it.

can't • might • must • should • shouldn't

1 I'm sure you had a good time.
You ______________________________.
2 I'm sure we didn't go to the same party.
We ______________________________.
3 Being rude to Liz was not a good idea!
You ______________________________.
4 It's possible that Gary forgot.
Gary ______________________________.
5 I wish you had phoned me!
You ______________________________.

4 Relationship patterns and phrases

Write one word in each gap to complete the letter.

Dear Miranda,

My brother's 22 years old. Two years ago, he fell (1) ____________ love with a girl called Sue. They started going out (2) ____________ each other and after only a couple of months he got engaged (3) ____________ her. He's only been married (4) ____________ her for about a year, but now he says he wants a divorce. I can't believe it! What can I do to stop them splitting (5) ____________? I don't have a very close relationship (6) ____________ my sister-in-law, so I can't really talk to her. Is there anything I can say to my brother to make him change his mind? Please help!
Julie

5 Phrasal verbs

Choose the correct word to complete each sentence.

1 My parents are planning to **do / make / set** up the attic and turn it into a spare bedroom.
2 I'm going to have to **take / give / let** up ballet classes – I just don't have the time.
3 That's not true! You're **turning / putting / making** it up!
4 I'll **pick / take / turn** you up outside the art gallery.
5 I'm thinking of **doing / setting / making** up a club on the internet for people who enjoy science fiction.
6 Would you be able to **put / set / take** me up for a couple of nights?
7 We arranged to meet at seven o'clock, but he didn't **make / give / turn** up until half past eight!

6 Tenses with time words

Each of the phrases in bold is grammatically incorrect. Rewrite the phrase correctly.

1 She'll let us know as soon **as she'll hear** some news. ____________________
2 I'll wait for you while **you'll finish** getting ready. ____________________
3 Keith will call us before **he is going to get** the tickets. ____________________
4 Let's stay until the museum **will close**. ____________________
5 I'll call you after we **are arriving** at the restaurant. ____________________
6 When **you'll see** Andy next week, say 'hi' from me! ____________________

7 Vocabulary

Choose the correct answer A, B, C or D.

1 The movie is __ in America in the 1940s.
A placed **B** set **C** put **D** taken
2 You should go to the local __ club.
A youth **B** young **C** teenage **D** child
3 My best friend gave me a really nice __ of Cameron Diaz for my birthday.
A note **B** warning **C** notice **D** poster
4 Could you pass me the __ control?
A mobile **B** remote **C** distant **D** moving
5 I don't need a TV __ because I usually watch programmes and DVDs on my computer.
A machine **B** engine **C** set **D** player
6 The __ of the film was so confusing that I couldn't understand what was happening.
A fiction **B** action **C** plot **D** movement

8 *-ing* form or full infinitive

Complete each sentence using the *-ing* form or the full infinitive.

1 I must remember ____________________ (**take**) the wedding rings with me!
2 I'll never forget ____________________ (**go**) to that circus in Madrid.
3 The band stopped ____________________ (**play**) after only half an hour – it was terrible!
4 We stopped ____________________ (**have**) something to eat on the way home from the concert.
5 I really regret ____________________ (**split**) up with Sophie.
6 Tony tried ____________________ (**get**) tickets for the opera, but they'd already sold out.
7 He started off as an editor, but then he went on ____________________ (**become**) a highly successful director.

9

It's the Way You Tell 'em!

Get warmed up!

Discuss the following. Work in pairs or in groups.

- Are you good at telling jokes?
- What's your favourite comedy programme on TV?

Reading 1.30

1 **Quickly read the article. What is the article about?**

a how funny the life of a doctor can be
b how laughing can make you healthier
c how to be happy about getting more exercise
d why people find certain jokes funny

2 **Match each paragraph with a picture A–E.**

Laughter is the Best Medicine!

A

B

We all enjoy a good laugh, but did you know it is actually good for you? Amy Cameron tells us more!

1

We see or hear something funny and we laugh. It seems simple, doesn't it? Well, if I hadn't written this article, I wouldn't have learned just how interesting laughter is! When was the last time you laughed? The answer probably depends on how old you are! Some people say that young children smile 300 times a day and laugh 150 times. As we get older, our brains change and we start to think more before we laugh out loud. By the time we're adults, the number of times we laugh has fallen to about 20 a day. For many of us, something has to be absolutely hilarious before we start laughing.

2

It might be time to laugh more because guess what? Laughter can be good for you! When we feel unhappy, it affects our bodies. We don't seem to have any energy, and we notice any pain we have more. Being down even affects the way we sit – our head and shoulders drop and we don't feel like doing anything. Researchers have found that having a sense of humour doesn't just make you feel better. It also has a positive effect on your body! So how does it work?

3

We laugh much more when we are with other people. It brings us together and makes our relationships stronger. We tell each other jokes and then we can't keep a straight face when we hear the punch line. We feel good because we are sharing something with friends and it means they understand us. Scientists think laughter developed to bring groups of people closer together. If we hadn't developed laughter, we wouldn't have had an easy way of showing how close we are.

3 Read the article again and decide if the statements are true (T) or false (F).

1 The writer always knew how interesting laughter was. T/F
2 Adults laugh less because they're less healthy than children. T/F
3 Your body works better when you are unhappy. T/F
4 Laughter is a sign that we have good relationships. T/F
5 Laughing can help to stop you getting ill. T/F
6 Laughing is bad for your heart and makes it work too hard. T/F

HOMEWORK!

Do the Reading exercise on page 57 of your Workbook.

C

4

But we also feel good because our bodies produce chemicals that relax us and help us fight illness. And it's a form of exercise! As you laugh, you take in more oxygen, which makes you feel better. Your heart works harder and pumps blood around your body. In fact, one minute of laughing can get your heart working as hard as 10 minutes in the gym! Doctors are beginning to see that laughter brings many benefits.

D

5

So how can you bring more laughter into your life? Go to the cinema and watch a comedy, or get a DVD starring your favourite comedian. Or perhaps you prefer to watch a sitcom, with funny characters and situations. Find something funny and let yourself laugh! You'll feel better, and you'll be doing something healthy at the same time!

E

DICTIONARY CORNER

Complete each sentence using a word or phrase from the box.

comedian • comedy • hilarious • humour • laughter • loud • punch line • sitcom • straight face

1 I think Jim Carrey is ________________. He always makes me laugh.
2 Although the film is a ________________, there are some very sad scenes too.
3 Being a professional ________________ is actually very hard work.
4 The ________________ of a joke is the final, funny line.
5 You have to have a sense of ________________ to work here. Things are always going wrong!
6 A ________________ is a TV comedy series, like *Friends*, where a particular group of characters deal with situations in a humorous way.
7 I don't know how he can keep such a ________________ when he's telling jokes.
8 The book was so funny that I couldn't stop laughing out ________________.
9 The audience's ________________ was so loud, you could hear it outside the theatre!

Have your say!

Do you know any good jokes that you can tell in English? Tell your classmates a joke and see if they laugh!

HOMEWORK!

Do exercises 1 and 2 on page 58 of your Workbook.

G Grammar 1

Third conditional

Look at *Grammar database 17* page 189 before you do the exercises.

1 Read the joke and choose the correct answers to complete the sentences.

Yesterday, Bill went up in an aeroplane for the first time. Unfortunately, he fell out. Fortunately, he had a parachute. Unfortunately, it didn't open. Fortunately, there was a haystack below. Unfortunately, there was a pitchfork in the haystack. Fortunately, Bill missed the pitchfork. Unfortunately, he also missed the haystack.

1 If Bill **had / hadn't** opened the door, he **would / wouldn't** have fallen out of the plane.
2 If he **had / hadn't** fallen out of the plane, he **would / wouldn't** have been fine.
3 If he **didn't have / hadn't had** a parachute, he would **face / have faced** certain death.

2 Put the verbs in brackets into the correct form.

1 If his parachute ______________ (**open**), he would have landed quite safely.
2 If there hadn't been a haystack below, he ______________ (**be**) very worried.
3 If someone ______________ (**not put**) the pitchfork in the haystack, it ______________ (**be**) a great place to land.
4 If he ______________ (**not miss**) the pitchfork, he ______________ (**hurt**) himself really badly.
5 If he ______________ (**land**) on the haystack, he ______________ (**not break**) his leg.

3 Write sentences about these situations using the third conditional.

1 You didn't laugh at your friend's joke because he forgot the punch line.
If my friend ______________ the punch line, I ______________.
2 You didn't know your favourite sitcom was on so you didn't watch it.
If I ______________ my favourite sitcom was on, I ______________ it.
3 We knew the film was funny because we had seen it.
If we ______________ the film, we ______________ it was funny.
4 You got into trouble at school because you laughed in class.
If I ______________ in class, I ______________ into trouble at school.

HOMEWORK!
Do exercises 1, 2, 3 and 4 on pages 58 and 59 of your Workbook.

Listening

1 1.31 **You are going to listen to part of a radio programme. As you listen, circle the correct option to complete this notepad.**

1 Who probably listens to this programme?
young people / adults
2 Richard Wiseman's occupation:
journalist / scientist
3 Number of jokes received:
over 14,000 / 40,000
4 Gurpal Gosall's occupation:
psychiatrist / comedian
5 Number of people mentioned in joke:
2 / 3

2 Complete each sentence with one word in each gap. Try to remember what you heard.

1 Name of radio programme: ________ *Newsround*
2 Discovery: *world's* ________ *joke*
3 LaughLab: *a scientific* ________
4 Purpose of LaughLab: *investigate our sense of* ________
5 We laugh at: *people doing* ________ *things*
6 Joke involves: *two* ________
7 People in the joke speak on: *a* ________

3 1.31 **Listen again and check your answers.**

HOMEWORK!
Do the Listening exercise on page 62 of your Workbook.

DICTIONARY CORNER

1 Complete the phrases with the words from the box.

allow • be capable • depend • let
manage • prevent • succeed

1 ________ to do something
2 ________ in (doing) something
3 ________ of (doing) something
4 ________ someone from doing something
5 ________ on someone/(doing) something
6 ________ someone do something
7 ________ someone to do something

2 Match to make sentences.

1 The comedian didn't manage ___
2 The audience prevented ___
3 They didn't let ___
4 They didn't allow ___
5 They succeeded ___
6 I'm not sure he's capable ___
7 Being funny often depends ___

a on getting your timing right.
b him tell any more bad jokes.
c to make the audience laugh.
d of performing to such large audiences.
e him from finishing his act.
f in booing him off the stage.
g him to stay on stage.

Soundstation

1.32 **Listen to these sentences and circle the numbers you hear.**

1	**13 / 30**	5	**17 / 70**
2	**14 / 40**	6	**18 / 80**
3	**15 / 50**	8	**19 / 90**
4	**16 / 60**		

HOMEWORK!
Do exercises 1 and 2 on page 60 of your Workbook.

G Grammar 2

Relative clauses

Look at *Grammar database 18* pages 189–190 before you do the exercises.

1 Choose the correct relative pronoun to complete these jokes.

1 Did you hear the one about the guy **which / who** walked into a bar? He had to go to hospital. It was an iron bar.

2 Did you hear the one about the book **which / where** was called *How to Make a Million Euros*? It was written by Ivor Lottov Cash!

3 – That's the place **which / where** they have lots of old cows.
– What is it?
– A moo-seum!

4 Did you hear the one about the guy **who / whose** parents came from Iceland and Cuba? He was an Ice Cube!

2 Complete the jokes with a relative pronoun. Don't use *that*.

1 Did you hear about the big hole ______________ suddenly appeared in our street? The police are looking into it!

2 Do you know the reason ______________ Nino threw his clock out of the window? Because he wanted to see time fly!

3 Do you know what the person ______________ invented the door knocker got? A Nobel Prize!

4 What do you call a person ______________ toes are growing out of his knee? Tony!

3 Which of the gaps in exercise 2 could also be completed with *that*?

A

B

HOMEWORK!

Do exercises 1, 2, 3, 4, 5 and 6 on pages 60 and 61 of your Workbook.

Speaking

1 Look at these two pictures and answer the questions.

Picture A:

1 What is this a picture of?

2 What might the comedian they are watching be doing?

3 What is the audience doing?

4 How do you think the people in the audience feel?

Picture B:

5 What is this a picture of?

6 What are the people in the picture doing?

7 What do you think might be on TV?

8 How do you think the people in the picture feel?

9 What are the main similarities between the two pictures?

10 What are the main differences between the two pictures?

11 Which situation would you prefer to be in? Why?

2 Work in pairs. Student A, read these instructions to your partner and then listen to your partner's answer. Student B, follow these instructions. Then, swap over.

I'd like you to compare and contrast these two pictures and tell me which situation you would prefer to be in and why.

Phrase Bank!

I'd prefer to be … because …
I'd rather be … because …
I really like …, so I'd prefer/rather …
I'm not very keen on … , so I'd prefer/rather …

3 Look at these two pictures. Make brief notes about them and then do exercise 2 with these pictures.

____
____
____
____
____
____

Use your English!

Read the text and choose the correct answer A, B, C or D to complete it.

the pirate

I don't really have a very good sense of (1) ___ but I do love this (2) ___. It made me laugh so much, I've never forgotten it: Jake and Ben, (3) ___ were two old pirates, met for the first time. Jake had a wooden leg, a metal hook on the end of his arm and a black patch over one eye. They started talking about the days (4) ___ they had been at sea. Ben asked Jake how he'd got his wooden leg. 'I fell overboard,' said Jake. 'The other pirates (5) ___ to rescue me, but as they were pulling me out, a shark (6) ___ was rather (7) ___ on eating me for dinner bit my leg off.'

'And how did you get the hook?' asked Ben. 'I was having a sword fight with someone,' said Jake. 'I was trying to prevent him (8) ___ stealing all my money – well, I couldn't (9) ___ him to do that, could I? – but he cut my hand off with his sword in the fight.' 'And how did you lose your eye?' asked Ben. 'I'd (10) ___ not say. It's embarrassing.'

'Go on, tell me.'

'Well, I got a bit of sand in it,' said Jake.

'But you can't lose your eye because you get a bit of sand in it!' said Ben. 'Usually that's true, but it was my first day with the hook!'

	A	B	C	D
1	**A** punch line	**B** laughter	**C** comedy	**D** humour
2	**A** laugh	**B** joke	**C** fun	**D** comedian
3	**A** which	**B** whose	**C** that	**D** who
4	**A** which	**B** when	**C** where	**D** why
5	**A** managed	**B** succeeded	**C** allowed	**D** failed
6	**A** which	**B** whose	**C** where	**D** when
7	**A** happy	**B** interested	**C** fond	**D** keen
8	**A** to	**B** with	**C** from	**D** by
9	**A** accept	**B** let	**C** allow	**D** agree
10	**A** prefer	**B** like	**C** rather	**D** want

4 Turn to page 169. In pairs, do the role-play activity in unit 9.

See *Speaking database* on page 174.

Writing

Developing a narrative

1 **Read the short story below and write one sentence to say briefly what happens in the story.**

____

2 **Think of the story as having three parts – a beginning, a middle and an end. What happens in each part?**

At the beginning: ____________________________

In the middle: ____________________________

At the end: ____________________________

The Practical Joke

It was April 1st, so I decided to play a practical joke on my brother Dan. He is always playing jokes on me, so I thought it was a great opportunity to get my own back.

Early in the morning, while Dan was asleep, I crept into his room and put his watch and clock forward two hours. Then I changed the clocks in the living room and kitchen. I changed my own watch too.

When Dan woke up, he ran downstairs. 'What time is it?' he asked in a panic. 'It's quarter past 10,' I said. 'Why?' I found it difficult not to laugh, because I knew he had arranged to meet his girlfriend at 10 o'clock.

'I can't believe it. I've overslept! Debbie will kill me!' He immediately called Debbie on her mobile phone. 'Debbie, I'm really sorry,' he said. 'You've just woken me up,' said Debbie. 'It's quarter past eight!'

I started laughing, and Dan realised what I had done. He seemed rather annoyed, but I thought it was a great joke.

3 **Work in pairs. With your books closed, retell the story. Take it in turns to say what happens next.**

Student A: First of all, the writer decides to play a joke on his brother. He changes all the clocks in the house so they show the wrong time.

Student B: Then, …

HOMEWORK!

Do exercises 1, 2 and 3 on page 62 of your Workbook.

Get ready to write

Short story

1 Read the story on page 86 again and answer the questions.

1 What is the main tense used to tell the story?
2 Is the language in direct speech formal or informal?
3 What happens when you have direct speech from two people in the same paragraph?
  a the second person's follows straight on from the first person's
  b the second person's is on a new line
4 Is the story definitely true?

2 Read the writing task and make notes. Use your imagination!

> You have decided to enter a short story competition.
> The rules of the competition state that your story must **begin** with the words:
>
> *It was April 1st, so I decided to play a practical joke.*
>
> Write your **story** for the competition.

1 Write a brief summary of the plot in one or two sentences.
____
____

2 Now divide your story into three parts. Write what happens …
at the beginning: ______________________________
in the middle: ______________________________
at the end: ______________________________

3 Make a plan in *Composition Planner 9* on page 160.

HOMEWORK!
You are now ready to write the first draft of your story. Write between 120 and 180 words. When your teacher has commented on your story, write the final version.

10

Fair Play

Get warmed up!

Discuss the following. Work in pairs or in groups.

- Think of as many sports as you can in half a minute.
- Which ones have you done?
- Which sports that you've never done before would you like to try? Why?
- Should sport be more about winning or having fun?

Reading 2.01

1 **Read this information about courses at a sports centre. Match each course A–F with one of the photos 1–6.**

A ____ B ____ C ____

D ____ E ____ F ____

SPORTS CENTRE COURSES

A Diving for Beginners

There's a whole new world under the sea. Time passes very quickly as you explore rocks and watch fish. This course is perfect for people trying diving for the first time. You will learn the basic skills and go to different parts of the country every weekend to dive. Please note that you must be over 18 and in good physical health for this course.

B Volleyball

If you like to spend your time having fun playing sports with other people, then volleyball is for you. You'll join one of our teams of six players and practise at the sports centre twice a week in the afternoon. We provide all the equipment, so it doesn't cost you a penny!

C Basic Hang-gliding

It takes a long time to master hang-gliding, but you can learn the basics very quickly. It might be expensive, but the experiences will stay with you for the rest of your life. With classes on Thursdays and Sundays, you need to have some time available, and you need to be fit, but it's worth it! Hang-gliding will give you a whole new view of the world!

D Running for Fitness

If you wish you could find the time to get more exercise, look no further. Running is the perfect way to get yourself in shape. And it's so convenient – you can do it any time, anywhere! All you need is a big open space. Too many people, though, run incorrectly and risk their health. We'll teach you everything you need to know about this fun activity. Unfortunately, for the time being this course is adults only.

E Tennis for Beginners

Unlike many other sports, tennis can be fun for all the family to play together. You buy your own equipment and we provide the court and the lessons, which take place on Saturdays. If you have the time, why not take part in our Sunday Family Tournaments? Fun and prizes for old and young.

F Learn to Play Pool

Pool is a very popular game, and you don't need to be fit to play it! In fact, pool is perfect for anyone who is disabled, or who has difficulty with physical sports. Our classes take place in Hall 5 on Wednesday evenings, and we teach you everything you need to know. It's a great way to make friends, so what are you waiting for?

1

2

3

4

5

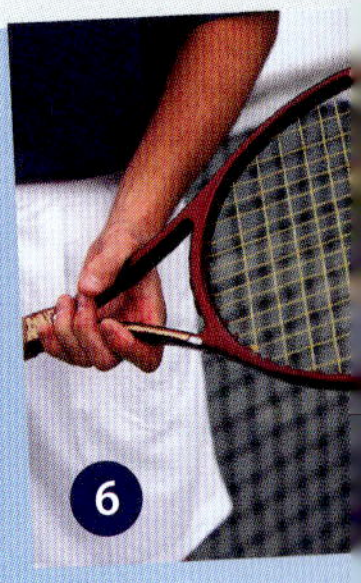
6

2 **Read the information again. For each course (A–F), decide which is a main point and which is a minor point and write *main* or *minor*.**

A 1 You can learn the basics of diving, which is an enjoyable hobby. ______
2 You can see fish when you go diving. ______

B 1 There are six people in a volleyball team. ______
2 Volleyball is a fun team sport. ______

C 1 Hang-gliding costs quite a lot of money. ______
2 Hang-gliding gives you memorable experiences. ______

D 1 You can go running where and when you choose. ______
2 Children can't take this course. ______

E 1 You can win prizes in the tournaments. ______
2 This is a good sport for people of all ages. ______

F 1 People with physical problems can do this sport. ______
2 You go to Hall 5 for the pool classes. ______

HOMEWORK!

Do the Reading exercise on page 63 of your Workbook.

3 **The people below are looking for a course to do. Decide which course would be the most suitable for each person.**

1 Jill should do ______________.
2 Hiro should do ______________.
3 Crystal should do ______________.
4 Mahesh should do ______________.

1

Jill works in an office and would like to get more exercise. Work takes up a lot of her time so she doesn't have much spare time during the week. She'd like to do something where she can take her two young daughters along.

2

Hiro loves team sports, and is looking for a new hobby. He likes learning new skills and has plenty of time, although he doesn't have much money to spend. He isn't able to travel far.

3

Crystal is interested in sport, but being in a wheelchair means that she isn't able to take part in some activities. She works part-time, so she is free in the evenings, but not at the weekend.

4

Mahesh is looking for a sport that he can do whenever he has a little free time. He works near a park, and he would like to be able to get some exercise there during his lunch break.

DICTIONARY CORNER

Complete the paragraph using a word from the list of courses or the descriptions of the people. Use the words in bold to help you.

I love skateboarding in my (1) **s**__________ **time**. I wish I **could** (2) **f**__________ **the time** to do it every day but unfortunately, homework (3) **t**__________ **u**__________ most of my **time** at the moment, so I don't usually (4) **h**__________ **the time** to go skateboarding after school. In fact, **for the time** (5) **b**__________, until I've taken all my exams, I can only do it at the weekend. But I (6) **s**__________ hours every Saturday and Sunday practising new tricks. I find that **time** (7) **p**__________ so **quickly** when you're having fun. **It** usually (8) **t**__________ quite a long **time** to become a really good skateboarder. I kept falling off when I tried it **for the** (9) **f**__________ **time**!

Have your say!

Which courses would/wouldn't you like to do? Why?

HOMEWORK!

Do exercises 1 and 2 on page 64 of your Workbook.

G Grammar 1

Revision of conditionals and *unless*

Look at *Grammar database 19* pages 190–191 before you do the exercises.

1 Match to make sentences.

1 The match would have been a draw
2 It'll be too dangerous to go cycling
3 I'd buy some Rollerblades
4 Why don't you try fishing
5 People often join a gym
6 I'll come swimming with you tomorrow

a unless I'm busy.
b if I had enough money.
c if the roads are still icy.
d if the goalie hadn't scored an own goal.
e if you don't like team sports?
f if they want to get fit.

2 Match each sentence you made in exercise 1 with a description.

a a general truth ______
b a suggestion ______
c a hypothetical present situation ______
d real, possible future situations ______ ______
e a hypothetical past ______

3 Rewrite each sentence beginning with *If*.

1 We won't go skiing tomorrow unless there's a lot of snow.
____
____

2 I don't go horse-riding more often because I don't have a horse.
____
____

3 I didn't play cricket with them because I didn't know the rules.
____
____

4 Golfers who win a professional tournament usually win a lot of money.
____
____

HOMEWORK!
Do exercises 1, 2, 3, 4 and 5 on pages 64 and 65 of your Workbook.

DICTIONARY CORNER

1 Complete each sentence using a verb from the box.

beat • draw • lose • play • score • win (× 2)

1 You ________ / ________ / ________ a game or a match.
2 You ________ another team if you win.
3 You ________ a prize or a trophy.
4 You ________ a goal.
5 If two teams get the same score, they ________ .

2 Complete the sentences using the information below and the words in the box. Put the verbs in the past simple.

FOOTBALL RESULTS
Premier League
Chelsea **2** – Arsenal **4**
Manchester United **3** – Liverpool **3**

beat • draw • lose • play • score • win

1 Arsenal and Chelsea ________ a very exciting game.
2 Arsenal ________ Chelsea by four goals to two.
3 Arsenal ________ the match and Chelsea ________ .
4 Both Manchester United and Liverpool ________ three goals.
5 Manchester United and Liverpool ________ three all.

HOMEWORK!
Do the Dictionary Corner exercise on page 66 of your Workbook.

Listening

1 Label the pictures with a word from the box.

commentator • jockey • player • referee • spectator

a ______________

b ______________

c ______________

d ______________

e ______________

2 2.02 Listen to five people talking about sport. As you listen, match each person with a picture.

Speaker 1: ______ Speaker 2: ______ Speaker 3: ______
Speaker 4: ______ Speaker 5: ______

3 2.03 Now listen again. Circle the correct word or phrase to complete each statement. The extracts are in a different order this time.

1 Speaker 1 believes his role is to ________ the team.
 A criticise
 B lead
 C support

2 Speaker 2 talks about having to ________ different things.
 A say
 B watch
 C learn

3 Speaker 3 mentions the different ________.
 A people he works with
 B horses he rides
 C sounds he hears

4 Speaker 4 is ________ the team's record.
 A pleased with
 B disappointed with
 C surprised by

5 Speaker 5 describes players ________ him.
 A cheating
 B respecting
 C disagreeing with

HOMEWORK!

Do the Listening exercise on page 68 of your Workbook.

Grammar 2

so, such, too, enough

Look at *Grammar database 20* pages 191–192 before you do the exercises.

1 Choose the correct word or phrase to complete the paragraph.

They've just opened a huge sports shop near the town centre. It's (1) **such / so / too** big that you need at least two hours to look round it properly. In fact, it's probably (2) **enough big / big enough** to put an athletics track inside! And it's got (3) **such / so / too** a wide range of sporting equipment. It's not (4) **enough / too / such** expensive either. I went there with my dad. He loves fishing and he bought (5) **such / so / too** much stuff we had to have two trolleys!

They had a great table tennis table but I didn't have (6) **enough money / money enough** for that. I'll have to save up!

2 Write a word or phrase from the box in each gap to complete the sentences.

enough • many • much • so • so many
such • too • too much

1 There are ________ bikes that I don't know which one to choose!
2 This one's ________ expensive for me, unfortunately.
3 There's so ________ choice! I don't know where to start!
4 There are just too ________ bikes to choose from! It's impossible!
5 I haven't got ________ money to buy that bike.
6 That one costs ________ money.
7 This bike's ________ heavy that it's difficult to pick up.
8 This is ________ a nice bike!

3 Complete each sentence using the word given so that it means the same as the sentence before it.

1 These trainers aren't big enough for me. **too**
These …
2 It was such an expensive tracksuit that I didn't buy it. **so**
The …
3 That wetsuit is so cool! **such**
That …
4 I've got so many baseball caps
I never know which one to wear! **such**
I've got …
5 It's too cold to wear a bikini! **enough**
It's …
6 There were too few ice skates for all of us. **enough**
There …
7 They were such cheap swimming costumes that I bought two. **so**
The …

HOMEWORK!
Do exercises 1, 2, 3, 4, 5 and 6 on pages 66 and 67 of your Workbook.

Soundstation

1 Play the Soundstation Game. Your teacher will explain the rules to you.

13 / 30	15 / 50	17 / 70	19 / 90
14 / 40	16 / 60	18 / 80	

I scored ________________ goals this season!

2 Can you say these numbers in English?

- 113
- 11615
- 6552370
- 2440
- 819918

3 2.04 Listen and check if you were right.

Speaking

1 Imagine you are a journalist. You are going to interview a professional sportsperson. Try to think of at least three questions to add to the list below.

Questions

1 What was your greatest professional moment?
2 And what was your worst moment?
3 How do you feel when you are running/racing, etc?
4 What are your hopes and ambitions for the future?
5 Do you do any other sports?
6 ______
7 ______
8 ______

3 In pairs, interview each other. One of you is the journalist and the other is the sportsperson. When you have finished, swap roles.

Phrase Bank!

That was when I won/lost …
I really like the feeling of excitement from …
I'd love to …
Well, I do … as well.

See *Speaking database* on page 174.

2 Imagine you are a professional sportsperson and fill in this information card.

INFORMATION CARD

Name: ______
Sport: ______
Current team (if applicable): ______
Greatest professional moment: ______
Worst professional moment: ______
Feelings when doing sport: ______
Future ambitions/hopes: ______
Other sports/hobbies: ______

Use your English!

Complete each sentence using the word given, so that it means the same as the sentence before it. Use no more than five words.

1 I didn't see the match because my TV was broken. **if**
I would ______ my TV hadn't been broken.
2 If you don't obey the rules, I'm not going to play. **unless**
I'm not going to play ______ the rules.
3 The weights were so heavy that Sam couldn't lift them. **too**
The weights were ______ lift.
4 You're too young to take up free diving! **enough**
You're ______ up free diving!
5 We've got too few people to make a team. **enough**
We ______ to make a team.
6 The race was so exciting that I forgot to call you. **such**
It was ______ that I forgot to call you.
7 They're such talented gymnasts that I think they'll be in the Olympics®. **so**
Those gymnasts ______ that I think they'll be in the Olympics®.
8 Mario trains for three hours every evening. **spends**
Mario ______ every evening.

Writing

Awareness of purpose

1 **Look at these extracts from students' compositions. Match each extract 1–5 with what the writer is doing.**

1 Not all children get enough exercise at home. Because of this, I believe that all children should do a sport at school at least three times a week. __

2 Costs
A monthly subscription to the gym costs €30. Non-members can use the gym for €8 per day. __

3 I would be grateful if you could let me know what time the race starts. __

4 It was a cold, dark night, and Mr Jenkins was reading in bed. Suddenly, the lights went off. __

5 I loved the photo you sent me of your dog. Here's a photo of my cat! She's called Twinkle. __

a presenting information so it's easy to find
b responding to and giving personal information
c discussing a subject in a logical and formal way
d trying to interest and entertain
e asking for information in a polite and formal way

2 **Look at the model compositions in units 1–7 and tick (✔) the appropriate boxes in the table.**

The writer wants to …	ask for information …	interest and entertain the reader	present information so it's easy to find	respond to and give personal information	discuss a subject in a logical and formal way
unit 1 page 15 informal letter					
unit 2 page 23 short story					
unit 3 page 33 essay					
unit 4 page 41 informal email					
unit 5 page 51 formal letter					
unit 6 page 59 report					
unit 7 page 69 article					

HOMEWORK!
Do exercises 1 and 2 and on page 68 of your Workbook.

Get ready to write

Informal letter

1 Read the letter and answer the questions.

1 What sporting event is Jackie talking about?
2 Which races is she in?
3 How does she feel about them?
4 Why does she feel this way?
5 Does she only talk about these events in her letter?
6 What reason does she give for ending the letter?

Dear Jill,

Hi! How's it going? Thanks for your last letter. I'm really glad you did well in your guitar exam. Who knows? One day, you might be in a pop group!

I'm fine, but I've got a very busy week ahead. Next Saturday, we've got our school Sports Day and I'm in the 100m and 200m races. I REALLY want to win – you know I won both of them last year – so I'm training really hard all week. I'm actually a bit worried about it, as there's a new girl at school this year, Belinda Johnson, and she's a really good runner. I think it's going to be a tough race.

I've got some other very important news too. My mum and dad say you can definitely come and stay this summer if it's OK with your parents. I really hope they say yes!

Well, I'd better go now. I've got to do some more training – I don't want to lose on Saturday!!! I'll let you know how it goes. Wish me luck!

Take care, and write back soon!

Lots of love,
Jackie

2 Read the writing task and make notes to answer the questions below.

You're getting ready to take part in an important sporting event. Write a **letter** to an English-speaking friend about the event. Say how you are preparing for it and how you feel about it. Mention any other news you have as well.

1 What's the sporting event?
______
2 When is it?
______
3 What exactly are you doing in the event?
______
4 How are you preparing for it?
______
5 How do you feel about it?
______
6 Why?
______
7 What other news do you have?
______

3 Make a plan in *Composition Planner 10* on page 161.

HOMEWORK!

You are now ready to write the first draft of your letter. Write between 120 and 180 words. When your teacher has commented on your letter, write the final version.

Revision Units 9–10

1 Conditionals

Each of the words or phrases in bold is grammatically incorrect. Rewrite the word or phrase correctly.

1 If you **had been** a comedian, what kind of jokes would you tell? ____________
2 You **laugh** out loud if you watch this film! ____________
3 If I **wasn't** nervous, my comedy act would have been better. ____________
4 If people find jokes funny, they usually **will laugh**. ____________
5 If his performance **won't improve**, he'll never be famous. ____________
6 If you **will get** the punch line wrong, the joke's a disaster. ____________
7 We **would have** more fun if we'd gone to see a comedy. ____________
8 I **would have shown** more sitcoms if I worked in TV. ____________

2 *so, such, too, enough*

Write *so*, *such*, *too* or *enough* in each gap to complete this paragraph.

my gym

The gym I go to – 'Frank's Keep-Fit Centre' – is (1) ____________ a nice place and Frank and his wife are (2) ____________ kind-hearted people. In fact, all the staff there are (3) ____________ friendly. And that's the problem. The gym is (4) ____________ good that everyone wants to go there, and there just isn't (5) ____________ room for everyone. I don't think Frank thought carefully (6) ____________ about how successful it was going to be. Last year was fine, but this year there are (7) ____________ many members to fit in one small gym. You have to wait (8) ____________ a long time to get to use the equipment. A 20-minute wait to use the bench press is just (9) ____________ long for me! I don't have (10) ____________ time to stand around. So, I'm going to have to go to another gym. It's (11) ____________ a shame, but if I find a gym that no-one else likes, I'll be able to use the equipment whenever I want!

3 Relative clauses

Choose the correct word to complete each sentence.

1 Charlie Chaplin, **which** / **who** / **where** is really respected, has never really made me laugh.
2 This is the joke book **which** / **who** / **whose** I told you about.
3 That's the cinema **which** / **who** / **where** we saw that Steve Martin movie.
4 Do you remember that time **who** / **when** / **which** I entered that joke-telling competition?
5 There are many reasons **that** / **where** / **why** I could never be a professional comedian.
6 Did you hear about the man **whose** / **who** / **which** nose ran and feet smelled? He was standing upside down!

4 Patterns

Tick (✔) the correct pattern in each pair. Put a cross (✘) next to the incorrect one.

1 **a** manage to do ___ **b** manage doing ___
2 **a** be capable to do ___ **b** be capable of doing ___
3 **a** allow someone do ___ **b** allow someone to do ___
4 **a** let someone do ___ **b** let someone to do ___
5 **a** prevent someone from doing ___ **b** prevent someone to do ___
6 **a** succeed to do ___ **b** succeed in doing ___
7 **a** depend on doing ___ **b** depend to do ___

5 Time patterns and phrases

Write a word from the boxes in each gap to complete the sentences.

finds • passes • spends • takes

1 Time __________ so quickly when you're having fun!
2 Dina __________ about two hours every evening working out.
3 Training for the Olympics® __________ up most of my time at the moment.
4 I don't know how he __________ the time to go sailing so often.

being • spare • long • first

5 It can take a __________ time to become good at a sport.
6 What do you like doing in your __________ time?
7 I went free diving for the __________ time in my life last weekend. It was fantastic!
8 I'm quite happy being an amateur rugby player for the time __________.

6 Sport vocabulary

Match to make sentences.

1 We played ___
2 I thought we were going to draw ___
3 Then we scored ___
4 We beat ___
5 We won ___ / ___

a another goal.
b the other team!
c the competition.
d football last week.
e the trophy.
f two all.

7 *if* and *unless*

Complete each second sentence so that it means the same as the sentence before it.

1 If I don't get some exercise soon, I'll get fat.
Unless __________.
2 If I didn't like making people laugh, I wouldn't be a comedian.
I wouldn't be a comedian unless __________.
3 She wouldn't have won unless she'd been the best player.
If __________.
4 We'll go diving at the weekend unless the weather's bad.
If the weather's bad, __________.
5 We'll go hang-gliding at the weekend unless the weather's bad.
If the weather's not bad, __________.

11

The Land of Plenty?

Get warmed up!

Discuss the following. Work in pairs or in groups.

- Think of as many geographical features as you can, eg *mountain, lake,* etc.
- Is it important to care about protecting the environment? Why?
- In what ways can people damage the environment?
- Is there anything we can do to stop this happening?

Reading 2.05

1 Read the leaflet quickly and answer the questions. Ignore the gaps in the text for now.

1 When was the world's first landfill site opened?
2 How much European rubbish will be put in the ground next year?
3 How much European rubbish will be recycled next year?
4 How long does it take for plastic to degrade?
5 What are the 3 Rs?
6 What number can you call for more information?

WE'RE TALKING RUBBISH!

You're hungry, so you buy a packet of crisps. You eat the crisps and throw away the packet. No problem, right? Wrong!

The disposal of rubbish has been a social and environmental problem for thousands of years. The first landfill site in history was opened by the Ancient Greeks in about 2500BC. They realised they had a problem with rubbish in Athens, so they dug a big hole several kilometres outside town, where all the rubbish was thrown. 1 ______ Next year, over 80% of Europe's rubbish will be dumped in landfill sites and less than 20% will be recycled. So what's the problem with that?

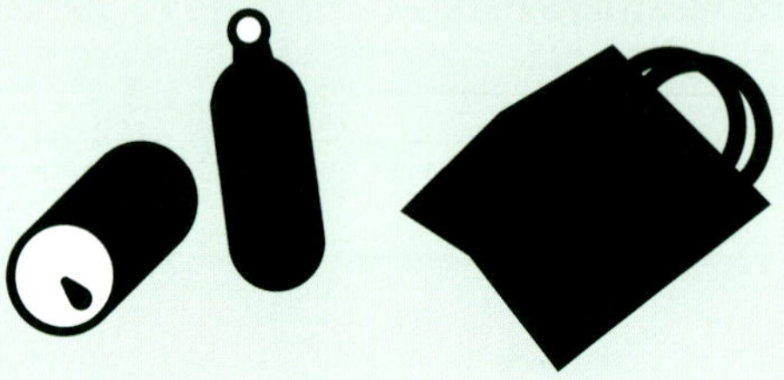

Landfill Sites

The main problem is that we're producing a huge amount of rubbish each year – millions and millions of tons of it – and the existing landfill sites are nearly full. Where are we going to put all our rubbish in the future? Finding new sites isn't easy. Farmland and the countryside have to be destroyed – and that's bad for the environment and for the farming industry. And remember that crisp packet that was thrown away? That's made of plastic. Plastic takes about 450 years to degrade. 2 ______ That's also bad for the environment. We can't burn a lot of it, because the gases that are given off pollute the air. So what can we do?

Remember the 3Rs

We can all do our bit to help solve the problem by remembering the 3Rs: reduce, reuse and recycle.

Reduce! Reuse! Recycle!

Reduce: We've all got to try to reduce the amount of rubbish we throw away. We can do that by buying unpackaged goods, like fruit and vegetables, rather than goods which are wrapped and packaged in plastic. 3 ______ The less that's thrown away, the more we help the environment.

2 Five sentences have been removed from the leaflet. Write the letter of the missing sentence in each gap. There is one sentence you don't need to use.

A In other words, a crisp packet takes hundreds of years to disappear.

B Because of this, millions of tons of rubbish are thrown into the sea.

C Try to use things as many times as possible before you throw them away.

D That means there's less pollution going into the atmosphere from the factories.

E And we still generally use the same solution today.

F Also, try not to buy disposable products like single-use cameras and non-rechargeable batteries.

HOMEWORK!

Do the Reading exercise on page 70 of your Workbook.

Reuse: 4 ______ For example, you're given some plastic bags at the supermarket to carry your food home in. Do you use them again? Most people don't. It would be much better for the environment if they did. Your kids have grown out of their old clothes. Don't just put them in the bin – think about giving them to charity. Somebody probably wants them.

Recycle: Glass, paper, plastic – they can all be recycled. Recycling cuts down the waste going to landfill sites and also means factories need to produce fewer new bottles and packets and paper. 5 ______ It also leads to fewer trees being cut down to make paper.

Protecting the environment is not a load of old rubbish!

For further information on your nearest Recycling Centre and Bottle Bank, phone 08081234567 free of charge **NOW!**

3 Look at these sentences from exercise 2 again and say what the words in bold refer to.

1 **That** means there's less pollution going into the atmosphere from the factories.

____

2 And we still generally use **the same solution** today.

____

DICTIONARY CORNER

Match the words 1–9 with their definitions a–i .

1 disposal ____
2 countryside ____
3 environment ____
4 factory ____
5 pollution ____
6 bin ____
7 recycling ____
8 waste ____
9 bottle bank ____

a the area outside towns and cities with fields, etc

b a building where large quantities of things are made with machines

c chemicals, etc that damage air, water and land

d a container to put bottles in for recycling

e the process of getting rid of something

f a more formal and scientific word for *rubbish*

g a container for putting rubbish in

h the world around us, especially the natural world

i the process of turning rubbish into new products

Have your say!

- Do you agree that the problem of rubbish disposal is very serious?
- What do you think of the 3 Rs? Are they a good idea?
- What other solutions can you think of?

HOMEWORK!

Do exercises 1 and 2 on page 71 of your Workbook.

G Grammar 1

The passive

Look at *Grammar database 21* pages 192–193 before you do the exercises.

1 Find the mistake in each sentence and write the word correctly.

1 The recycling scheme has introduced last year. ________________
2 The scheme is running by the local council. ________________
3 It is supported from the government. ________________
4 Millions of trees in the world's rainforests have being cut down. ________________
5 Less than 20% of rubbish will have recycled this year. ________________

2 Put the verbs in brackets into the passive.

Every spring, before the summer season starts, our local beach (1) ________________ (**clean**) by volunteers. All the rubbish (2) ________________ (**pick up**) and (3) ________________ (**put**) into big bags. Later, it (4) ________________ (**separate**) into things that can (5) ________________ (**recycle**), like glass and paper, and things that have to (6) ________________ (**throw**) away. Last year, 10 large bin bags (7) ________________ (**take**) to the local recycling centre. I always help with the cleaning. The beach (8) ________________ (**make**) safer and cleaner for all of us and it's good for the environment if some of the rubbish (9) ________________ (**recycle**) too.

3 Rewrite each sentence in the passive. If there's a star (*) at the end of the sentence, don't use *by*.

1 They dumped a lot of rubbish into the sea last year.*
2 Exhaust fumes from cars pollute the atmosphere.
3 Loud motorbikes annoy many people.
4 They have introduced a new recycling scheme.*
5 Factories are pumping a lot of waste into rivers.*
6 They're going to build a new airport here next year.*

4 Read the text and find eight mistakes. Underline them and rewrite them correctly.

RECYCLING

What happens to the stuff you recycle? First of all, it has taken to a special place called a Materials Recovery Facility (MRF). At the MRF, the material is sort into different types, such as plastic, paper, card and glass. Let's look at what happens to the plastic. The plastic must is sorted again because there are many different kinds of plastic and you can't mix them together for recycling. You might be surprised to learn that plastic bottles not used to make more plastic bottles! Drinks bottles, for example, is made of PET. The PET melted at high heat and is turned into a thread, which is use in new clothes. The plastic in milk bottles is different. They be made out of HDPE. HDPE is used to make a kind of 'plastic wood' and becomes plastic fences and garden furniture.

1 ________________
2 ________________
3 ________________
4 ________________
5 ________________
6 ________________
7 ________________
8 ________________

HOMEWORK!

Do exercises 1, 2, 3 and 4 on pages 71 and 72 of your Workbook.

Listening

1 Write a word from the box in each gap to complete the sentences.

CFCs • environmentally • green • rural • surroundings • urban

1 If you are ________________, you care about the environment.
2 If you live in beautiful ________________, you live in a beautiful place.
3 If you live in a(n) ________________ environment, you live in the countryside.
4 If you live in a(n) ________________ environment, you live in a town or a city.
5 If a product is ________________ friendly, it is designed not to damage the environment.
6 ________________ are a type of gas which can damage the ozone layer.

2 2.06 You are going to listen to a programme about the environment. For each person, choose the main point they make. Be careful! They might mention both ideas.

1 Tom
  A CFCs weren't very dangerous.
  B We will find a way to solve our problems.
2 Jackie
  A It's hard to be green because it's expensive.
  B People in the countryside blame people in the town.
3 Oliver
  A We should think more carefully about how we live.
  B We should eat more fruit and vegetables.

3 2.06 Now listen again and decide if the statements are true (T) or false (F).

1 Tom believes that recycling is a waste of time. T/F
2 Tom says that scientists will solve environmental problems. T/F
3 Jackie says it's difficult for people in the country to protect the environment. T/F
4 Jackie says that we don't need to worry about recycling paper. T/F
5 Oliver thinks fruit is more environmentally friendly than meat. T/F
6 Oliver says that we would waste less food if we planned better. T/F

HOMEWORK!
Do the Listening exercise on page 75 of your Workbook.

DICTIONARY CORNER

Complete each sentence using the correct form of the phrasal verbs.
Look at the *Phrasal verb database* on page 172 to help you.

break out • bring out • fall out • hand out • look out • make out • put out • turn out

1 I can't ________________ what that sign says. Can you read it from here?
2 The forest fire ________________ by local firemen.
3 An elephant ________________ of the zoo last night.
4 ________________! Don't stand on that broken glass!
5 Have you two ________________ again? You're always arguing!
6 The new road ________________ to be a disaster for the local environment.
7 Why don't they ________________ a cheap, solar-powered car?
8 I'm going to ________________ some leaflets in the town centre.

HOMEWORK!
Do exercises 1 and 2 on page 73 of your Workbook.

Grammar 2

The causative

Look at *Grammar database 22* pages 193–194 before you do the exercises.

1 Match to make sentences.

1 We've had
2 Our neighbours get
3 Kathy's having
4 Are you going to have

a that wasps' nest removed?
b her car repaired at the moment.
c their food delivered by the local supermarket.
d a solar-powered water heater installed on our roof.

2 Choose the correct answer A, B or C.

1 We ___ once a week and our rubbish collected once a fortnight.
A collect our recycling
B have our recycling collected
C have collected our recycling

2 My mum ___ so they're more environmentally friendly.
A is having changed the lights
B has the lights changed
C is having the lights changed

3 We are going ___ and it's made of plastic wood!
A to have new garden furniture delivered
B to deliver new garden furniture
C to have delivered new garden furniture

4 Our neighbours ___ on their roof to provide all their electricity.
A install solar panels
B get installed solar panels
C have had solar panels installed

5 I didn't ___ last year and now it's producing a lot of smoke.
A get serviced my car
B get my car serviced
C get my car to service

3 Rewrite each sentence in the causative form. If there's a star (*) at the end of the sentence, don't use *by*.

1 An expert tested their drinking water.
____

2 An electrician checks her smoke alarms once a year.
____

3 Someone is redecorating our flat at the moment.*
____

4 A vet has examined Megan's pet tarantula.
____

5 Someone's going to cut down the tree in my grandparents' garden.*
____

HOMEWORK!
Do exercises 1, 2, 3, 4 and 5 on pages 73 and 74 of your Workbook.

Speaking

1 A new airport has just been built in your area. The local council aren't sure yet what to do with the old airport. Look at the suggestions they have made and, for each one, think of one benefit and one drawback.

A create a landfill site
one benefit: ______________
one drawback: ______________

B create a park
one benefit: ______________
one drawback: ______________

C build new houses
one benefit: ______________
one drawback: ______________

2 Work in pairs or in groups. Discuss what should be done with the site. Use your ideas from exercise 1 and the phrases below to help you.

3 Turn to page 169. In pairs, do the role-play activity unit 11.

See *Speaking database* on page 174.

Phrase Bank!

P

Agreeing

I (completely) agree (with you, Tony) because/as …

I (completely) agree that …

Exactly!

Absolutely!

That's a very good point.

Disagreeing

I'm afraid I disagree/don't agree (with you, Tony) because/as …

I have to disagree because/as …

But what about …?

Surely, though, …

Soundstation

2.07 You are going to listen to nine sentences. As you listen, circle the words you hear.

1 **sight / site**
2 **sun / son**
3 **meet / meat**
4 **where / wear**
5 **not / knot**
6 **write / right**
7 **sure / shore**
8 **one / won**
9 **ate / eight**

Use your English!

Read the quiz and choose the correct answer A, B, C or D to complete it.

How (1) ________ are you?

Do this quick quiz to find out how much ***you*** *help to protect the environment!*

- Do you (2) ________ all your used bottles, packets, boxes and paper?
- Do you just throw your rubbish in the (3) ________ (or on the floor!) and not worry about it?
- Do you buy environmentally (4) ________ products, even if they're a bit more expensive?
- Do you frequently buy (5) ________ razors, cameras, etc?
- Do you care about the rainforests being cut (6) ________?
- Do you think that an urban (7) ________ is always better than a (8) ________ one?
- Do you think that cars (9) ________ the atmosphere with their exhaust (10) ________?
- Do you think that the car is the best invention ever?

If you answer 'yes' to most of the green questions, you're a real friend of the Earth.
If you answer 'yes' to the red ones, you've got a lot to learn!

	A	B	C	D
1	blue	green	red	yellow
2	recycle	reduce	repeat	recharge
3	box	container	basket	bin
4	friendly	kind	caring	nice
5	disposing	disposal	disposed	disposable
6	off	up	down	out
7	environment	surroundings	countryside	farmland
8	real	royal	regal	rural
9	annoy	injure	pollute	hurt
10	fumes	gas	air	clouds

Writing

Complex sentences

1 Which word or phrase in bold in the sentences 1–5 introduces …

- **a** a reason?
- **b** a result?
- **c** an example?
- **d** a suggested solution?
- **e** a contrast between two different ideas?

1 Recycling bottles, paper and plastic **leads to** a reduction in the amount of waste which is dumped in landfill sites.

2 Those people who travel everywhere by car **should be** encouraged to use public transport more often.

3 **Although** people often talk about recycling, too few people recycle on a regular basis.

4 Many people continue to buy and use harmful products **because** they do not realise that the environment is in danger.

5 Many household products, **such as** deodorants and fridges, used to contain harmful CFCs.

2 Write a word or phrase from exercise 1 in each gap to complete the sentences.

1 There are several organisations, ________________ Greenpeace and Friends of the Earth, which campaign to protect the environment.
2 Recycling in some areas is difficult ________________ recycling bins are not provided by the local council.
3 The government ________________ do more to encourage factories not to pollute rivers.
4 An increase in the number of cars on our roads ________________ an increase in the amount of air pollution.
5 Landfill sites are still in use in many areas, ________________ we are trying to find alternative ways to dispose of rubbish.

3 Join each pair of sentences to make one sentence. Use the word in bold.

1 There was an Environmental Awareness campaign.
More people started to recycle their rubbish. **led**

____

2 The animal's habitat was destroyed. It became extinct. **because**

____

3 Some products have become more environmentally friendly in recent years.
Deodorants and fridges are examples of these. **such**

____

4 There are many bins in the city centre. People still throw rubbish on the ground. **Although**

____

5 Environmental studies is not a subject at school. I think that is a shame. **should**

____

HOMEWORK!

Do exercises 1 and 2 on page 75 of your Workbook.

Get ready to write

Essay

1 Read the essay and answer the questions.

1 Which word(s) or phrase(s) in the essay:
   a introduces two contrasting ideas?
   ____
   b links a cause and an effect?
   ____
   c introduce an example?
   ____
   ____
2 Is the essay formal or informal?
3 Does the writer use short forms (*don't*, *won't*, etc)?

Although we live on the Earth and have control over much of our environment, the Earth does not belong to us. It is also home for plants, animals, insects, birds and fish, and it will be home for future generations of humans. Because of this, we have a responsibility to protect the environment.

Most of the Earth's major environmental problems, such as the holes in the ozone layer, have been caused by humans and we are the only ones able to solve the problems. We have to start recognising that our actions can lead to environmental damage.

Education is extremely important. For example, if people learn to recycle their waste, instead of just throwing it away, we will not have to destroy the countryside. Landfill sites will not have to be constructed, and factories, which pollute the atmosphere, will not have to produce so many new products.

In conclusion, I believe that all of us must do our best to be as green and as environmentally friendly as possible. The whole future of the planet is in our hands.

2 Read the writing task and make notes to answer the questions below.

> Your class has been doing a project on the environment.
> Your teacher has asked you to write an **essay** on the following statement:
> *Although most people would like to be green, it is not possible in today's modern world. Do you agree or disagree?*
> You should state whether you agree or disagree with the statement .

1 What does 'being green' mean to you? Give an example.
2 Do you think most people are already green enough?
3 Do you think most people would like to be green but are not?
4 Do you think it is possible to be green in today's modern world? Why?/Why not? Give an example.
5 What is the result of this situation?
6 What do you think about most people's attitudes to protecting the environment?

3 Make a plan in *Composition Planner 11* on page 162.

HOMEWORK!

You are now ready to write the first draft of your essay. Write between 120 and 180 words. When your teacher has commented on your essay, write the final version.

12

C U @ 8!

Get warmed up!

Discuss the following. Work in pairs or in groups.

- Do you have a mobile phone? How often do you use it?
- How often do you send and receive text messages or emails?
- Has modern technology changed the way people communicate? How?

Reading 2.08

1 **Read the article quickly and underline all the different means of communication mentioned.**

2 **Read the article more carefully and find a word or phrase which …**

1 shows that a piece of information is surprising. (paragraph 1) ________
2 contrasts the present with the past. (paragraph 2) ________
3 shows that something is better than something else. (paragraph 2) ________
4 shows that something is very likely. (paragraph 3) ________
5 shows that something is successful a lot of the time. (paragraph 6) ________

communication breakdown!

Before mobile phones took off in the mid-1990s, no-one had predicted that they'd create a new means of communication: the text message. In fact, not long before email and text messages came along, some people had said that writing was dying and that in the future, speech would be king. We won't write letters anymore, we were told. We'll just make phone calls and video calls.

But now, writing is back on top. Why call someone when you can email them? Every second, millions of emails are sent around the world. (That's billions of emails every day, and trillions every year!) It's the same with text messages. And millions of people are posting on social networking sites such as Facebook and Twitter, or using instant messaging, or chatting away with friends or strangers in online chat rooms or forums, or commenting on articles in online newspapers and magazines. They're all communicating using a written form of the language.

If they're sending text messages, the chances are they're using software on their mobile phone that provides some kind of 'predictive text' or 'auto-correct' facility.

Older mobile phones allow users to type their message using a traditional telephone keypad. This has several letters on each number key. For example, the 2 key has the letters A, B and C on it. If you want to type a word beginning with A or B, you press the same key. So let's say you want to type the word *gone*. Which keys do you press? 4-6-6-3. But these are the same numbers for the word *home*. And this can lead to problems. Your phone 'predicts' the word you want to write, and it sometimes gets it wrong. If you don't check your message carefully before you send it, it might get sent with the wrong word!

More modern mobile phones which have touch screens, often known as smartphones, usually provide a keyboard with each of the 26 English letters on a separate key. This solves many of the problems of predictive text. However, problems can still occur.

3 Read the article again and choose the correct answer A, B, C or D. Underline the sentences in the article which give you the answers.

1 What did people fail to predict?
A the mobile phone
B text messages
C email
D the end of writing

2 What does the writer emphasise in paragraph 2?
A that writing helps us meet new people
B that writing is now as popular as speaking
C that we waste a lot of time writing
D that we do a lot of writing these days

3 What do the words *home* and *gone* have in common?
A They're the most common words used in text messages.
B Many people have problems spelling them correctly.
C The same keys are pressed to produce both words.
D Mobile phones are good at predicting words like these.

4 In the final paragraph, what does the writer mean by 'communication breakdown'?
A not understanding what someone else means
B not receiving an important text message or email
C finding something funny that wasn't meant to be
D receiving a message that was meant for someone else

Many people write text messages or emails on smartphones very quickly, and don't read what they've written before pressing 'send'. Let's say someone had wanted to write the word *good* but by mistake pressed *g-o-i-d*. Smartphones have software that automatically corrects mistakes like this. It often works, and in a case like this the phone would almost certainly change the word to *good*. But it doesn't always work, because sometimes there's more than one choice. For example, if the writer had meant to type the word *kitten* but in fact typed *k-o-t-t-o-n*, the phone will probably think they meant *cotton*. Or if you meant to type *t-y-p-e* but typed *t-i-p-e* instead, your phone may well auto-correct that to *ripe*. This can lead to some very funny text messages – and sometimes complete communication breakdown, where the person receiving the message has absolutely no idea what the sender had intended to say.

HOMEWORK!
Do the Reading exercise on page 76 of your Workbook.

DICTIONARY CORNER

Complete each phrase using the verbs in the box. You can use more than one verb for each phrase.

call • chat • get • have • hear • listen • make • receive • ring • send • speak • talk • type • write

1 ___get/make/receive___ a phone call
2 ________________ an email
3 ________________ a text message
4 ________________ on the internet
5 ________________ about something
6 ________________ on a keyboard
7 ________________ a conversation
8 ________________ someone
9 ________________ to someone
10 ________________ a letter

Have your say!

- Do you ever have problems when you're sending text messages, for instance with the auto-correct facility?
- Do you ever have problems understanding text messages you receive?

HOMEWORK!
Do exercises 1 and 2 on page 77 of your Workbook.

G Grammar 1

Past perfect simple and past perfect continuous

Look at *Grammar database 23* pages 194 –195 before you do the exercises.

1 Each of the sentences mentions two actions. Underline the action that happened first.

1 I sent the email after I'd called you.
2 They'd spoken to Sam before he told me about the problem.
3 When I got into the chat room, she'd already left.
4 She left after I'd got into the chat room.
5 She had been learning to type for ages before she joined the class.

2 Choose the correct word or phrase to complete the paragraph.

I (1) **had / had been** studying French for six years before I first (2) **had gone / went** to France, and I'd also (3) **pass / passed** all my French exams, so I thought I wouldn't have any problems communicating. How wrong I was! On the ferry, before I even landed in France, a French woman (4) **had come / had been coming** up and asked me something and I didn't have a clue what she (5) **had / had been** said. Then, after we'd actually (6) **been arriving /arrived** in France, I went into a cheese shop and (7) **asked / had asked** for some cheese. The assistant behind the counter just (8) **looked / had looked** at me blankly. She clearly (9) **hasn't / hadn't** understood a word I'd (10) **say / said**.

3 Put the verbs in brackets into the correct form, past perfect simple or past perfect continuous.

1 I got a reply about four weeks after I ____________ (**send**) the email.
2 Tina ____________ (**try**) to send a text message for hours before she finally worked out how to do it.
3 ____________ (**he/ever/speak**) to you like that before?
4 It was the first time she ____________ (**have to**) use sign language.
5 I ____________ (**wait**) for the letter all morning, so I was very relieved when it finally arrived.

4 Look again at exercise 3. In some of the gaps we can also use past simple or past continuous. If it's possible, write the verbs on the line in the correct tense (past simple or past continuous). If it isn't, put a cross (✗).

1 ____________
2 ____________
3 ____________
4 ____________
5 ____________

HOMEWORK!

Do exercises 1, 2, 3, 4 and 5 on pages 77 and 78 of your Workbook.

Listening

1 **You are going to listen to a radio programme about gestures. First match gestures 1–5 with the pictures A–E. Do you know what each gesture means for British people?**

1 shaking hands
2 shrugging your shoulders
3 nodding your head
4 shaking your head
5 crossing your fingers

2 **2.09 Now listen to the radio programme about gestures and choose the correct answer A, B or C.**

1 What was last week's episode about?
A written and spoken English
B formal and informal English
C old and modern English

2 What does Adam say has changed?
A the way we shake hands
B how often we shake hands
C the reason for shaking hands

3 In what way is nodding your head the same as shaking hands?
A Both of them are only used in some places.
B They both have the same meaning in some countries.
C Both gestures confuse people on holiday.

4 Adam believes that some of his listeners might
A not know why they shrug their shoulders.
B use gestures without thinking about them.
C have used the wrong gesture.

HOMEWORK!
Do the Listening exercise on page 81 of your Workbook.

DICTIONARY CORNER

1 **The nouns below are all incorrect. Rewrite them all correctly.**

	Adjective	**Noun**	
1	able	ablety	____________
2	high	hight	____________
3	long	longth	____________
4	strong	strongth	____________
	Verb	**Noun**	
5	believe	beliefe	____________
6	choose	choise	____________
7	decide	decidion	____________
8	describe	describtion	____________
9	explain	explaination	____________
10	practise	practise	____________
11	see	site	____________
12	speak	speach	____________
13	think	thowt	____________

2 **Complete the sentences with six of the nouns from exercise 1.**

1 I'd like you all to write a ____________ of your best friend.
2 Text messages usually have a maximum ____________ of about 160 characters.
3 We did lots of ____________ putting verbs into the past perfect continuous.
4 She had an incredible ____________ to learn foreign languages easily.
5 Do you think my ____________ to do Latin instead of geography was sensible?
6 I hate giving a(n) ____________ in public. I get really nervous.

HOMEWORK!
Do exercises 1 and 2 on page 79 of your Workbook.

Grammar 2

Reported speech

Look at *Grammar database 24* pages 195–197 before you do the exercises.

1 **When we write text messages, we sometimes use 'cyber-English'. Look at these text messages and match them with their meanings.**

1. c u @ 8 2nite! ☐
2. am gonna b a bit 18! ☐
3. we r listening to music at the mo! ☐
4. u'll love my new shoes when you c them 18r! ☐
5. i wanna have a party next sat night! ☐

a I'm going to be a bit late!
b I want to have a party next Saturday night!
c I'll see you at eight o'clock tonight!
d We're listening to music at the moment!
e You'll love my new shoes when you see them later!

2 **Write four text messages starting with the words in bold. Imagine they're from different people.**

(Aiden to Bill) **c u @** : *c u @ 10 2nite!*
1 (Carol to Dave) **amgonna** : ______
2 (Ed to Fiona) **we r** : ______
3 (Greg to Harry) **u'll** : ______
4 (Imran to Jack) **i wanna** : ______

3 **Imagine that the person receiving the text message tells a person in the same room what it says. Write what they say. Use direct speech.**

Bill says to his friend:
'Aiden *will see us at 10 o'clock tonight*.'
1 Dave says to his friend:
'Carol ______.'
2 Fiona says to her friend:
'Ed ______.'
3 Harry says to his friend:
'Greg ______.'
4 Jack says to his friend:
'Imran ______.'

4 **Write what happened in exercise 3. Use reported speech.**

Bill told his friend that *Aiden would see them at 10 o'clock that night*.
1 Dave told his friend that Carol ______.
2 Fiona told her friend that Ed ______.
3 Harry told his friend that Greg ______.
4 Jack told his friend that Imran ______.

HOMEWORK!
Do exercises 1, 2, 3 and 4 on pages 79 and 80 of your Workbook.

Soundstation

1 **Look at these pairs of words. Underline the syllable which is stressed in each word.**

1	communicate	communication
2	photograph	photography
3	library	librarian
4	advert	advertisement
5	science	scientific
6	economy	economical
7	secretary	secretarial
8	Italy	Italian

2 2.10 **Listen and check your answers.**

3 **Now say each pair of words.**

Speaking

1 **Choose one of the statements from 1–6 below and answer the questions. Do not write full sentences.**

1 Learning Latin and ancient Greek is very useful.

2 We should all learn at least two foreign languages.

3 It is impossible to communicate with animals.

4 Email and text messages make communication much easier.

5 It would be better if everyone in the world spoke the same language.

6 Children should learn to read when they are about three years old.

I have chosen statement number:
***I completely agree/partly agree/completely disagree** with the statement.*

- Give two reasons.
- Can you think of an example to support your opinion?
- What arguments would someone use to disagree with you?
- Why do you disagree with them? Is there anything you're not sure about?
- What other points could you make about the statement?

Phrase Bank! P

I'd also like to add that …
The first/second reason I agree is that …
For example, …
For instance, …
One thing I'm not sure about is …

2 **Play the Keep Talking Game. Your teacher will explain the rules to you.**

See *Speaking database* on page 174.

Use your English!

Use the word given in capitals to form a word that fits in the space in the same line.

BRITISH ACCENTS AND DIALECTS

Before I went to the UK for the first time, I'd never (1) ______________ about	THINK
different accents and dialects. People's (2) ______________ varies across the	SPEAK
(3) ______________ and breadth of Britain, sometimes making	LONG
(4) ______________ difficult, even for native speakers. This is because	COMMUNICATE
their (5) ______________ of vocabulary differs from region to region,	CHOOSE
and also because the way they (6) ______________ say words differs.	ACTUAL
I met someone from Glasgow. The (7) ______________ of his accent made it	STRONG
(8) ______________ to work out what he said. So I asked a friend from	POSSIBLE
London who was with me, and he hadn't (9) ______________ either!	UNDERSTAND
Luckily, (10) ______________ English doesn't have the same kind of problems	WRITE
as spoken English.	

Writing

Selecting the appropriate style

1 **Read the extracts 1 – 6 from different types of writing and answer the questions.**

1 As requested, I have visited the new shopping complex and examined the security system. My findings are outlined below.

Find three examples of formal vocabulary.

2 **Oh, by the way, I forgot to tell you. I got a really cool mobile for my birthday! Great, eh? We'll be able to send loads of text messages to each other from now on!**

Find three examples of informal vocabulary.

3 *Should you have any further enquiries, please do not hesitate to contact me.*

Is the language very polite or very friendly?

4 Have you ever thought about putting on a play with your friends? It's great fun, and it's not as difficult as you might think.

Is the style very formal or quite informal?

5 For this reason, I strongly believe that it is very important for us all to learn at least one foreign language.

a Is the language formal or informal?
b Find two expressions common in essays.

6 Sonia nodded her head enthusiastically. 'You're absolutely right,' she said. 'What's more, I'd like to offer you the job. Come and work for me!' Sonia stood up, and extended her arm to shake hands with Paul.

a Find one example of descriptive language.
b Is the direct speech formal or informal?

2 **Match each of the extracts in exercise 1 with a text type.**

____ **a** an essay for your teacher
____ **b** a letter applying for a job
____ **c** a report
____ **d** a story
____ **e** an article for a young people's magazine
____ **f** a letter or email to your friend

HOMEWORK!
Do exercises 1 and 2 on page 81 of your Workbook.

Get ready to write

Informal email

1 Read the email and answer the questions.

1 Is the style conversational and chatty?
2 Are the vocabulary, grammar and punctuation formal or informal?
3 Underline two examples of incomplete sentences.
4 Does Francesca use paragraphs in her email?

write reply send

From: Francesca <fran123@freemail.it>
To: Joanne <jps@uk/net.uk>
Subject: Hi!!!!

Hi, Joanne,

Thanks for your email. Glad you've sorted out the problem with your computer virus!

Yes, I have been to Greece before. I don't think you'll have any problems. The Greeks are really friendly and most of them speak English well. They do like it, though, if you try to speak a bit of Greek, so I'd suggest getting a phrase book and learning a few things before you go. You know, just things like 'hello' and 'How much does this cost?' and things like that. You'll really impress the Greek boys if you speak to them in their own language! You're going to have a great time!

Oh, by the way, I've got some great news. I've just got the leading part in the school play. Rehearsals start next week. Should be fun!

Well, got to go now. Homework :-(
Send me an email again soon!

Love,
Francesca

2 Read the writing task and make a plan in *Composition Planner 12* on page 163.

You have received an email from an English-speaking friend. Read the extract from the email and the notes that you have made on the printout and then write an **email** responding to your friend's questions. Mention any other news you have as well.

yes – Angelo (one of my best friends)

Oh, by the way, I think you said you had a friend who was deaf, didn't you? Well, a deaf girl's just moved in next door and I'd like to make friends with her but I'm not sure what to do. Any ideas? Will it be really difficult to communicate with her?

try and learn sign language – not difficult and great fun!

deaf people are just like everyone else!

most can lip-read

HOMEWORK!

You are now ready to write the first draft of your email. Write between 120 and 180 words. When your teacher has commented on your email, write the final version.

Revision
Units 11–12

1 Environment vocabulary

Write a verb from the box in each gap to complete the sentences.

degrade • destroy • dispose • pollute • recycle • reduce • solve

1 You should ________________ that paper rather than throw it away.
2 We've got to ________________ the amount of rubbish we throw away.
3 Cars ________________ the atmosphere far more than factories do.
4 How are you supposed to ________________ of batteries?
5 They'll completely ________________ the natural beauty of the area if they build a motorway through the hills.
6 How long does it take a plastic bag to ________________ ?
7 The hole in the ozone layer is a problem we've got to ________________ soon.

2 The passive

Complete each second sentence so that it means the same as the sentence before it.

1 People send millions of emails every day.
Millions of emails ________________________________ every day.
2 Trisha answered the phone in the end.
The phone ________________________________ Trisha in the end.
3 We've set up the website to educate people about the environment.
The website ________________________________ to educate people about the environment.
4 We're going to hold an Environment Day next week at school.
An Environment Day ________________________________ next week at school.
5 You mustn't throw that away!
That ________________________________ away!

3 The causative

Each of the words or phrases in bold is grammatically incorrect. Rewrite the word or phrase correctly.

1 My mum usually **have** her emails answered by her secretary.
____
2 Have you had **tested your eyes** recently?
____
3 We're having the house **redecorating** while we're on holiday.
____
4 I have to **got** my computer fixed next week.
____
5 They **had had** their swimming pool cleaned last week.
____
6 Don't you get your rubbish collected **from** the local council?
____

4 Phrasal verbs

Choose the correct phrasal verb to complete each sentence.

1 I expected their website to be really interesting but it __________ to be quite disappointing.
A brought out **B** fell out **C** turned out **D** made out

2 A gorilla managed to __________ of the zoo last night.
A put out **B** break out **C** hand out **D** turn out

3 It took the firefighters four hours to __________ the fire.
A look out **B** bring out **C** turn out **D** put out

4 That could be an eagle in the distance, but it's difficult to __________ exactly what kind of bird it is from here.
A make out **B** look out **C** break out **D** hand out

5 I hope we're not going to __________ over this. I know we both have very different opinions.
A fall out **B** make out **C** break out **D** turn out

6 __________! There's a car coming!
A Put out **B** Turn out **C** Look out **D** Bring out

5 Past perfect simple and continuous

Put the verbs in brackets into the correct form, past perfect simple or past perfect continuous.

1 She __________________ (**wait**) for him to call all week, so she was very pleased when he rang on Friday morning.
2 __________________ (**you/send**) a text message to her before?
3 Alan and Pete __________________ (**try**) to connect to the internet for ages before they finally managed it.
4 I __________________ (**not finish**) typing the letter when my computer crashed.
5 Kim __________________ (**just/started**) writing you an email when you called.
6 We __________________ (**just/talk**) about him when he walked into the room!

6 Reported speech

Complete each second sentence using reported speech so that it means the same as the sentence before it.

1 'I'm hoping to work for an environmental organisation,' said Ellie.
Ellie said ______________________________.
2 'I'll meet you in the chat room tomorrow night, Dave,' said Phil.
Phil told Dave ______________________________.
3 'I sent the information yesterday,' said Fiona.
Fiona said ______________________________.
4 'We really must start recycling our rubbish,' said Jon.
Jon said ______________________________.
5 'Plastic takes an extremely long time to degrade,' said the scientist.
The scientist said ______________________________.

7 Word formation

Complete the text using the correct form of the words in brackets.

Communication skills

The (1) __________ (**able**) to communicate effectively is a great (2) __________ (**strong**). Sometimes, it's the difference between getting a job or not. When you're asked a question in a job interview, for example, you don't have long to turn your (3) __________ (**think**) into (4) __________ (**speak**). You may have to give an (5) __________ (**explain**) or a (6) __________ (**describe**). Your choice of words will affect how the person who you are communicating with sees you.

13

Getting By

Get warmed up!

Discuss the following. Work in pairs or in groups.

- Think of a member of your family. What is their job? Where do they work?
- Have you ever worked during your summer holidays? Which job would you like to do this summer? Why?

Reading 2.11

1 **Quickly read the information about the four jobs A, B, C and D. Which job would you most like to do, and why?**

A

Name	**Craig McFarland**
Age	**42**
Position	**Sales representative**

'As a sales rep, a lot of my working day is spent on the road or in the air. I work in telecommunications, so I mainly sell telecoms equipment to other companies. The salary's excellent – I get around €100,000 a year, plus commission – but I usually end up working about 60–70 hours per week, so I don't get to see my family very much. To do this job well, you have to be outgoing, patient, persuasive and polite and you also have to be prepared to do a lot of travelling.'

B

Name	**Daniel Thompson**
Age	**21**
Position	**Waiter**

'I've just finished my second year at university. I didn't have any studying to do over the summer holidays and I didn't have any money, so I decided to get a temporary job. So, for the next two months I'm working in a café not far from the university. It's not bad. I work every lunchtime and evening, except weekends – that comes to 40 hours per week – and the customers are generally university professors or graduate students, so they're quite interesting people. The wages aren't great, of course. I get €7.50 an hour, but it's enough for me to get by, and the job's not difficult. I wouldn't want to be a waiter for the rest of my life, though!'

C

Name	**Jessica Murray**
Age	**34**
Position	**Civil servant**

'I've been working in local government since I left university and I find it very rewarding. I started working part-time after I had my first child. I love it! I have enough time to do things like go to the kids' Sports Day at school. I earn about €20,000 a year – that's for 20 hours a week. My husband works full-time, so together we bring in quite a good income. At the moment, I'm working in the City Council Planning Department, so I spend a lot of my time dealing with building regulations and planning applications. It might sound boring but actually it's not. I think to be a successful civil servant, you have to like working with people, you probably need a sense of social responsibility and you shouldn't have dreams of becoming rich!'

2 Which of the people might make these statements? Write A, B, C or D. Give reasons for your answers. You will need to use one of the letters twice.

1 I've got big plans for the company. ___
2 I couldn't do my job without a driving licence. ___
3 This is definitely not my chosen career. ___
4 I'm glad I don't have a full-time job. ___
5 I like being in control. ___

3 Which of the positions …

1 does not involve selling a product? ___
2 is not permanent? ___
3 does not require at least eight hours work a day, five days a week? ___
4 involves a long break during the working day? ___
5 involves paying the salaries of employees? ___
6 brings in more money if you are successful? ___ ___
7 involves working with politicians? ___
8 is it not possible to be sacked from? ___

HOMEWORK!

Do the Reading exercise on page 83 of your Workbook.

D

Name	**Devi Sohanta**
Age	**29**
Position	**Magazine publisher**

'I used to work in the advertising department of a women's magazine and gained a lot of experience there, so, about two years ago, I decided to start my own business. It's extremely hard work being self-employed, but at least there's no-one telling you what to do! I only have two people working for me, which means I have to do lots of different things: writing articles, getting advertisers, dealing with the printers, getting the magazine distributed. You name it, I do it! We're only a small local magazine at the moment but I'm hoping to expand soon. How much do I earn? It depends on how many copies we sell! How many hours a week do I work? A lot! And every day, including weekends, usually.'

DICTIONARY CORNER

Complete each sentence using a word or phrase from the article.

1 If you have a ______________ job, you don't work a full working week.
2 If you have a ______________ job, you work a full working week – usually at least 40 hours per week.
3 If you have a ______________ job, you only do that job for a few days, weeks or months.
4 If you are ______________, you work for yourself rather than for someone else.
5 If you earn a ______________, you get a certain amount of money per year and you are usually paid at the end of every month.
6 If you earn ______________, you get a certain amount of money per hour and you are usually paid at the end of every week.
7 If you are on ______________, how much you earn depends on how much you sell.
8 If you don't earn enough to ______________, you don't earn enough money to buy food, pay the bills, etc.
9 If you work ______________ advertising, your job is something to do with the advertising industry.

Have your say!

What do you want from a job? Put these factors in order (1: most important – 4: least important) and explain why.

- a good salary ___
- working with other people ___
- lots of time off ___
- being my own boss ___

HOMEWORK!

Do exercises 1 and 2 on page 84 of your Workbook.

G Grammar 1

Reported questions

Look at *Grammar database 25* pages 197–198 before you do the exercises.

1 Choose the correct word or phrase to complete the text.

It was a disaster! When I went in, they asked me if I (1) **want / wanted** some coffee and I stupidly said yes. When it came, I spilt it all over the desk. Then one of the interviewers asked me why (2) **had I applied / I had applied** for the job. I was so nervous that I started talking about the job I've got at the moment. I soon realised my mistake and started sweating. So then they asked me (3) **if / when** I was feeling all right and (4) **whether / weather** I wanted to carry on with the interview. I asked if (5) **we could / could we** start again but they just laughed and asked me what (6) **did I know / I knew** about the (7) **company? / company**.

2 Complete each sentence using reported questions so that it means the same as the sentence before it.

1 'Why did you apply for the job, Claire?' asked the interviewer.
The interviewer asked Claire ______________________________.

2 'And what skills do you have?'
She was also asked ______________________________.

3 'Will you be able to work on Saturday mornings, Claire?'
They wanted to know ______________________________.

4 'Do you have any questions?'
Claire was asked ______________________________.

5 'Can you start tomorrow?'
The interviewer asked her ______________________________.

3 Read this dialogue between Claire and her husband and choose the correct answer A, B or C.

Ben: So how was your first day at work, Claire?

Claire: When I got to the entrance, the security guard asked me who (1) ____ . I told him my name and he asked if (2) ____ an ID card.

Ben: And did you?

Claire: No, it was my first day! I asked him whether (3) ___ a list of new employees and he said he did. He looked on the list and I wasn't there! He asked me who (4) ____ the job. I couldn't remember the interviewer's name!

Ben: Oh, no! What did he do?

Claire: He rang upstairs and asked if they (5) ____ me. They said yes and he let me in. I asked him where (6) ____ an ID card and he said: 'From me!' And he gave me one straight away! The rest of the day was fine after that.

	A	B	C
1	A I am	B was I	C I was
2	A I did have	B I had	C had I
3	A he had	B had he	C did he have
4	A did give me	B had given me	C am I giving
5	A expect	B did expect	C were expecting
6	A could I get	B I can get	C I could get

HOMEWORK!
Do exercises 1, 2, 3 and 4 on pages 84 and 85 of your Workbook.

Listening

1 **You are going to listen to a woman talking to someone about her new job. Before you listen, look at the sentences in exercise 2. Can you think of any words or phrases that might fit in the gaps?**

2 **2.12 Listen to the conversation and complete the sentences with a word or short phrase.**

- Amy is supposed to be at work by (1) ________________ in the morning.
- Amy's (2) ________________ is called Mrs Collins.
- The (3) ________________ is on the fifth floor.
- Amy wasn't given an (4) ________________ .
- The employees there are allowed to work at any (5) ________________ they like.
- Most of Amy's colleagues are also graphic (6) ________________ .
- Amy's company is doing an (7) ________________ campaign for a computer company.
- Amy spent her first day working on one of the newspaper (8) ________________ .

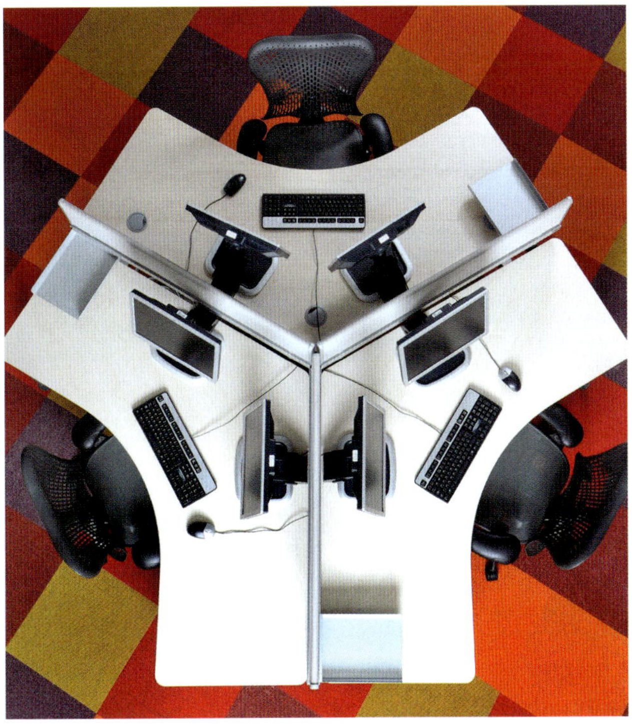

3 **How many of your guesses in exercise 1 were right?**

HOMEWORK!
Do the Listening exercise on page 88 of your Workbook.

DICTIONARY CORNER

1 **Choose the correct word(s) to complete the word patterns.**

1 apply **to** / **for** a job
2 make someone **do** / **to do** something
3 cause someone **do** / **to do** something
4 approve **for** / **of** (doing) something
5 complain **for** / **about** something
6 be interested **in** / **on** (doing) something
7 be made **do** / **to do** something
8 be involved **in** / **at** (doing) something
9 apologise **for** / **of** (doing) something
10 insist **on** / **for** (doing) something

2 **Write one word from exercise 1 in each gap to complete the sentences. You may need to change the form of the word.**

1 I don't ________________ of people wearing casual clothes to work.
2 Pedro is ________________ in applying for the job of Hotel Manager he saw advertised in the local paper.
3 Melissa's going to ________________ about being ________________ to work three weekends in a row.
4 I don't think they should ________________ you go on the training course if you don't want to.
5 They ________________ for making me do so much overtime but they didn't offer to pay me any more money!
6 We ________________ on your having a clean driving licence.
7 At the moment Jo's heavily ________________ in a project to redesign the town centre.

HOMEWORK!
Do exercises 1 and 2 on page 86 of your Workbook.

Grammar 2

Indirect questions

Look at *Grammar database 26* page 198 before you do the exercises.

1 **Match to make indirect questions.**

1	Would you mind	**a**	tell me what experience you have.
2	Could I ask	**b**	much the pay is per hour?
3	Do you know where	**c**	when I would be expected to start?
4	I wonder if you could	**d**	what qualifications you have.
5	I'd like to know	**e**	telling me what the salary is?
6	Could you tell me how	**f**	the job interview is?

2 **Choose the correct word or phrase to complete each indirect question.**

1 Could you **tell / say** me what **do you want / you want** to do when you leave **school. / school?**
2 Can I ask if **you are planning / are you planning** to go to **university? / university.**
3 I'd like to **tell me / know** whether **you would / would you** be happy to work **abroad. / abroad?**

3 **Complete each sentence so that it means the same as the sentence before it.**

1 Where are you working at the moment?
Can you tell me ______
2 What are your plans for the future?
Do you know ______
3 When did you decide to be a teacher?
I wonder if you could ______
4 Is a large salary important to you?
Would you mind ______
5 Why have you quit your job?
Do you think you could explain ______

HOMEWORK!
Do exercises 1, 2, 3, 4 and 5 on pages 86 and 87 of your Workbook.

Soundstation

1 2.13 **Listen to these pairs of words. Can you hear the difference between them?**

shake / sake
shoe / Sue
ship / sip
show / so
short / sort

2 2.14 **Now listen to these sentences. For each one circle the word you hear.**

1 **shack / sack**
2 **shine / sign**
3 **shaving / saving**
4 **sheet / seat**
5 **shell / sell**
6 **shock / sock**
7 **shed / said**

Speaking

1 Read the question and the answers different students gave during an English exam interview. Tick (✔) the answers you think are successful, cross (✘) next to the ones you think are not so successful.

Phrase Bank! P

Have you decided yet what job you'd like to do when you're older?

1 No, I haven't really decided yet but I think I'd like to work in the media – maybe writing for a magazine or for TV.

2 No, I haven't.

3 Well, I definitely want to study English at university. After that? I'm not really sure yet, to be honest.

4 Yes, I really want to be an actor. I've been in several school plays and everyone said I was very good. I just love being on the stage. I can't imagine doing anything else.

5 Yes, I want to be a lawyer.

2 Make notes about yourself to answer these questions. Give reasons for your opinions.

- Have you decided yet what job you'd like to do when you're older?
- Would you like to do the same job that someone in your family does now?
- Would you like to go to university? If so, what do you think you would study?
- Can you imagine yourself running your own business one day?
- Do you think you'll ever go abroad to work?

Use your English!

Complete each sentence using the word given so that it means the same as the sentence before it. Use no more than five words.

1 'What do you do for a living, Darren?' asked Yussuf. **know**
Yussuf wanted ____________________
for a living.

2 'Can I take the day off tomorrow?' asked Emma. **if**
Emma ____________________
the next day off.

3 Where are you working at the moment? **ask**
Could I ____________________
working at the moment?

4 What did you say to the boss? **know**
I'd like ____________________
to the boss.

5 They made Costas apologise when he was late. **made**
Costas ____________________
being late.

6 I don't like it when shop assistants are rude to customers. **approve**
I don't ____________________
rude to customers.

7 Narinder was late for the meeting because of a traffic jam. **caused**
A traffic jam ____________________
for the meeting.

8 I would like to find out more about the position. **interested**
I ____________________
more about the position.

3 In pairs, ask and answer the questions in exercise 2

4 Turn to page 169. In pairs, do the role-play activity unit 13.

See *Speaking database* on page 174.

Writing

Using set phrases

1 **Write a word from the box in each gap to complete the phrases.**

advertised • apply • attend • contact • experience
forward • grateful • position • require • wonder

1 I am writing to ________ for the ________ of … as ________ in …
2 I have ________ at/in …
3 I ________ if you could let me know/tell me …
4 I would (also) be ________ if you could let me know/tell me …
5 Please do not hesitate to ________ me if you ________ any further information.
6 I would be more than happy to ________ an interview.
7 I look ________ to hearing from you.

2 **Underline the phrases from exercise 1 in the letter of application on page 123.**

3 **We often use indirect questions in a letter applying for a job. Rewrite each of the questions as indirect questions. Use appropriate indirect question beginnings.**

How much is the salary?
Could you tell me how much the salary is?

1 Where is the shop?

2 How much is the pay per hour?

3 Would I have to wear a uniform?

4 When would you want me to start?

5 What responsibilities would I have?

6 Would I be able to work part-time?

7 Do you need a reference?

8 Which days would I be expected to work?

HOMEWORK!
Do exercises 1 and 2 on page 88 of your Workbook.

Get ready to write

Letter of application

1 Read the letter and answer the questions.

1 Is the job full-time?
2 Where was it advertised?
3 When?
4 How old is Harvey?
5 Where is he studying at the moment?
6 What word does he use to mean 'at the moment'?
7 What is he studying?
8 Has he got any previous experience?
9 How many questions does he ask?
10 Are his questions direct or indirect?
11 Is the letter formal or informal?

Dear Mrs Singh,

I am writing to apply for the position of part-time kitchen assistant, as advertised in 'The Evening Gazette' last Tuesday.

I am an eighteen-year-old student currently studying French at Tyfold College. I have experience in food preparation, as I worked in a restaurant last summer.

I wonder if you could let me know how many hours a week I would be expected to work. I would also be grateful if you could tell me what the pay per hour is.

Please do not hesitate to contact me if you require any further information. I would be more than happy to attend an interview.

I look forward to hearing from you soon.

Yours sincerely,

Harvey Goldman

2 Read the writing task and make notes to answer the questions below.

You have seen this advertisement for a job in a local sports shop and are interested in applying.
Write your **letter of application**.

Part-time shop assistant
required for local sports shop

- Job involves serving customers and helping Manager
- Previous experience an advantage
- Good rate of pay

Please apply in writing to:
Dave Parker, Southam Sports

SS

1 What's the name of the person who's going to apply for this job?
2 How old is he/she?
3 What is he/she doing at the moment? (unemployed? at university?)
4 What experience does he/she have?
5 Where did he/she see the advert?
6 When?
7 What two questions does this person need to ask?

3 Make a plan in *Composition Planner 13* on page 164.

HOMEWORK!

You are now ready to write the first draft of your letter. Write between120 and 180 words. When your teacher has commented on your letter, write the final version.

14

Away from Home

Get warmed up!

Discuss the following. Work in pairs or in groups.

- How many means of transport can you think of?
- Do you like travelling? Why?/Why not?
- Which types of transport have you travelled in or on?
- Which countries would you like to visit? Why?

MEDITERRANEAN TEENAGE
Summer Cruise

You're aged 16–19. You believe that travel broadens the mind. You want to do something interesting and different with people your own age this summer. You don't want to go on another boring package holiday with Mum and Dad. Is that you? If it is, then we've got the perfect solution to your problem. And your mum and dad will let you go, because they'll know you're in safe hands. And having fun. And learning a lot. And it's not costing them too much!

Reading 2.15

1 **Read the advertisement for a holiday. Choose what the underlined words and phrases are talking about.**

1 your problem what to do this summer / how to see different countries
2 go on this cruise / wherever you like
3 back again returning to the city you came from / Bristol Airport
4 in the best possible way by plane, bus, coach and ship / on a luxury cruise ship

PACKAGE INCLUDES:

- Coach from any major UK city to Bristol Airport, and back again at the end of the cruise
- Flights to and from Majorca (meals included)
- Short bus rides between Palma Airport and port
- 14 nights aboard our luxury cruise ship (4 teenagers in each cabin)
- Visits to and guided tours around (in alphabetical order): Ajaccio, Corsica (France), Athens (Greece), Barcelona (Spain), Cadiz (Spain), Casablanca (Morocco), Gibraltar (UK), Lisbon (Portugal), Nice (France), Rome (Italy)

Join us on our two-week Mediterranean Teenage Summer Cruise. All you need is a current passport (and some money from your parents!). Think about it! In a few weeks, you'll be travelling around the Mediterranean in the best possible way with people your own age. And by the end of the summer, you'll have had an experience you'll never forget.

Call 07000700 or visit our website for details.

2 Read the advertisement again and decide if the statements are true (T) or false (F).

1 This holiday is designed for all teenagers. T/F
2 The advertisement says the holiday is educational. T/F
3 The cost of the holiday includes transport to the airport. T/F
4 From the advert, we can understand that Palma Airport is in Majorca. T/F
5 On the ship, you can choose not to share a room with other people. T/F
6 The places are listed in the order in which you visit them. T/F

3 Read these notices from the cruise ship. For each one, choose the statement that means the same as the notice.

1 **Please note: As the ship departs at 5pm, there will not be time for those leaving the ship to cross the border from Gibraltar into Spain.**

A Make sure you're back from Spain by 5pm.
B You cannot take a trip to Spain today.
C Only those people staying on the ship can go to Spain.

2 ***Digital camera found!***

If you've lost yours, come and describe it to me and tell me about the photos you've taken. If it's your camera, I'll give it back!
Helen – Cabin 307
(come between 6 and 7pm)

A You have to show me that it's yours.
B You have to show me where you lost it.
C You have to show me when you lost it.

3 **FUN QUIZ!**
Tonight – 8.30 pm – Topsiders Lounge
Free entrance!
(Latecomers will not be admitted, so be on time!)

A You mustn't get there before 8.30pm.
B You must be there by 8.30pm.
C The doors open at 8.30pm.

4 **Always give your name and cabin number to a member of staff before leaving the ship**

A Tell us if a member of staff leaves the ship.
B Remember your name and cabin number when you are not on the ship.
C Don't get off the ship without telling us.

HOMEWORK!
Do the Reading exercise on page 89 of your Workbook.

DICTIONARY CORNER

Complete each sentence using a word from the advertisement and notices.

1 You often need to show your ______________ when you enter another country.
2 A ______________ is a journey on a plane.
3 A ______________ is a holiday on a ship.
4 The ______________ is the line between two countries.
5 A ______________ is a bedroom on a ship.
6 A bus ______________ is a journey on a bus.
7 A ______________ is a comfortable bus.
8 A ______________ holiday is a holiday where transportation, accommodation and sometimes food are arranged for you by a travel company.
9 '______________' is an uncountable noun that means 'going on journeys'.
10 If you go on a ______________ tour, someone shows you round a place and gives you information about it.

Have your say!

- Would you like to go on the Mediterranean Teenage Summer Cruise? Why? / Why not?
- Which aspects of the cruise would you enjoy most/least? Why?

HOMEWORK!
Do exercises 1 and 2 on page 90 of your Workbook.

G Grammar 1

Future perfect simple and future continuous

Look at *Grammar database 27* page 199 before you do the exercises.

1 Match to make sentences.

1 At eight o'clock tomorrow night, I'll
2 By this time next week, you'll
3 This time next week, we'll be
4 In a couple of days, they'll have

a arrived back home and will feel a lot better!
b have travelled over 10,000 kilometres.
c be flying across the Atlantic on an Airbus.
d climbing Mount Everest.

2 Tick (✔) the correct sentences. Rewrite those that are incorrect.

1 The travel agent will have sent us the tickets by the end of next week.
____

2 I'm afraid we'll have leaving by then.
____

3 You'll be sunbathe on a golden beach in a few days.
____

4 They will are arriving at around six o'clock.
____

3 Put the verbs in brackets into the correct form, future perfect simple or the future continuous.

1 By the end of this century, they _______________ (**introduce**) three-hour flights from Europe to Australia.
2 Do you think that, by the time we're adults, someone _______________ (**invent**) a time travel machine?
3 In a few hundred years, we _______________ (**all/go**) on holiday to other planets every year.
4 I hope that we _______________ (**not/still/use**) petrol in cars in 50 years' time.
5 I hope they _______________ (**find**) a more environmentally friendly fuel by then.

DICTIONARY CORNER

Choose the correct word to complete each sentence. Use the circled words to help you.

1 Dad's away on a (**business**) **trip / journey** at the moment.
2 We're going on a (**school**) **excursion / trip** next week.
3 I've always wanted to go on a (**luxury**) **voyage / cruise** round the Caribbean.
4 We were given a (**guided**) **tour / trip** of the palace.
5 If you don't hurry up, we'll **miss / lose** (**the plane!**)
6 Go (**straight**) **forward / ahead** and turn left at the traffic lights.
7 We (**made**) our **journey / way** to the departure lounge.
8 If you're backpacking through France, you (**should plan**) your **route / direction** carefully before you set off.
9 Irene (**gave**) us very good **directions / ways** so we didn't get lost.
10 Our neighbours are (**on**) **holiday / holidays** in South America at the moment.

HOMEWORK!
Do exercises 1, 2, 3, 4 and 5 on pages 90 and 91 of your Workbook.

HOMEWORK!
Do the Dictionary Corner exercise on page 92 of your Workbook.

Listening

1 **Match the people on the left with the people who they usually deal with. You will only use six of the letters.**

1 travel agents	___	**a**	visitors
2 flight attendants	___	**b**	passengers
3 hotel receptionists	___	**c**	children
4 tour guides	___	**d**	viewers
5 parents	___	**e**	customers
6 radio presenters	___	**f**	listeners
		g	guests

2 2.16 **Listen to extracts from six situations. For each situation, choose the correct picture to show who is speaking.**

1

2

3

4
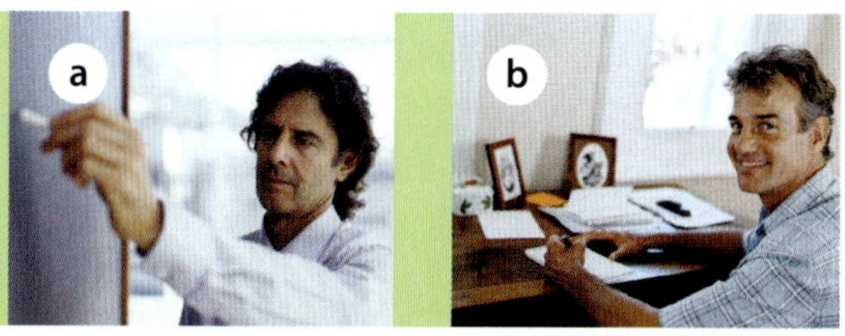

5
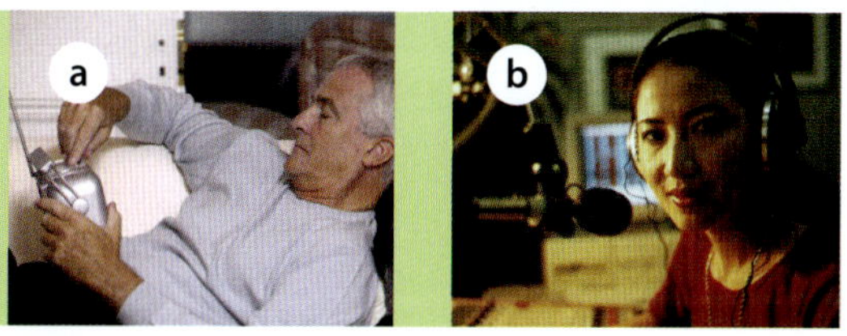

6

3 2.17 **Listen to the complete situations and choose the correct answer A, B or C.**

1 One of the people mentions the number 7. What does it refer to?
A a room number
B a phone number
C a time

2 What will they collect soon?
A food trays
B rubbish
C bags

3 What does the customer and his family NOT need?
A special food
B plane tickets
C meals on the plane

4 What do we NOT learn from the conversation?
A how long the trip lasts
B how much the trip costs
C how many teachers are involved

5 Who will hear this message?
A Todd and his family
B Just Todd
C Todd's neighbours

6 Which of these does NOT exist right now?
A the castle gift shop
B the castle hotel
C the castle café

HOMEWORK!
Do the Listening exercise on page 94 of your Workbook.

Grammar 2

wish and *if only*

Look at *Grammar database 28* pages 199–200 before you do the exercises.

1 What do the words in bold refer to?

1 If only **we'd booked** the tickets in advance!
A the past **B** the present

2 I wish **you'd come** and visit us more often.
A a general situation **B** the present

3 If only **we had** a map with us.
A the past **B** the present

4 I wish **we were leaving** on Tuesday and not Thursday.
A the past **B** the future

5 If only **you could join** us in Paris. We'd have a great time.
A the past **B** the future

6 I wish **you hadn't invited** them to come with us next week.
A the past **B** the future

2 Each of the words in bold is incorrect. Rewrite them correctly.

1 I wish I **haven't** bought such an expensive ticket. ________
2 If only you **are** coming with us. ________
3 Do you sometimes wish you **can** travel back in time? ________
4 If only they **will** tell us why there's a delay. ________
5 Sarah wishes **she's** invited Tony to come on the trip too. ________
6 I **wish** you can come with us on Saturday. ________

3 Complete the second sentence so that it means the same as the first. Use no more than three words.

1 Why didn't you remember to pack our swimming costumes?
I wish ________________ to pack our swimming costumes.

2 'I shouldn't have eaten the seafood,' said Joanne.
Joanne wished she ________________ the seafood.

3 It really annoys me when Dan videos everything we do on holiday.
I wish Dan ________________ everything we do on holiday.

4 It's a shame we can't stay another week.
If only ________________ another week.

5 The problem is that I don't have my phrase book with me.
If only ________________ my phrase book with me.

HOMEWORK!
Do exercises 1, 2, 3, 4 and 5 on pages 92 and 93 of your Workbook.

Speaking

1 Look at the photos and make notes to answer the questions for both of them.

1 What is this a picture of?
2 What things can you say for sure about the situation?
3 What things are probably true about the situation?
4 What things can't you tell about the situation from the photo?
5 Would you like to go on a holiday like this? Why?/Why not?

Soundstation

Play the Soundstation Game. Your teacher will explain the rules to you.

ship / sip
shine / sign
shack / sack
shock / sock
sheet / seat

What an amazing/incredible ____________ !

2 In pairs, make points about the photos using these phrases.

Phrase Bank!

Expressing certainty	Expressing possibility
It/They must be …	It/They might/could be …
It/They can't be …	I would imagine that …
I'm sure it is/ they are …	I'm not really sure, but perhaps …
It's/They're definitely	It's/They're probably …

3 Now do the task below.

Look again at the two pictures of different types of holiday and the notes that you made. Compare the pictures. Then say which holiday you would prefer to go on and why. Try to keep talking for at least one minute.

4 Turn to page 169. In pairs, do the role-play activity unit 14.

5 Imagine you are on a camping holiday like the one shown in the photo on page 128. Write a postcard to a friend at home. In your postcard, you should:

- describe what you have done on your holiday
- describe how you feel about your holiday
- say what plans you have for tomorrow
- write 35–45 words.

See *Speaking database* on page 174.

Use your English!

Complete the text with one word in each gap.

Our Day Out

When our teacher told us we were going (1) ____________ a school trip, I was really excited. Well, a whole day away (2) ____________ boring lessons sounds exciting. Now, I wish I (3) ____________ stayed at home. We set (4) ____________ from school at 9am and the drive to Warwick Castle took about two hours. When we arrived, I was really hungry, so I (5) ____________ my way to the café to buy a sandwich. When I got back, all my classmates had disappeared. I thought they were probably on a guided (6) ____________ of the castle, so I went to try and find them. I got completely lost. I couldn't even find the way out. Someone (7) ____________ me directions but I think I turned left instead of going straight (8) ____________ and I ended up at the top of the castle. I looked down and saw everyone (9) ____________ into the coach. I shouted: 'Wait for me!' but they didn't hear me and drove off. I (10) ____________ missed the coach! 'Don't panic,' I thought. 'They'll (11) ____________ coming back for you very soon. In a few minutes they'll (12) ____________ realised you're not on the coach.' But they didn't (13) ____________ back. I had to call my dad, who came to pick me (14) ____________. He was so angry! If (15) ____________ I hadn't gone to buy a sandwich!

Writing

Making recommendations

1 **Choose the correct word or phrase.**

Traveller's Reviews

1 This is the perfect guide book **to / for** anyone travelling on a small budget.
2 I **would / must** definitely recommend this hotel to anyone.
3 If you like travel magazines, **you'll / you** love *Out & About*.
4 If you go to London, you must **visit / to visit** the Tower of London.
5 If you enjoy travel programmes, don't **lose / miss** *Here We Go*!
6 This novel's not for younger children, **so / but** teenagers will love it!
7 I wouldn't recommend this island **to / at** people who don't like beach holidays.
8 If you're looking for an easy-to-use travel website, **so / then** this is the site for you!

2 **For each sentence in exercise 1, answer the question.**

1 Who would find the book useful?
- **a** people on holiday without much money
- **b** anybody who is on holiday

2 Could we write 'advise' instead of 'recommend'?
- **a** yes **b** no

3 Does the writer recommend *Out & About*?
- **a** yes **b** no

4 Who has probably written this sentence?
- **a** someone who has visited the Tower of London
- **b** someone who wants information about the Tower of London

5 What is the writer suggesting?
- **a** *Here We Go* is the same as all other travel programmes.
- **b** *Here We Go* is a great travel programme.

6 Does the writer recommend the book to everyone?
- **a** yes **b** no

7 Who should visit the island?
- **a** people who like beach holidays
- **b** people who don't like beach holidays

8 Who would find this recommendation useful?
- **a** someone who wants to find travel information on the internet
- **b** someone who wants to start a website about travel

HOMEWORK!

Do exercises 1 and 2 on page 94 of your Workbook.

Get ready to write

Review

1 Read the review and answer the questions.

1 Where is the Tower of London?
2 What can people do there?
3 According to the writer, who should visit the Tower?
4 In what ways is the review similar/different to:
  a a report?
  b an article?
  c an essay?

THE TOWER OF LONDON

The Tower of London is almost a 1,000 years old and is one of the most famous attractions in London. The Tower is on the River Thames, next to the famous Tower Bridge.

There are guards at the Tower called 'Beefeaters', who wear red and black costumes and strange hats! They look after the Tower, and the ravens (black birds) that live there. The Beefeaters give guided tours, and they tell you about all the exciting things that happened there, and several ghost stories too!

One of the main attractions at the Tower is the 'Crown Jewels'. This is the jewellery of the Kings and Queens of England, including the world's most famous diamonds. Visitors can look at the jewels but they can't touch them. They're too valuable for that!

If you go to London, you must visit the Tower of London. It's extremely interesting and educational. There's plenty to see and do, and it's perfect for families with children.

2 Read the writing task and make notes to answer the questions below.

> **Reviews needed!**
>
> Have you been to a local tourist attraction recently? If so, could you write us a **review** of the place? Include information on where it is and what there is to do there, and say whether you would recommend the place to other people.
>
> The best reviews will be published next month.

1 Which local tourist attraction will you write about?
2 Where is it?
3 What can people do there?
4 Would you recommend it to everyone?
Why? / Why not?

3 Make a plan in *Composition Planner 14* on page 165.

HOMEWORK!

You are now ready to write the first draft of your review. Write between 120 and 180 words. When your teacher has commented on your review, write the final version.

Revision
Units 13–14

1 Travel and transportation vocabulary

Each of the words or phrases in bold is in the wrong sentence. Write a word or phrase in bold from another sentence to replace the incorrect one.

1 I felt very nervous when we took off, but in fact the **coach** was great. ____________
2 Let's not go on a **cabin** this year. Let's just get there and then find accommodation. It'll be more fun! ____________
3 We don't need a **border** on that ferry as we're not going to be on board during the night. ____________
4 I've got to get a new **flight** so I'd better get a photo taken. ____________
5 It took us hours to cross the **passport** from Canada into the USA. ____________
6 I decided to go by **package holiday** rather than by train as the ticket was a lot cheaper. ____________

2 Patterns

Choose the correct words or phrases to complete the text.

THE JOB INTERVIEWER

I work in the Personnel Department of a big company and I'm involved (1) **in** / **at** all aspects of the job application process. When someone applies (2) **for** / **to** a job with us, I look at their application form. If I think they are suitable, I invite them to come to an interview. In the interview, I ask them lots of different questions. I usually ask why they are interested (3) **to work** / **in working** for the company and why they want to work (4) **in** / **at** this industry. I often also make them (5) **do** / **to do** some tasks, like problem-solving activities. If someone's made (6) **do** / **to do** a task like that, we can see how they react under stress. Stress can cause people (7) **to behave** / **behaving** very strangely! I personally don't approve (8) **for** / **of** people wearing casual clothes to interviews. I think you should be very smartly dressed. The other thing I would insist (9) **of** / **on** is that candidates are on time for the interview. If you have to apologise (10) **for** / **at** being late as soon as you get into the room, it creates a very bad impression. You almost certainly won't get the job!

3 Future perfect simple and future continuous

Put the verbs in brackets into the correct form, future perfect simple or future continuous.

1 This time tomorrow, you ____________ (**travel**) to Cardiff for your job interview.
2 By this time next week, I ____________ (**hear**) whether I've got the job or not.
3 I imagine Tammy ____________ (**earn**) a very high salary in five or 10 years' time.
4 Do you think you ____________ (**work**) for the same company this time next year?
5 We ____________ (**not finish**) setting up the business by next month.

4 Travel phrases

Complete each sentence with one word in each gap.

1 A local historian is going to take us on a guided ____________ of the castle.
2 Last summer we went on a luxury ____________ around the Greek islands. The ship was huge!
3 There was so much traffic on the way to the airport. We nearly ____________ our plane!
4 Mrs Williams is away on a business ____________ at the moment and won't be back in the office until next Tuesday.
5 All students going on the school ____________ to Manchester should meet outside the main doors at 9am.
6 Go straight ____________ and turn left at the traffic lights.

5 Reported questions

Rewrite each direct question as a reported question, beginning with the words given.

1 'Are you self-employed, Ben?' asked Alex.
Alex asked Ben ____________.
2 'Has Danny been paid his commission yet?' Jan asked Roula.
Jan asked Roula if ____________.
3 'Do you want to come in to the office tomorrow morning, Vic?' asked Alicia.
Alicia asked Vic ____________.
4 'What's the salary?' the applicant asked the interviewer.
The applicant asked the interviewer ____________.
5 'When can I expect a pay rise?' asked Jill.
Jill asked ____________.

6 Indirect questions

Rewrite each direct question as an indirect question, beginning with the words given.

1	What does 'departure' mean?	Do you know ____________
2	How much is the bus ticket?	I wonder if you could tell me ____________
3	Will you be leaving on Friday?	We'd like to know ____________
4	Is it a single or a return?	Could you tell me ____________
5	Which airline did you fly with?	Can I ask ____________

7 *wish* and *if only*

The words or phrases in bold are grammatically incorrect. Rewrite each one correctly.

1 I wish my wages **are** higher! ____________
2 If only I **can** start my own business. ____________
3 I wish you **will** work a bit harder! ____________
4 I wish I **didn't quit** my job last month. ____________
5 Tim wishes he **is** self-employed. ____________
6 If only you **haven't** been rude to your boss yesterday! ____________

15

Make or Break

Get warmed up!

Discuss the following. Work in pairs or in groups.

- What does success mean to you?
- What job would you like to do when you are older?
- How ambitious are you?

Success means doing something that makes you happy!

To me, success means having a well-paid job.

Reading 2.18

1 Read the article and answer the questions.

1 What did James Dyson invent?
2 How was his invention different?

A success story: James Dyson

Sir James Dyson is worth a fortune. It is estimated that he has made over £1 billion (almost €1.5 billion) from his career as an inventor and businessman. In a recent public lecture, he described himself as someone 'whose recipe for success has been to make things that people want to buy. Not because they look better – although of course I hope they do – but because they work better.'

Getting to where he is today wasn't easy, though. After school, he went to art college, where he got qualifications in furniture and design before he became interested in engineering. In the late 1970s, he realised that the vacuum cleaner he was using lost power as it got full of dust. He made up his mind to invent a new kind that didn't have this problem.

He had to be very determined. At the time, he and his wife didn't have much money. Her salary as an art teacher helped them live while Dyson worked on his invention. It took him five years to succeed. Along the way, he had to make 5,127 models to test his ideas. However, once he had a working model, that wasn't the end of his struggle.

Even though he had managed to achieve his first aim, to build a better vacuum cleaner, companies were not interested in helping him. They were already making a lot of money from selling vacuum cleaner bags that people regularly had to buy for their vacuum cleaners. Dyson's cleaner didn't need a bag and they thought they would lose money. Dyson realised that the only way he could achieve his ambitions was to start his own company.

He started selling his vacuum cleaners in Japan and won the International Design Fair prize in 1991. Using the money he earned in Japan, Dyson set up a company in Britain, which started producing his vacuum cleaners in 1993.

2 Match the figures to the statements.

1 £1 billion	a Dyson sells vacuum cleaners in this many countries.
2 the 1970s	b Dyson has made this much money.
3 5,127	c Dyson has built this many models of his vacuum cleaner.
4 1991	d Dyson thought of his invention then.
5 1993	e Dyson started his company then.
6 22	f Dyson won an award for his invention then.

3 Read the article again and decide if the statements are true (T) or false (F).

1 James Dyson thinks he's successful because he improves things. T/F
2 Dyson studied engineering and then studied design. T/F
3 He decided on an invention because of his experiences with housework. T/F
4 He had a lot of money to help him develop his ideas. T/F
5 He made a fortune as soon as he had a model that worked. T/F
6 At first, companies tried to buy his ideas from him. T/F
7 His success in Japan helped him to be successful in Britain. T/F
8 People prefer vacuum cleaners without bags. T/F
9 Dyson thinks teachers should make sure that students don't make mistakes. T/F
10 Dyson thinks it's important to experience failure in your life. T/F

HOMEWORK!

Do the Reading exercise on page 96 of your Workbook.

His product became more and more popular as people realised they would rather not buy new bags every few weeks. Today, Dyson sells vacuum cleaners in 22 countries around the world and he continues to work on new inventions.

Dyson has some interesting ideas about how to help the next generation of young people to achieve the same kind of success as he has. 'We need to encourage children to be different at school. In subjects such as design and technology, I think students should be marked by how many mistakes they make. It's what they learn from those mistakes that's important. Not how quickly and neatly they complete the task,' he said. He also believes that it's not always the best students at school who succeed in later life. 'The fact is, the B grade students are the most successful in life. They're not scared of failure.'

James Dyson proves that it's possible to succeed, even when everyone else is telling you that your ideas are wrong. 'When I was at school,' he said, 'my teachers told me that if I failed my exams I'd end up in a factory … Well, I proved them wrong. Somehow I passed most of my exams. And yet I still ended up in a factory. In fact, I built one.'

DICTIONARY CORNER

Complete each sentence using a word from the article.

1 If you are **d**__________ to do something, you won't let anything stop you doing it.
2 Your **q**__________ are the exams that you have passed.
3 The opposite of 'success' is '**f**__________'.
4 The opposite of 'fail' is '**s**__________'.
5 If you **a**__________ something, you manage to do it successfully after a lot of effort.
6 Our **a**__________ are the things that we want to do in our life.
7 A **f**__________ is a very large amount of money.
8 If you make up your **m**__________, you decide to do something.

Have your say!

- James Dyson says we should mark students on how many mistakes they make and that B grade students often succeed the most.
- Do you agree?
- Do you think making mistakes is important?

HOMEWORK!

Do exercises 1 and 2 on page 97 of your Workbook.

G Grammar 1

prefer, would rather, had better

Look at *Grammar database 29* pages 200–201 before you do the exercises.

1 Decide if the statements are true (T) or false (F).

1 We use *prefer* for general preferences and *would prefer* for specific decisions. T/F
2 *Prefer* is never followed by the *-ing* form. T/F
3 The opposite of *prefer to do* is *prefer not to do*. T/F
4 The opposite of *I would rather do* is *I wouldn't rather do*. T/F
5 *Would rather* has a similar meaning to *should* or *ought to*. T/F
6 The opposite of *You'd better* is *You wouldn't better*. T/F

2 Choose the correct word or phrase to complete the paragraph.

Although my parents and teachers (1) **would / had** prefer me (2) **to go / going** to university, I (3) **would / had** rather get a job as soon as I leave school. Generally, I prefer (4) **to do / doing** something active (5) **to / from** studying so I (6) **would rather not / wouldn't rather** spend another three or four years after leaving school taking more exams. I know getting a job is not easy these days though, and I'd definitely (7) **prefer / rather** not to be unemployed, so I suppose I (8) **had / would** better work hard at school for the next couple of years, get some qualifications and then I'll be able to find a job.

3 Find the extra word in each sentence and cross it out.

1 Sara prefers to work fewer hours would rather than earn more money.
2 I prefer to working out of doors to sitting behind a desk in an office.
3 Would you rather than have a highly paid job or a happy family life?
4 You'd better to decide what you want to do with your life.
5 I would rather you had waited until you are a bit older before you decide.
6 I'd rather prefer to have a job I enjoyed rather than a well-paid boring job.

4 Complete each sentence using the word given so that it means the same as the sentence before it. Use no more than five words.

1 I suggest checking your lottery ticket again. **better**
You ______________________ your lottery ticket again.
2 I don't want you to leave school at 16. **would**
I ______________________ leave school at 16.
3 Would Christine rather be happy than rich and famous? **prefer**
Would Christine ______________________ than rich and famous?
4 Sean would rather take risks than play it safe. **taking**
Sean ______________________ playing it safe.

HOMEWORK!

Do exercises 1, 2, 3, 4 and 5 on pages 97 and 98 of your Workbook.

Listening

1 2.19 **You are going to listen to five people talking about their ambitions for the future. As you listen, note down each speaker's main ambition.**

Speaker 1

Speaker 2

Speaker 3

Speaker 4

Speaker 5

2 2.19 **Listen again. Choose from the list A–F what each speaker says. There is one extra sentence that you do not need to use.**

A I would work with a professional.
B A lot of people have the same ambition.
C I'm young enough to succeed.
D I might need to study first.
E I've dreamt of this since I was a child.
F I'm not happy with my current situation.

Speaker 1 ☐
Speaker 2 ☐
Speaker 3 ☐
Speaker 4 ☐
Speaker 5 ☐

HOMEWORK!

Do the Listening exercise on page 101 of your Workbook.

DICTIONARY CORNER

1 Choose the correct word to complete each sentence.

1 They've made me an offer to go to America for a year but I think I'm going to turn it **off** / **down**.
2 He put **up** / **on** a lot of weight when he became famous.
3 She said that she was a successful actress but I think she made the whole story **up** / **out**!
4 The team intends to carry **out** / **on** winning for as long as possible.
5 He turned **in** / **into** a really arrogant person when he became rich.
6 I don't usually get **on** / **out** well with very ambitious people.
7 I'd love a job where I can look **after** / **on** children.
8 The researchers are looking **into** / **out** whether money can buy you happiness.

2 Write each of the phrasal verbs in exercise 1 in the bare infinitive next to its definition.

1 become: ____________
2 continue: ____________
3 gain: ____________
4 have a (good) relationship: ____________
5 investigate: ____________
6 not accept, reject: ____________
7 take care of: ____________
8 invent: ____________

HOMEWORK!

Do exercises 1 and 2 on page 99 of your Workbook.

G Grammar 2

Direct and indirect objects

Look at *Grammar database 30* page 201 before you do the exercises.

1 Complete each sentence with *to* or *for* if necessary.

1 Karen gave ________ me some advice about setting up my own business.
2 I sent an email ________ Grant congratulating him on his success.
3 They're going to give a trophy ________ the winning team.
4 They've bought a consolation prize ________ the losing team.
5 Justine asked me to lend ________ her the CD player I won in the competition.
6 I've decided not to lend it ________ her.
7 They sent ________ me my exam results by post.
8 The school has bought ________ the best student in each class a book token.

2 Rewrite each sentence without using the words in bold.

1 I made a promise **to** my dad to try harder at school.
2 We'll send the certificate **to** you next week.
3 Did you get a present **for** Mandy?
4 I'm going to make an effort to write a letter **to** my pen friend every week.
5 My mum made a cake **for** the team when they won the match.

3 Rewrite each second sentence so that it means the same using the word in bold.

1 Amy showed me the new office computer system. **to**
Amy ______________________________.
2 Could you lend me some money? **to**
Could ______________________________.
3 I've made you a birthday card! **for**
I've ______________________________.
4 Let me play you a video online. **for**
Let ______________________________.
5 Send me the email you got from Jake. **to**
Send ______________________________.

HOMEWORK!
Do exercises 1, 2, 3, 4 and 5 on pages 99 and 100 of your Workbook.

Soundstation

1 2.20 Listen to these words. Can you hear the difference between the vowel sounds?

caught • cut

2 2.21 Now listen to these words. Circle the words you hear.

1 **short / shut**	3 **warn / won**	5 **bought / but**
2 **dawn / done**	4 **born / bun**	6 **bored / bud**

3 Now say each pair of words. Be careful with the vowel sounds.

Speaking

1 You and your friends recently represented your local youth club in a general knowledge quiz. Your team won. The prize is €700 to spend on equipment for the youth club. You can only afford one of the possibilities shown above. Answer the questions.

1 Which do you think would be the most useful? Why?
2 Which would be the least useful? Why?
3 Would any of the other items be useful? Why?/Why not?

2 In pairs, discuss which equipment you should choose for the youth club. Give reasons for your opinions. Use the phrases below to help you.

Phrase Bank!

Giving and asking opinion

- I don't think … would be very useful because …
- I think … would be more useful than … because …
- What do you think about getting … ?
- I don't think … is as useful as … because
- Maybe we should get … because …
- I think … would be the most useful because …

3 Turn to page 169. In pairs, do the role-play activity unit 15.

See *Speaking database* on page 174.

Use your English!

Complete the text with one word in each gap.

MAKING MISTAKES

Most of us would prefer (1) _________ to fail. We try hard to succeed at what we do and aim to do our best. Whether you are a student, carefully checking your mark for an essay when your teacher gives (2) _________ back to you, or whether you have a job, you probably hate making mistakes. Often, we (3) _________ rather not admit our mistakes, and sometimes even hide (4) _________ from other people. However, that might not be the best attitude towards mistakes. In fact, once you make (5) _________ your mind to see mistakes as learning opportunities, they become something completely different.

You have to ask yourself why you have failed. Is it because someone gave (6) _________ something to do that you didn't understand? In that case, you (7) _________ better make sure next time that you know exactly what is expected. Or was it because you weren't determined enough (8) _________ succeed? In that case, you need to focus more on what you are doing.

Each of our mistakes can teach (9) _________ something. Although we would often (10) _________ to ignore them, they show us what we need to succeed next time. Our mistakes send important messages (11) _________ us, so carry (12) _________ making them and listening to them!

Writing

Using the correct register

1 Read the two short texts and answer the questions.

QUIZ

A

Are you the kind of person who likes competing with your friends? I am, so I decided to organise a regular general knowledge quiz at our local youth club. It's great fun, popular with everybody, educational and it's not as difficult to organise as you might think. If you'd like to run your own quiz, here's how to do it.

B

Humans are by nature very competitive. On the one hand, this is positive as the desire to win encourages us to do our best and to succeed. On the other hand, competition produces losers as well as winners and that can lead to disappointment, a sense of failure and a loss of confidence.

Which extract …

1 asks the reader a question to interest him/her?
2 uses short forms (*don't, can't,* etc)?
3 is the more formal one?
4 presents an argument in a logical way?
5 is conversational and chatty?
6 uses essay phrases and expressions?
7 promises to give the reader information he/she might find useful?
8 could be from an essay written by a student?
9 is from an article for a young people's magazine?

2 Rewrite each sentence so that it is more appropriate for an article for a young people's magazine.

It is sensible to purchase a large quiz book.
It's a good idea to buy a big quiz book.

1 Ensure that you know the correct answer to each question.
______

2 Answer sheets need to be produced beforehand.
______

3 A decision must be made as to how many questions will be asked.
______

4 Consider whether you wish teams or individuals to participate.
______

5 Remember that not every contestant will bring writing equipment to the event.
______

6 The winning team should be presented with an inexpensive prize.
______

HOMEWORK!

Do exercises 1, 2 and 3 on page 101 of your Workbook.

Get ready to write

Article

1 **Read the article and underline one example of:**

1 a short form (*mustn't, haven't*, etc)
2 informal punctuation
3 a question to interest the reader
4 a verb in the imperative
5 chatty and conversational English

Successful Revision

Are you about to start revising for exams? Are you worried you're studying in the wrong way? Then take a look at the tips below. They might be useful!

First, make a list of all your exams and their dates. Add to this list all the books you have to study for each exam. Then, you can begin to work out how much revision time you have for each exam. Give yourself as much time as possible. Don't imagine you'll be able to do it all the night before. You won't!

People revise in different ways. Find out the way that suits you best. When I'm revising, I underline all the important points. I then write out my own list of points and make tests based on my notes. I don't cheat (that's important!) and I keep testing myself until I get the answers right.

Most importantly, stay calm throughout the whole revision period and get a good night's sleep before each exam. Exams aren't much fun but if you revise in the right way you can succeed. Good luck!

2 **Read the writing task and make notes to answer the questions below.**

You saw the advertisement below in a young people's magazine. Write your **article** for the magazine.

Have you ever organised a successful event (a party, a barbeque, a quiz, an outing)?

Could you give our readers some advice and tips on how they could organise something similar?

We'd love to hear from you. Send us your articles.

The best ones will be published in the next issue.

1 What kind of event will you write about?
2 Can you think of five pieces of advice or tips?

3 **Now make a plan in *Composition Planner 15* on page 166.**

HOMEWORK!

You're now ready to write the first draft of your article. Write between 120 and 180 words. When your teacher has commented on your article, write the final version.

16

Buy, Buy, Buy!

Get warmed up!

Discuss the following. Work in pairs or in groups.

- What's the most expensive thing you've ever bought?
- Is there anything you would really like to buy if you had enough money?
- How important is money to you?

Reading 2.22

1 **Do the questionnaire and find out what kind of shopper you are.**

2 **Now read the score on page 143 and choose the correct answer, A, B, C or D.**

1 What would the writer of this questionnaire probably say to someone with a score of 47?
   - A You've got nothing to worry about.
   - B If you're not careful, you might be in trouble.
   - C You need to change your habits immediately.
   - D Make sure you've got enough money.

2 What do the comments at the end of the questionnaire imply?
   - A Boys and girls often have different shopping habits.
   - B Most people these days like shopping.
   - C The higher your score, the better.
   - D It is dangerous not to go shopping.

3 What is the tone of the comments at the end of the questionnaire?
   - A scientific and serious
   - B academic and professional
   - C light-hearted and humorous
   - D formal and persuasive

HOMEWORK!

Do the Reading exercise on page 102 of your Workbook.

What kind of shopper are you?

We're all citizens of the consumer society these days, but what kind of shopper are YOU? Do our quick questionnaire to find out the truth about yourself and your shopping habits!

1 Do you have your own credit card?
- ☐ **a** yes
- ☐ **b** I use my parents' card.
- ☐ **c** no

2 Do you try on clothes before you buy them?
- ☐ **a** always
- ☐ **b** sometimes
- ☐ **c** never

3 Do you keep receipts in case you have to take back what you've bought?
- ☐ **a** always
- ☐ **b** sometimes
- ☐ **c** never

4 Do you look forward to the summer and winter sales?
- ☐ **a** always
- ☐ **b** sometimes
- ☐ **c** never

5 Do you shop around for the cheapest price?
- ☐ **a** always
- ☐ **b** sometimes
- ☐ **c** never

6 When was the last time you ordered something over the internet?
- ☐ **a** last week
- ☐ **b** about three months ago
- ☐ **c** can't remember/never

7 When was the last time you ordered something from a catalogue?
- ☐ **a** last week
- ☐ **b** about three months ago
- ☐ **c** can't remember/never

8 When was the last time you looked through a catalogue?
- ☐ **a** last week
- ☐ **b** about three months ago
- ☐ **c** can't remember/never

9 How important are brand names to you?
- ☐ **a** very
- ☐ **b** not very
- ☐ **c** not at all

10 Do you ever ask for money for your birthday and Christmas presents?
- ☐ **a** always
- ☐ **b** sometimes
- ☐ **c** never

11 **How long would you usually spend in a clothes shop?**

☐ **a** more than one hour
☐ **b** about 30 minutes
☐ **c** as little time as possible

12 **How long would you usually spend in a music shop?**

☐ **a** more than one hour
☐ **b** about 30 minutes
☐ **c** as little time as possible

13 **How would you rather spend next Saturday?**

☐ **a** at a new shopping centre
☐ **b** doing sport
☐ **c** hanging out at home

14 **How often do you buy things that you don't really want just because they are a bargain?**

☐ **a** all the time
☐ **b** sometimes
☐ **c** never

15 **Do you look forward to Christmas shopping?**

☐ **a** very much
☐ **b** a little
☐ **c** not at all

16 **How much money would you take with you on a shopping trip?**

☐ **a** more than €100
☐ **b** about €50
☐ **c** less than €50

17 **Do you have different wallets/purses to match your clothes?**

☐ **a** yes, lots
☐ **b** a few
☐ **c** no

18 **How many hours a week do you spend shopping?**

☐ **a** more than five
☐ **b** between two and five
☐ **c** less than two

19 **Do you know the opening hours of your favourite shops?**

☐ **a** absolutely!
☐ **b** some of them
☐ **c** no

20 **Do you ever watch a TV shopping channel/programme and think 'That looks like a good product'?**

☐ **a** all the time
☐ **b** occasionally
☐ **c** never

DICTIONARY CORNER

Complete each sentence using a word or phrase from the questionnaire.

1 If you ______________ something ______________, you put it on to see if it fits.
2 To ______________ something ______________ means to return something to the shop where you bought it.
3 If you use a ______________ ______________, you don't pay cash and you pay for what you've bought at a later date.
4 A ______________ is a piece of paper that shows you have paid for something.
5 When shops have ______________, they reduce their prices for a certain period of time.
6 A ______________ is a type of book or magazine which shows products and their prices.
7 If you ______________ something, you say you want to buy it and you pick it up or receive it at a later date.
8 If you think something is a ______________, you think its price is very low.
9 ______________ ______________ are the names of companies that make products, eg Reebok.

Have your say!

- Did you enjoy answering the questionnaire?
- Do you think the scoring comments are accurate and sensible?
- Can you think of other questions to include in the questionnaire?

HOMEWORK!

Do exercises 1 and 2 on page 103 of your Workbook.

What kind of shopper are YOU?

Give yourself 3 points for every **a** you ticked, 2 points for every **b** and 1 point for every **c**.

Score

51–60: You're clearly addicted to shopping! Are you sure it's healthy? Are you sure you've got enough money??? Try doing something else for a change.

35–50: You're a sensible shopper at the moment, but if your score is above 45, you're in danger of becoming a shopaholic. Take care – there are other things in life too!

20–34: Have you ever heard of the consumer society? Maybe you should get out more! You're definitely not addicted to shopping. That's good, of course, but you might be in danger of being called old-fashioned and boring by many of the people round you.

Grammar 1

Question tags

Look at *Grammar database 31* pages 201–202 before you do the exercises.

1 Match to make sentences.

1 You're not going to buy those jeans,
2 Stacy used her credit card,
3 They will give you a refund,
4 I'm allowed to try these on,
5 Dan's got the new *Sarks* catalogue,
6 Don't spend too much money,

a didn't she?
b aren't I?
c hasn't he?
d are you?
e will you?
f won't they?

2 Underline the mistake in each sentence and write the word or phrase correctly.

1 Let's go to that new shopping centre tomorrow, will we?
____

2 That new department store hasn't opened yet, hasn't it?
____

3 I'm going to regret buying this, amn't I?
____

4 Dana never pays back the money she borrows, doesn't she?
____

5 Shop assistants should never be rude to customers, shouldn't they?
____

3 Complete each sentence with a question tag.

1 Your dad works in a bank, ______________
2 It isn't a bank holiday today, ______________
3 Sarah has her food delivered by the supermarket, ______________
4 We haven't been into town for ages, ______________
5 Nobody uses cheque books anymore, ______________
6 Let's see if we can order it online, ______________
7 I'm not a shopaholic, ______________
8 Don't forget to ask about the guarantee, ______________
9 We could always get the cheaper one, ______________

HOMEWORK!
Do exercises 1, 2, 3 and 4 on page 104 of your Workbook.

Listening

1 Label the pictures with the words in the box.

cash • cash card • cash machine
cheque book

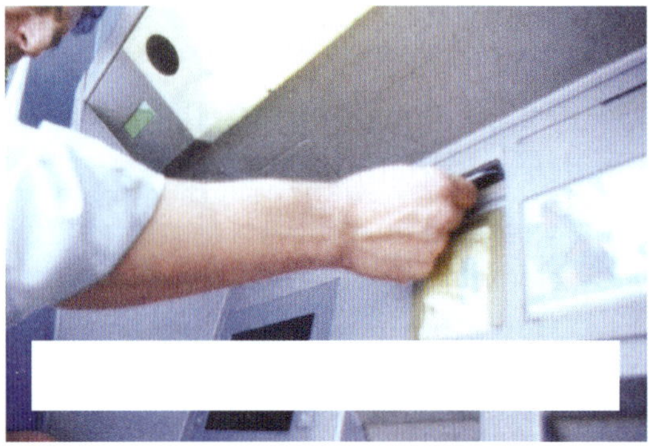

2 2.23 **You are going to listen to Adriana talking to her friends Buck and Claire about money. As you listen, decide if the statements are true (T) or false (F).**

1 Adriana has already opened a bank account. T/F
2 Adriana sometimes writes cheques. T/F
3 Adriana will be given a credit card. T/F
4 Adriana is worried she'll lose her cash card. T/F
5 Adriana decides that a cash card is unnecessary. T/F

3 2.23 **Now listen again and write a short phrase in each gap.**

1 If she wants one, Adriana can get a ______________ from her bank.
2 Buck usually pays with his ______________ when he doesn't want to use cash.
3 Cheques: useful for phone bills and ______________.
4 Banks closed: at the weekend and ______________.
5 Claire thinks Adriana should get a ______________.

HOMEWORK!
Do the Listening exercise on page 107 of your Workbook.

DICTIONARY CORNER

Complete the table with one word on each line.

Verb	Person	Other nouns	Phrases
______	______	shop ______	______ centre go ______
produce	______	______	fresh ______
______	______	consumption	______ rights ______ society
✗	salesperson	______	on ______ for ______ buy something in the ______
deliver	✗	______	pay cash on ______ free ______
manage	______ director	______	✗
______	advertiser	______	______ agency

HOMEWORK!
Do exercises 1 and 2 on page 105 of your Workbook.

G Grammar 2

although, even though, despite, in spite of

Look at *Grammar database 32* page 202 before you do the exercises.

1 Choose the correct word or phrase to complete each sentence.

1 **In spite / Despite** of the convenience, we rarely order things online.
2 **Although / Despite** the price was reduced, I decided not to buy it.
3 **Even though / In spite of** it's only October, Emma's already done her Christmas shopping.
4 **Despite / Even though** complaining to the manager, I still couldn't get a refund.
5 **Despite the fact that / In spite of** it was Sunday, most of the shops were open.
6 I bought the top **in spite of / although** the price.

2 If a word or phrase in bold is correct, put a tick (✔). If it's incorrect, rewrite it correctly.

1 Although my dad **has** a credit card, he doesn't often use it.
____
2 Even though the top **being** in the sale, Justine decided not to buy it.
____
3 Despite **I looked** in several shops, I couldn't find any jeans I liked.
____
4 Jen bought the shoes in spite of the fact they **being** a bit expensive.
____
5 Even though I **ordered** it three weeks ago, my bike still hasn't arrived.
____

3 Complete each sentence so that it means the same as the sentence before it.

1 The shop is a long way from the city centre but it is popular.
Although ______________________________________.
2 We've got a car but we prefer to take the bus into town.
Even ______________________________________.
3 The jeans were the right size but they didn't feel comfortable.
Despite being ______________________________________.
Despite the fact that ______________________________________.
4 There was a big queue but I decided to wait.
In spite of there being ______________________________________.
In spite of the fact ______________________________________.

HOMEWORK!
Do exercises 1, 2, 3, 4 and 5 on pages 105 and 106 of your Workbook.

Soundstation

1 2.24 Listen to this sentence. You will hear it twice.

You've got the receipt, haven't you?

- First time: The speaker wants the listener to agree. She expects the answer 'Yes, I have.' Her voice goes down at the end.
- Second time: The speaker wants to check that the listener has got the receipt. It's more like a real question. Her voice goes up at the end.

2 2.25 Listen to these sentences. For each one, decide if the speaker wants the listener to agree or if the speaker wants to check that what she thinks is true.

1 You haven't got a bank account, have you? **agree / check**
2 Dave needs some new trainers, doesn't he? **agree / check**
3 They're having it repaired, aren't they? **agree / check**
4 You paid the bill, didn't you? **agree / check**
5 You can come with me, can't you? **agree / check**

3 Now say each sentence both ways. Make sure you make your voice go up or down at the end of the sentence, depending on what you mean.

Speaking

1 **Make notes to answer the questions and give reasons for your opinions.**

1 Do you like going shopping on your own, with friends or with your family?

____

2 Do you ever buy second-hand clothes? Why?/Why not?

____

3 Would you rather pay for something in cash or with a credit card?

____

4 Would you prefer to get money rather than presents for Christmas?

____

5 Which do you think is better, ordering things from a catalogue or buying them from a shop?

____

6 Would you be happy to buy something over the internet?

____

7 Which do you prefer: saving money or spending money?

____

Phrase Bank!

I really like going shopping with … because …

No, I don't. I suppose it's because …

Yes, I do. It's a good idea because …

That's a good question. I think that …

I would rather get presents/money because …

I prefer to save/spend money because …

2 **In pairs, ask and answer the questions in exercise 1. Use your notes to help you, and remember to give reasons.**

3 **Turn to page 169. In pairs, do the role-play activity unit 16.**

See *Speaking database* on page 174.

Use your English!

Use the word given in capitals to form a word that fits in the space in the same line.

KNOW YOUR RIGHTS!

If you're a regular (1) __________, you ought to make sure you know your — SHOP
(2) __________ rights. For example, did you know that TV and radio and newspaper — CONSUME
(3) __________ have to tell the truth? If they say something about a — ADVERTISE
(4) __________ that isn't true, they can be taken to court. Also, if you order something — PRODUCE
and you are promised (5) __________ before a certain date, you should get some money back if it doesn't come in time. — DELIVER

The general rule is: don't be afraid to make a (6) __________. And if a — COMPLAIN
shop (7) __________ is unhelpful or rude, always insist on speaking to the — ASSIST
(8) __________. The shop certainly doesn't want to lose one of its — MANAGE
(9) __________. Now more and more people are buying things — CUSTOM
(10) __________, shops have to try even harder to keep us happy. — LINE

Writing

Punctuation and capitalisation

1 Find the punctuation mistakes in each sentence and rewrite the sentence correctly on the line.

1 I got the new *Homeshopper* catalogue yesterday, its great.

2 This department store has it's own credit card.

3 I asked if I could return the top?

4 «I didn't buy anything.» said Chris.

5 The shop assistant, that served me, was very helpful.

2 Rewrite each of these pieces of writing, capitalising the correct letters and adding any necessary punctuation (full stops, commas, question marks, etc).

1 to mr deacon
from alison davis
subject improvements to deacons newsagents
date 24th February

2 dear charlie
hi how are you thanks for your email im really pleased youre coming to stay with us this christmas youre not going to spend a lot on presents for my family are you

write reply send

3 yours sincerely
jean prentice

4 hardy came into the room good morning he said he sat at the breakfast table and opened the newspaper I see the sales have started he remarked

HOMEWORK!
Do the Writing exercise on page 107 of your Workbook.

GO Get ready to write

Report

1 Read the report and answer the questions.

1 Who wrote the report?
2 Is the report formal or informal?
3 Find two words that introduce contrast.
4 What would be another possible heading for the final paragraph?
5 Find a word or phrase in the report that has a similar meaning to:
   a perfect
   b found out
   c fair, not too high (for prices)
   d the place we have at the moment

To: Mrs Peters
From: Amy Baxter

Subject: New location for 'Cards & Gifts'

Introduction

As requested, I have visited several possible new locations for 'Cards & Gifts'. My findings are outlined below.

24 High Street

Although this shop is in the town centre, it may not be an ideal new location for 'Cards & Gifts' as there is another gift shop next door. However, the shop is very large, and I discovered that the rent is only €500 per month. This is very reasonable for the centre.

18 Cartwright Avenue

This shop is not as large as 24 High Street, but it is larger than our current location. The building is in very good condition and is only five minutes' walk from the centre. The rent is €450 per month.

67 Fisher Lane

The shop is extremely small and in very poor condition.

Recommendation

Of the three shops I visited, I would recommend 18 Cartwright Avenue. It is large enough and near the centre. The rent is not expensive and there are no other gift shops nearby.

2 Read the writing task and make notes to answer the questions below.

You work part-time for a sports shop. Your manager has asked you to look at two or three other sports shops in the same area to see if they offer products and services that your sports shop doesn't. Write a **report** for your manager and recommend improvements to your shop based on what you have found.

1 What's the name of your boss?
2 What's the name of your sports shop?
3 How many other shops did you visit?
4 What are they called?
5 What was each shop like?
   What products or services did they offer that your shop doesn't offer?
6 What recommendations will you make?

3 Make a plan in *Composition Planner 16* on page 167.

HOMEWORK!

You are now ready to write the first draft of your report. Write between 120 and 180 words. When your teacher has commented on your report, write the final version.

Revision
Units 15–16

1 Direct and indirect objects

Tick (✔) the correct sentences. If a sentence contains an extra word, write the word on the line.

1 These shoes cost to me over a hundred euros. ______
2 I wrote a letter to the manager last week. ______
3 I've got a great present for Tina. ______
4 My grandma always gives to me a jumper for my birthday. ______
5 We'll send the things you've ordered to you next week. ______
6 I handed my credit card to the shop assistant. ______
7 Steve's bought for Jo a rabbit for Christmas. ______

2 Phrasal verbs

Write a word from the box in each gap to complete the sentences.

after • down • into • on (× 3) • up

1 Do you get ______ well with your boss?
2 He quit his job in order to look ______ his ageing parents.
3 How can you turn ______ such a great job offer?
4 Have you made ______ your mind what you want to do when you leave school?
5 I think I'll only carry ______ working here for another couple of years.
6 Our research is looking ______ why some people are more ambitious than others.
7 Elvis Presley put ______ a lot of weight in the last few years of his life.

3 Question tags

Complete each sentence using the correct question tag.

1 They haven't sent us their new catalogue yet, ______?
2 Rachel's dad works for a credit card company, ______?
3 You're not going to buy that one, ______?
4 We should find out if they're having a sale soon, ______?
5 I'm good at spotting bargains, ______?
6 It's not early closing today, ______?
7 No-one keeps their receipts, ______?

4 *although, even though, despite, in spite of*

Tick (✔) the correct sentences. Put a cross (✘) next to those that are incorrect.

1 Although her qualifications were good, they still didn't offer her the job. ______
2 Even though having a fortune, Howard didn't like wasting money. ______
3 Despite to be unemployed for so long, Gavin never got depressed. ______
4 He never became arrogant, despite the fact that he was so successful. ______
5 In spite being a very talented musician, Gordon never wanted to become a professional. ______
6 I don't mind not being rich, although I do dream about winning the lottery sometimes! ______

5 Shopping and money

Choose the correct words to complete the text.

I'm not a shopaholic!

I admit it. I hate shopping. In fact, I hate it so much I only go clothes shopping once a year. I wait for the (1) **selling / sales** to start, and then go into town to buy all my clothes for the year. I shop (2) **along / around** for the cheapest (3) **bargains / costs** rather than the things I like best. I try them (4) **over / on** and, as long as they fit, I buy them. I don't bother keeping the (5) **bill / receipt**, as I know I won't go back to the shop if there's a problem! Also, I always pay (6) **change / cash**, as I don't want to get a huge (7) **credit / cheque** card bill at the end of the month. And if I really need some new clothes later during the year, I order them from a mail order (8) **catalogue / menu**. It's so much easier – you can look (9) **for / through** it at home and make your decisions without a (10) **shopping / shop** assistant hanging around trying to get you to buy something you don't want!

6 Word formation

Complete each sentence using the correct form of the word in brackets.

1 I love the new __________ (**advertise**) on TV for Carlton's chocolate. It's really funny!
2 They're building a huge __________ (**shop**) centre on the outskirts of town.
3 Can I pay cash on __________ (**deliver**)?
4 He's the __________ (**manage**) director of a company that makes toilet rolls.
5 Everyone should know their __________ (**consume**) rights.
6 We produce over a hundred different __________ (**produce**) in this factory.

7 *prefer, would rather, had better*

Write *prefer, rather* or *better* in each gap to complete these sentences.

1 I'd __________ not pay by cheque, if you don't mind.
2 I __________ going to a travel agent rather than booking flights on the internet.
3 You'd __________ not spend any more money or you won't have enough for this evening.
4 I'd __________ you didn't invite your boss to dinner tomorrow night.
5 You'd __________ try on a bigger pair. Those are too small.
6 Would you __________ to go to another department store first?

8 Success vocabulary

Solve the clues and find the words in the wordsearch puzzle.

Q	F	A	F	E	L	A	K	F	Q	E	S	A	X
Z	U	F	I	U	B	M	L	A	M	E	U	J	Y
X	C	A	W	J	O	W	L	E	I	P	C	L	V
N	A	I	L	R	T	A	U	I	D	F	C	F	A
P	S	L	A	I	O	M	F	E	O	O	E	P	M
Y	Z	U	T	E	F	B	N	H	R	N	E	G	H
J	P	R	S	T	N	I	A	P	U	R	D	B	O
E	F	E	V	H	M	T	C	T	O	D	X	E	Z
G	A	R	F	R	Q	I	R	A	J	E	O	S	Q
I	D	G	E	B	A	O	K	R	T	L	A	I	S
T	U	T	P	E	F	U	A	C	H	I	E	V	E
Q	E	S	T	H	A	S	L	O	I	B	O	M	N
D	A	H	O	T	D	E	R	V	Z	O	P	N	Q
J	O	X	R	P	U	D	X	L	E	A	M	N	S

1 What is the adjective from 'ambition'? (9)
2 If you make a huge amount of money, you make a __________. (7)
3 What's the opposite of 'success'? (7)
4 If you are __________ to do something, you won't let anything stop you from doing it. (10)
5 If you __________ a lot, you manage to do lots of things successfully. (7)
6 Certificates and diplomas show what __________ you have. (14)
7 What's the verb from 'success'? (7)

Laser Composition Planner 1
Informal letter

1 Complete the chart.
Be careful! Do NOT write your letter until your teacher has seen your notes here.

Part	Purpose	Your notes	Useful expressions
First line	greet your pen friend	Dear ______________ ,	
Paragraph 1	thank pen friend for letter; mention something in their letter		Hi! How are you? / How's it going? / Thanks (a lot) for your (last) letter/postcard, etc / It was great to hear … / I'm glad …
Paragraph 2	give your main news (first day back at school) + how you feel about it		Today was … / I felt/feel … / think …
Paragraph 3	continue your news		By the way, … / Oh, yes, I forgot to tell you …
Paragraph 4	give a reason for ending the letter		(Well,) I'd better go now as … / I have to go now as …
Closing expressions (1)	final remarks		Write soon, / Take care, and I hope to hear from you soon. / See you soon!
Closing expressions (2)	express love		Love, / Lots of love, / All the best,
Final line	say who you are (first name only)		

2 When you have finished the first draft of your letter, and before you give it to your teacher, check that you haven't made any serious mistakes by ticking (✔) the checklist on the right.

- ☐ I have started with *Dear*.
- ☐ I have written four main paragraphs.
- ☐ I have used some short forms (*haven't, can't,* etc).
- ☐ I have used some informal vocabulary and punctuation.
- ☐ I have mentioned my pen friend's letter in the first main paragraph.
- ☐ I have given my news about the first day of school.
- ☐ I have said why I have to finish the letter.
- ☐ I have used some closing expressions.
- ☐ I have not written my surname at the bottom of the letter.

Laser Composition Planner 2

Short story

1 **Complete the chart.**
Be careful! Do NOT write your story until your teacher has seen your notes here.

Part	Purpose	Your notes	Useful expressions
Title	briefly tell us what the story is about		
Paragraphs 1 and 2	introduce main character(s), say when the story happened describe the dream		One night / A few months ago / strange /weird/bizarre/odd / While he was asleep / In the dream / He dreamed that …
Paragraphs 3 and 4	say what happened the next day / shortly afterwards, describe how the dream came true		The next morning, … / The next day, … / Later that week, …
Final paragraph	bring the story to a close, say how he felt and reacted, finish with the correct ending		His dream had come true! / It was just like in his dream. / … and he always believed in his dreams from that day on.

2 **When you have finished the first draft of your story, and before you give it to your teacher, check that you haven't made any serious mistakes by ticking (✔) the checklist on the right.**

- ☐ I have written at least four paragraphs.
- ☐ I have used some direct and some indirect speech.
- ☐ My direct speech is informal.
- ☐ The rest of the story is formal.
- ☐ The main tense is the past simple.
- ☐ I have tried to use descriptive language.
- ☐ The story finishes with the correct ending.

Laser Composition Planner 3
Essay

1 **Complete the chart.**
Be careful! Do NOT write your essay until your teacher has seen your notes here.

Part	Purpose	Your notes	Useful expressions
Paragraph 1	introduce the subject		There is no doubt that … / Schools cannot allow … / However,
Paragraph 2	present arguments in favour of permanent exclusion, give reasons		On the one hand, / Firstly, Secondly, etc / For example, / Because of this,
Paragraph 3	present arguments against permanent exclusion, give reasons		On the other hand, / … such as … / As a result,
Paragraph 4	come to a conclusion		In conclusion, / I believe that …

2 **When you have finished the first draft of your essay, and before you give it to your teacher, check that you haven't made any serious mistakes by ticking (✔) the checklist on the right.**

- ☐ I have written four paragraphs.
- ☐ I have used formal English.
- ☐ I have used key essay words and phrases.
- ☐ I have given some examples.
- ☐ I have given some reasons.
- ☐ I have expressed my opinion.

Laser Composition Planner **4**

Informal email

1 **Complete the chart.**
Be careful! Do NOT write your email until your teacher has seen your notes here.

Part	Purpose	Your notes	Useful expressions
First line	greet your friend	Dear ________ ,	
Paragraph 1	Thank friend for email; mention something in their email		Hi! How are you? / How's it going? / Thanks (a lot) for your email. It was great to hear … / I'm glad …
Paragraph 2	mention the project; say you'll be happy to answer their questions		Your project sounds interesting / I'd be happy to …
Paragraph 3	answer the questions and give a little more information		I like her because … / I've been a fan for … / My favourite song of hers is …
Paragraph 4	finish main part of email; give a reason for ending the email		Anyway, let me know … / I'd better go now as … / I have to go now as …
Closing expressions (1)	final remarks		Write soon! / Take care, and hope to hear from you soon. / See you soon!
Closing expressions (2)	express love		Love, / Lots of love, / All the best,
Final line	say who you are (first name only)	________	

2 **When you have finished the first draft of your email, and before you give it to your teacher, check that you haven't made any serious mistakes by ticking (✔) the checklist on the right.**

- ☐ I have started with *Dear.*
- ☐ I have written four main paragraphs.
- ☐ My email is informal.
- ☐ I have mentioned my friend's email in the first main paragraph.
- ☐ I have answered ALL my friend's questions.
- ☐ I haven't just copied the notes.
- ☐ I have added some information that is not in the notes.
- ☐ I have used some closing expressions.
- ☐ I have not written my surname at the bottom of the email.

Laser Composition Planner 5
Formal letter

1 **Complete the chart.**
Be careful! Do NOT write your letter until your teacher has seen your notes here.

Part	Purpose	Your notes	Useful expressions
First line	greeting	Dear Sir / Madam,	
Paragraph 1	reason for writing letter; where you saw advertisement		I am writing with regard to …, which I saw in …, / I am interested in …, / However, …
Paragraph 2	first question		I would be grateful if you could …, / I wonder if you could / would …,
Paragraph 3	second question		Could you …?, / Secondly, / further information,
Paragraph 4	third question		regarding, / let me know, / send me
Closing expressions (1)	final remarks		I look forward to hearing from you.
Closing expressions (2)	express respect		Yours faithfully,
Final line	say who you are (first name and surname)		

2 **When you have finished the first draft of your letter, and before you give it to your teacher, check that you haven't made any serious mistakes by ticking (✔) the checklist on the right.**

- ☐ I have started with *Dear Sir/Madam*,.
- ☐ My letter is formal.
- ☐ I have not used any short forms (*I'm*, *can't*, etc).
- ☐ I have used formal letter words, phrases and expressions.
- ☐ I have mentioned all the information in the notes.
- ☐ I have used the correct closing expressions.
- ☐ I have written my first name and my surname at the end.

Laser Composition Planner 6
Report

1 **Complete the chart.**
Be careful! Do NOT write your report until your teacher has seen your notes here.

Part	Purpose	Your notes	Useful expressions
First line	say who the report is for (first name or Mr/ Mrs/ Ms + surname)	To: ______________	
Second line	say who wrote the report (first name + surname)	From: ______________	
Third line	say what the report is about	Subject: ______________	
Paragraph 1	introduction	(heading) ______________	The aim of the report is to … / As requested, I interviewed … / My findings are presented below.
Paragraphs 2 and 3	main findings	(heading) ______________ (heading) ______________ (heading) ______________	Firstly, / However, / For example, / Furthermore,
Final paragraphs	conclusion and recommendations	(heading) ______________	I would recommend / suggest that … / We should/ could also consider …

2 **When you have finished the first draft of your report, and before you give it to your teacher, check that you haven't made any serious mistakes by ticking (✔) the checklist on the right.**

- [ ] I have started with *To:*, *From*: and *Subject*:.
- [ ] All my paragraphs have headings.
- [ ] I have used formal vocabulary and grammar.
- [ ] I have used some set report phrases.
- [ ] I have made some recommendations in my final paragraph.

Laser Composition Planner **7**

Article

1 **Complete the chart.**
Be careful! Do NOT write your article until your teacher has seen your notes here.

Part	Purpose	Your notes	Useful expressions
Title	briefly tell us what the article is about		
Paragraph 1	introduce the topic, get the reader's interest		Have you ever ...? I have. / It all started ...
Paragraph 2	say what you did and how you felt before the contest		On the day of the contest, / Before it started, / I felt really ...
Paragraph 3	describe the contest and how you felt during it		When I went out on stage, ... / Everyone clapped and cheered / I've never felt so ...
Paragraph 4	conclude and look to the future		It was the best / worst / most exciting, etc experience I've ever had. / I can't wait to enter ... / I'll never enter another ...

2 **When you have finished the first draft of your article, and before you give it to your teacher, check that you haven't made any serious mistakes by ticking (✔) the checklist on the right.**

- ☐ I have written at least four paragraphs.
- ☐ I have used a fairly informal style.
- ☐ I have used some short forms (*won't, can't,* etc).
- ☐ I have described what I did in the contest.
- ☐ I have said how I felt.
- ☐ I have said if I won or not.

Laser Composition Planner **8**

Letter of advice

1 Complete the chart.
Be careful! Do NOT write your letter until your teacher has seen your notes here.

Part	Purpose	Your notes	Useful expressions
First line	greet your pen friend	Dear ______________,	
Paragraph 1	thank pen friend for letter; mention something in their letter (but not their problem)		Hi! How are you? / How's it going? / Thanks (a lot) for your (last) letter. / It was great to hear … / I'm glad …
Paragraph 2	mention their problem; say whether you agree or disagree with their parents' view		I was sorry to hear about / that … / To be honest, … / If you ask me … / I tend to think that …
Paragraph 3	make your suggestions		If I were you, … / How about …? / I'd suggest … / My advice would be to … / Perhaps you should/could … / Why don't you …?
Paragraph 4	give a reason for ending the letter		(Well,) I'd better go now as … / I have to go now as …
Closing expressions (1)	final remarks		Write soon! / Take care, and hope to hear from you soon / See you soon!
Closing expressions (2)	express love		Love, / Lots of love, / All the best,
Final line	say who you are (first name only)	________	

2 When you have finished the first draft of your letter, and before you give it to your teacher, check that you haven't made any serious mistakes by ticking (✔) the checklist on the right.

- ☐ My letter is informal.
- ☐ I have started with *Dear* + first name.
- ☐ I have mentioned my pen friend's letter in the first paragraph.
- ☐ I have said whether or not I agree with my pen friend's parents.
- ☐ I have made some suggestions.
- ☐ I have written at least four main paragraphs.
- ☐ I have used some closing expressions.
- ☐ I have put my first name at the bottom of the letter.

Laser Composition Planner **9**

Short story

1 Complete the chart.
Be careful! Do NOT write your story until your teacher has seen your notes here.

Part	Purpose	Your notes	Useful expressions
Title	briefly tell us what the story is about		
Paragraph 1	say who you played the joke on; give a reason why		It was April 1st, so I decided to play a practical joke on … / X was a great person to choose because …
Paragraph 2	describe how you prepared the joke		I planned it carefully, / First, I … / Then, … / After that, …
Paragraph 3	describe how they reacted		When X came in, etc … /upset/annoyed /shocked/surprised
Final paragraph	bring the story to a close, say how you felt and they felt afterwards		Afterwards, … / X saw the funny side

2 When you have finished the first draft of your story, and before you give it to your teacher, check that you haven't made any serious mistakes by ticking (✔) the checklist on the right.

- ☐ I have started with the correct words.
- ☐ I have written at least four paragraphs.
- ☐ My story has a beginning, a middle and an end.
- ☐ I have used some direct speech.
- ☐ The direct speech is informal.
- ☐ The main tense is past simple.

Laser Composition Planner 10
Informal letter

1 Complete the chart.
Be careful! Do NOT write your letter until your teacher has seen your notes here.

Part	Purpose	Your notes	Useful expressions
First line	greet your friend	Dear ______________,	
Paragraph 1	thank friend for letter; mention something in their letter		Hi! How are you? / How's it going? / Thanks (a lot) for your (last) letter/postcard, etc / It was great to hear … / I'm glad …
Paragraph 2	give your main news (preparation for sporting event, + how you feel about it)		I'm really busy at the moment because … / Actually, I feel (a bit) nervous/ worried, etc
Paragraph 3	continue your news		By the way, … / Oh yes, I forgot to tell you …
Paragraph 4	give a reason for ending the letter		(Well,) I'd better go now as … / I have to go now as …
Closing expressions (1)	final remarks		Write soon! / Take care, and hope to hear from you soon. / See you soon!
Closing expressions (2)	express love		Love, / Lots of love, / All the best,
Final line	say who you are (first name only)		

2 When you have finished the first draft of your letter, and before you give it to your teacher, check that you haven't made any serious mistakes by ticking (✔) the checklist on the right.

- ☐ I have used informal grammar, vocabulary and punctuation.
- ☐ I have mentioned my friend's letter in the first paragraph.
- ☐ I have described my preparations and feelings in the second paragraph.
- ☐ I have said why I feel the way I do.
- ☐ I have mentioned some other news in the third paragraph.
- ☐ I've given a reason for ending the letter in the fourth paragraph.

Laser Composition Planner **11**

Essay

1 **Complete the chart.**
Be careful! Do NOT write your essay until your teacher has seen your notes here.

Part	Purpose	Your notes	Useful expressions
Paragraph 1	introduce the subject		Being green means … / For example, …
Paragraph 2	agree or disagree with the statement; give reasons		Although it is true that … / This is because …
Paragraph 3	explain the result(s) /effect(s) of the points you made in the second paragraph		Because of this, … / For this reason, … / As a result, …
Paragraph 4	come to a conclusion		In conclusion, / I believe that …

2 **When you have finished the first draft of your essay, and before you give it to your teacher, check that you haven't made any serious mistakes by ticking (✔) the checklist on the right.**

- ☐ I have written at least four paragraphs.
- ☐ I have used formal English.
- ☐ I have used essay words and phrases.
- ☐ I have given some examples.
- ☐ I have given some reasons.
- ☐ I have expressed my opinion.

Laser Composition Planner **12**
Informal email

1 **Complete the chart.**
Be careful! Do NOT write your email until your teacher has seen your notes here.

Part	Purpose	Your notes	Useful expressions
First line	say who wrote the email (name or email address or both)	From: ____________	
Second line	say who the email is for (name or email address or both)	To: ____________	
Third line	give your email a title	Subject: ____________	
First line of email	greet your friend	Dear ____________, Hi, ____________,	
Paragraph 1	thank your friend for their email and mention something in their email		Hi! How are you? / How's it going? / Thanks (a lot) for your email. It was great to hear … / I'm glad …
Paragraph 2	respond to their main questions		Yes, I do/have … / It's a great idea. I'd suggest …
Paragraph 3	mention any other news you have		Oh, by the way, … / I forgot to tell you …
Paragraph 4	give a reason for ending the email		Well, got to go now … / I've got to go now …
Closing expressions (1)	final remarks		Write soon! / Take care, and hope to hear from you soon. / See you soon!
Closing expressions (2)	express love		Love, / Lots of love, / All the best,
Final line	say who you are (first name only)		

2 **When you have finished the first draft of your email, and before you give it to your teacher, check that you haven't made any serious mistakes by ticking (✔) the checklist on the right.**

- ☐ I have used informal and conversational English.
- ☐ I have mentioned my friend's email in the first paragraph.
- ☐ I have responded to their questions.
- ☐ I have used all the notes I made on the printout.
- ☐ I have written at least four paragraphs.

Laser Composition Planner 13
Letter of application

1 **Complete the chart.**
Be careful! Do NOT write your letter until your teacher has seen your notes here.

Part	Purpose	Your notes	Useful expressions
First line	greet the person you are writing to	Dear Mr ________,	
Paragraph 1	say why you are writing: where and when you saw the advert		I am writing to apply for the position of … as advertised in …
Paragraph 2	give some information about yourself and your experience		I am … / currently / experienced at … as …
Paragraph 3	ask questions		I wonder if you could … / I would also be grateful if you could …
Paragraph 4	say you are happy to attend an interview; say you are happy to give more information if they need it		I would be more than happy … / Please do not hesitate …
Closing expressions (1)	ask them to reply		I look forward …
Closing expressions (2)	express respect		Yours sincerely,
Final line	first name + surname		

2 **When you have finished the first draft of your letter, and before you give it to your teacher, check that you haven't made any serious mistakes by ticking (✔) the checklist on the right.**

- ☐ I have started with *Dear Mr* + surname.
- ☐ I have written four main paragraphs.
- ☐ I have not used any short forms (*haven't, can't,* etc).
- ☐ My letter is formal.
- ☐ I have used all the information from my notes.
- ☐ I have asked some indirect questions.
- ☐ I have used the letter of application phrases.
- ☐ I have written a first name and surname at the bottom of the letter.

Laser Composition Planner **14**
Review

1 **Complete the chart.**
Be careful! Do NOT write your review until your teacher has seen your notes here.

Part	Purpose	Your notes	Useful expressions
Title	the name of the tourist attraction		
Paragraph 1	give basic information about the place, including where it is		… is very near … / … is not far from … / … is one of the most popular attractions in the area … / is famous for …
Paragraph 2	describe one or two of the main things you can do/see there		Most people who go there … / One of the best things to do is … / One of the main attractions is … / You can also … / You also have the chance to … / Visitors can …
Paragraph 3	mention one or two more things you can do/see there		
Final paragraph	say if you recommend or don't recommend the place and briefly explain why		I would definitely recommend … / If you go to …, you must visit … / It's perfect for … / I wouldn't recommend it to …

2 **When you have finished the first draft of your review, and before you give it to your teacher, check that you haven't made any serious mistakes by ticking (✔) the checklist on the right.**

- ☐ I have given my review a title.
- ☐ I have said where the attraction is.
- ☐ I have mentioned several things to do or see there.
- ☐ I have recommended visiting or not visiting the place.
- ☐ I have said why I recommend or don't recommend the place.
- ☐ I have written four main paragraphs.
- ☐ I have tried to interest the reader.

Laser Composition Planner **15**

Article

1 **Complete the chart.**
Be careful! Do NOT write your article until your teacher has seen your notes here.

Part	Purpose	Your notes	Useful expressions
Title	briefly tell us what the article is about		
Paragraph 1	introduce the subject to the reader		Have you ever …? / Would you like to …? / Here's how … / Have a look …
Paragraph 2	give first two or three pieces of advice		First, … / Remember to … / Don't forget to … / Then …
Paragraph 3	give final two or three pieces of advice		After that … / How about …? / You'd be better …
Paragraph 4	conclude; wish the reader luck		Good luck! / Good luck with organising your … / I hope it's a success!

2 **When you have finished the first draft of your article, and before you give it to your teacher, check that you haven't made any serious mistakes by ticking (✔) the checklist on the right.**

- ☐ I have used a chatty and conversational style.
- ☐ I have written at least four paragraphs.
- ☐ I have asked the reader a question in the first paragraph.
- ☐ I have mentioned what event I am talking about in the first paragraph.
- ☐ I have given four or five pieces of advice.
- ☐ I have wished the reader luck in the final paragraph.

Laser Composition Planner **16**

Report

1 **Complete the chart.**
Be careful! Do NOT write your report until your teacher has seen your notes here.

Part	Purpose	Your notes	Useful expressions
First line	say who the report is for (first name or Mr/Mrs/Ms + surname)	To: ______________	
Second line	say who wrote the report (first name + surname)	From: ______________	
Third line	say what the report is about	Subject: ______________	
Paragraph 1	introduction	(heading) ______________	The aim of this report is to … / As requested, I have looked at … / My findings are presented below.
Paragraph 2	present the information you found out about each shop	(heading) ______________ (heading) ______________ (heading) ______________	One service which X offers … / X sells … / X is very popular because …
Paragraph 3	conclusion and recommendations	(heading) ______________	I would recommend/ suggest that … / We should/could also consider …

2 **When you have finished the first draft of your report, and before you give it to your teacher, check that you haven't made any serious mistakes by ticking (✔) the checklist on the right.**

- ☐ I have started with *To:*, *From:* and *Subject:*.
- ☐ All my paragraphs have headings.
- ☐ I have used formal vocabulary and grammar.
- ☐ I have used some set report phrases.
- ☐ I have made some recommendations in my final paragraph.

Role-play activities

Unit 2

Friend A: You think you've just seen a UFO. Tell your friend what you saw and try to persuade him/her that you're telling the truth.

Friend B: You don't believe your friend. He/She is lying, playing a joke on you or maybe it was just the Moon, a planet or a plane. Try to find out exactly what happened.

Unit 3

Teacher: You're annoyed because the student is always late for class. What are you going to do about it?

Student: You're late for class again. Think of a good excuse and try to persuade the teacher not to punish you.

Unit 4

Journalist: You've just found the phone number of a famous person, so you decide to call him/her to ask for an interview. Be polite, but be persuasive. You want that interview!

Celebrity: (Before you start, decide which famous person you're going to be. Tell your partner.) You're at home when the phone rings. You don't like journalists calling you at home.

Unit 5

Teenager: It's the year 2050. You're 16 years old. You want to go on a trip to the Moon with your friends.

Parent: You're worried your son/daughter is too young to go to the Moon. It might be dangerous! Try to persuade him/her not to go.

Unit 6

Neighbour A: Your neighbour is always playing music really loud late at night. You knock on your neighbour's door to complain. Be polite but try to get them to promise to turn the music down. If they don't, threaten to call the police!

Neighbour B: You don't think the music you play is too loud. You don't like neighbours telling you what to do and you feel like having an argument!

Unit 7

Flatmate A: You want to go out tonight. You're bored with staying in. Try to persuade your flatmate to go out somewhere with you.

Flatmate B: You would rather stay in tonight. Try to persuade your flatmate to stay in with you. You could maybe watch some DVDs and get a pizza.

Unit 8

Brother/Sister A: You are annoyed because your brother/sister is always borrowing your things without asking first. Explain how you feel.

Brother/Sister B: You can't see what the problem is. Brothers and sisters don't have to ask each other first if they want to borrow something!

Unit 9

Friend A: You and your friend want to enter the school talent contest. You think you should do a comedy act.

Friend B: You think that a comedy act is not a good idea. Being funny is difficult! Try to persuade your friend that it would be a better idea to sing a song.

Unit 11

Teenager: You don't recycle anything at home. You think it's time to start. Explain the benefits of recycling to your parent and try to persuade him/her to start recycling.

Parent: You understand that recycling is a good idea, but it's easier just to put rubbish in the bin. You haven't got time to go to the bottle bank and the recycling centre. Explain the situation to your child.

Unit 13

Interviewer: (Before you start, decide with your partner what job this is an interview for.) You are holding a job interview. You want to make sure you get the best person for the job. Ask appropriate questions.

Interviewee: Use your imagination to answer the questions. You've got the right experience and qualifications for the job.

Unit 14

Parent: You're planning the family summer holiday. You really want to go on a camping holiday. You think it will be fun, and your family has never been camping together before.

Teenager: You don't want to go camping. You'd rather have a beach holiday in a resort with some nightlife. Try to persuade your parent that everyone will be happier in a hotel.

Unit 15

Reporter: You work for a local newspaper. You are interviewing a local teenager who won some money to buy equipment for the youth club in a quiz. Ask all the relevant questions.

Teenager: Answer the reporter's questions. Use your imagination!

Unit 16

Customer: You recently bought an item of clothing from a clothes shop. When you got it home, you discovered it had a hole in it. You want a replacement or your money back, but you can't find the receipt. You think the shop assistant will remember you buying the item.

Shop assistant: You remember the customer buying the item of clothing, but the shop policy is clear: No refund or replacement without a receipt. Be polite and explain the situation clearly.

Pattern and collocation database

able	be able to do something
ahead	(go/be) straight ahead
allow	allow someone to do something
apologise	apologise for (doing) something
apply	apply for a job
approve	approve of (doing) something
arrest	arrest someone for (doing) something; be under arrest
asleep	be fast asleep
awake	be wide awake
away	far away (from something)
bath	take/have a bath; be in the bath
beat	beat a person/team, etc
begin	begin (to do)
best	do your best; make the best of something
big	(be in) big trouble
business	(go/be on a) business trip
capable	be capable of doing
care	take care of someone
cause	cause someone to do something
commit	commit a crime; commit suicide
complain	complain about (doing) something
cruise	(go/be on a) luxury cruise
cut	(take/be a) short cut
decision	make a decision
deep	(in a) deep voice
depend	depend on (doing) something
directions	give someone directions
dream	have a dream
effort	make an effort
escape	(have/be a) narrow escape
far	far away (from something)
fast	be fast asleep
favour	do someone a favour
fond	be fond of (doing) something
forward	look forward to (doing) something
fun	have/be fun; make fun of someone
fuss	make a fuss
game	win/play a game/match, etc
goal	score a goal
good	be good at (doing)
good	do (someone) good
guided	(go/be on a) guided tour
help	help someone with something; help someone to do something
high	(have a) high temperature

holiday	be on holiday; have/take a holiday; school holidays; bank holiday
homework	do (your) homework
housework	do (the) housework
idea	have an idea
include	include (doing) something
insist	insist on (doing) something
interested	be interested in (doing) something
involve	be involved in (doing) something
job	apply for a job; have a job
law	be against the law; break the law
let	let someone do
likely	be likely to do; be likely that + clause
long	for a long time
look	look forward to (doing) something
luxury	(go/be on a) luxury cruise
make	make someone do; be made to do
manage	manage to do
mind	make up your mind (to do)
miss	miss a plane/ferry, etc
mistake	make a mistake
motion	(in) slow motion
narrow	(have/be a) narrow escape
part	take part in something
pass	time passes (quickly/slowly, etc)
pity	take pity on someone
plan	plan your route
prepare	prepare for something
prevent	prevent someone from doing
ready	be ready for something; be ready to do
responsible	be responsible for (doing) something
route	plan your route
school	(go/be on a) school trip
score	score a goal
short	(take/be a) short cut
slow	(in) slow motion
spare	spare time
spend	spend time doing; spend money on something
straight	(go/be) straight ahead
succeed	succeed in (doing) something
temperature	(have a) high temperature
time	for a long time; spare time; find/have (the) time to do; take up time; for the time being; spend time doing; time passes (quickly/slowly, etc); it takes time to do; for the first/last, etc time; have a good/nice, etc time (doing)
tour	(go/be on a) guided tour
trip	(go/be on a) business/school trip
trouble	(be in) big trouble
voice	(in a) deep voice
way	make your way
wide	be wide awake
win	win a game/match/competition, etc; win a prize/trophy, etc

Phrasal verb database

break out	escape	*Three prisoners **broke out** of the prison last night.*
bring out	start selling a new product	*We're **bringing out** a new CD next month.*
carry on	continue	*I'm just going out for a minute.* ***Carry on** working while I'm away.*
do up	renovate, redecorate	*We're going to **do up** the living room this weekend.*
fall out	stop being friends (usually because of a disagreement)	*Karen and Mike have **fallen out** again.*
get off	leave a plane, bus, train, etc	*We **got off** the plane and went into the airport.*
get on (well, badly, etc)	have a (good, bad) relationship	*I **get on** well with all my teachers.*
give up	stop, quit	*My dad **gave up** smoking last year.*
go off	explode	*The bomb **went off** at 3am.*
hand out	distribute	*The teacher **handed out** the tests and we started writing.*
let off	not punish	*The teacher decided to **let** us **off**.*
look after	take care of	*Can you **look after** my cat for me while I'm away?*
look out	be careful	***Look out**! There's a car coming.*
make off	escape	*The thieves **made off** on a motorbike.*
make out	see clearly	*I can't **make out** if that's Tracy or not over there.*
make up	invent (a story)	*He said he'd met Madonna but I think he **made** it **up**.*
pick up	meet someone in order to take them somewhere in your car, etc	*Will you **pick** me **up** outside the supermarket?*
put on	gain (usually for weight)	*I **put on** a few kilos while I was on holiday.*
put out	extinguish (a fire, cigarette, etc)	*Dad managed to **put out** the fire before the firemen got there.*
put up	provide accommodation	*Could you **put** me **up** for the night?*
set up	start (a club, organisation, etc)	*I'm thinking of **setting up** a youth club.*
take off	leave the ground (for planes, space rockets, etc)	*We watched the planes **taking off** and landing.*
take up	start (a new hobby, sport, etc)	*I'm thinking of **taking up** golf.*
turn down	not accept	*I was offered the job but I **turned** it **down**.*
turn into	become	*The holiday started well, but it **turned into** a nightmare when I lost my passport.*
turn off	stop a piece of equipment from working by pressing a button or turning a switch (switch off)	*I **turned off** the computer and left the room.*
turn out	be in the end, have as a result	*I thought the party was going to be a disaster, but it **turned out** to be a great success.*
turn up	arrive (often unexpectedly)	*I couldn't believe it when John **turned up** at my door last night.*

Irregular verb database

Bare infinitive	Past simple	Past participle
be	was/were	been
beat	beat	beaten
become	became	become
begin	began	begun
bet	bet	bet
bite	bit	bitten
bleed	bled	bled
blow	blew	blown
break	broke	broken
bring	brought	brought
build	built	built
buy	bought	bought
catch	caught	caught
choose	chose	chosen
come	came	come
cut	cut	cut
dig	dug	dug
do	did	done
drink	drank	drunk
drive	drove	driven
eat	ate	eaten
fall	fell	fallen
feel	felt	felt
find	found	found
fly	flew	flown
forecast	forecast	forecast
forget	forgot	forgotten
get	got	got
give	gave	given
go	went	gone
grow	grew	grown
have	had	had
hear	heard	heard
hide	hid	hidden
hit	hit	hit
hold	held	held
keep	kept	kept
know	knew	known
leave	left	left
lend	lent	lent
let	let	let
lie	lay	lain
lose	lost	lost
make	made	made

Bare infinitive	Past simple	Past participle
mean	meant	meant
meet	met	met
mistake	mistook	mistaken
pay	paid	paid
put	put	put
read	read	read
ride	rode	ridden
ring	rang	rung
run	ran	run
say	said	said
see	saw	seen
sell	sold	sold
send	sent	sent
set	set	set
shake	shook	shaken
shine	shone	shone
shoot	shot	shot
show	showed	shown
shut	shut	shut
sing	sang	sung
sink	sank	sunk
sit	sat	sat
sleep	slept	slept
speak	spoke	spoken
spend	spent	spent
split	split	split
spring	sprang	sprung
stand	stood	stood
steal	stole	stolen
stick	stuck	stuck
sting	stung	stung
strike	struck	struck
swim	swam	swum
take	took	taken
teach	taught	taught
tear	tore	torn
tell	told	told
think	thought	thought
throw	threw	thrown
understand	understood	understood
wake	woke	woken
wear	wore	worn
win	won	won
write	wrote	written

Speaking database

Giving personal information

- My name is …
- I'm … years old.
- I'm still at school and I go to …
- There are … of us in my family.
- I've got … brothers and sisters.
- My dad's a … and my mum's a …
- I enjoy …-ing and …
- When I have free time, I like …-ing and …

Comparing

- A is (much) better/etc than B.
- A is good/etc but B isn't.
- A is not as good as B.
- A is almost as good as B.
- Although A is …, B is …
- On the one hand, …
- On the other hand, …

Expressing preferences

- I like/love …-ing … because …
- I prefer …-ing to …-ing because …
- I'd rather … than …
- I think … is more interesting than …
- because …

Agreeing/Disagreeing

- I completely agree.
- Yes, you're right.
- Yes, that's right.
- I agree with you.
- That's true, but …
- I'm not sure I agree with you.
- I don't agree because …
- I completely disagree.

Giving/Asking for opinion

- I think (that) …
- In my opinion, …
- As far as I'm concerned, …
- If you ask me, …
- I (believe) that …
- My view is that …
- What do you think?
- Do you agree?
- We should …, shouldn't we?
- What do you think of …?
- How/What about …?

Asking for clarification

- Could you say that again, please?
- Could you explain it again, please?
- Could you say that again more slowly, please?
- I'm sorry. Would you mind repeating that?
- Do you mean …?
- What do you mean?
- What does … mean?

Grammar database

1 Present simple and present continuous

We use present simple for:

- actions that happen always, usually, often, regularly, every day/week/month/year, etc, sometimes, rarely, never
  *She usually **goes** to bed at 10 o'clock.*
- states
  *His hair **is** quite long at the moment.*
- general truths and facts
  *Water **freezes** at 0°C.*

Present simple: the verb *to be*

Positive	Negative	Question
I **am** tall. (I'**m**)	I **am not** tall. (I'**m not**)	**Am** I tall?
You **are** tall. (You'**re**)	You **are not** tall. (You **aren't**,You'**re not**)	**Are** you tall?
He **is** tall. (He'**s**)	He **is not** tall. (He **isn't**, He'**s not**)	**Is** he tall?
She **is** tall. (She'**s**)	She **is not** tall. (She **isn't**, She'**s not**)	**Is** she tall?
It **is** tall. (It'**s**)	It **is not** tall. (It **isn't**, It'**s not**)	**Is** it tall?
We **are** tall. (We'**re**)	We **are not** tall. (We **aren't**, We'**re not**)	**Are** we tall?
You **are** tall. (You'**re**)	You **are not** tall. (You **aren't**, You'**re not**)	**Are** you tall?
They **are** tall. (They'**re**)	They **are not** tall. (They **aren't**, They'**re not**)	**Are** they tall?

NOTE See *Grammar database 10* for information on use of present simple to talk about the future.

Present simple: regular verbs

Positive	Negative	Question
I **like** pizza.	I **do not like** pizza. (**don't**)	**Do** I **like** pizza?
You **like** pizza.	You **do not like** pizza. (**don't**)	**Do** you **like** pizza?
He **likes** pizza.	He **does not like** pizza. (**doesn't**)	**Does** he **like** pizza?
She **likes** pizza.	She **does not like** pizza. (**doesn't**)	**Does** she **like** pizza?
It **likes** pizza.	It **does not like** pizza. (**doesn't**)	**Does** it **like** pizza?
We **like** pizza.	We **do not like** pizza. (**don't**)	**Do** we **like** pizza?
You **like** pizza.	You **do not like** pizza. (**don't**)	**Do** you **like** pizza?
They **like** pizza.	They **do not like** pizza. (**don't**)	**Do** they **like** pizza?

! BE CAREFUL!
I have – he/she has
I go – he/she goes
I do – he/she does

Emphatic present simple

We can use the emphatic present simple to emphasise an action or state, particularly to emphasise that it is true, or that it's different from what someone else thinks.

Emphatic present simple = subject + do/does + bare infinitive

present simple: *Pete **knows** the answer.*
emphatic present simple: *Pete **does know** the answer.*

NOTE We CANNOT use the emphatic present simple with the verb *be*.

We use present continuous for:

- actions happening at the moment of speaking
  *Tracy **is having** a bath at the moment.*
- temporary situations and actions in the present
  *This week, we **are learning** about the present continuous.*

BE CAREFUL!

We can also use present continuous for repeated actions (with *always*) to emphasise that the action is annoying or unexpected.

*You are **always complaining**!*
*He is **always giving** me little surprise presents.*

We can also use present continuous for changing situations (usually with *more and more, better and better*, etc).

*The weather **is getting** worse and worse every day.*

NOTE See *Grammar database 10* for information on use of present continuous to talk about the future.

Present continuous

Positive	Negative	Question
I **am doing** it now. (I'**m**)	I **am not doing** it now. (I'**m not**)	**Am** I **doing** it now?
You **are doing** it now. (You'**re**)	You **are not doing** it now. (You **aren't**, You'**re not**)	**Are** you **doing** it now?
He **is doing** it now. (He'**s**)	He **is not doing** it now. (He **isn't**, He'**s not**)	**Is** he **doing** it now?
She **is doing** it now. (She'**s**)	She **is not doing** it now. (She **isn't**, She'**s not**)	**Is** she **doing** it now?
It **is doing** it now. (It'**s**)	It **is not doing** it now. (It **isn't**, It'**s not**)	**Is** it **doing** it now?
We **are doing** it now. (We'**re**)	We **are not doing** it now. (We **aren't**, We'**re not**)	**Are** we **doing** it now?
You **are doing** it now. (You'**re**)	You **are not doing** it now. (You **aren't**, You'**re not**)	**Are** you **doing** it now?
They **are doing** it now. (They'**re**)	They **are not doing** it now. (They **aren't**, They'**re not**)	**Are** they **doing** it now?

2 Stative verbs

Some verbs are not usually used in their continuous form, ie in present continuous, past continuous, etc.
These are called stative verbs.

✔ ***I understand** now.*
✘ ~~*I am understanding now*~~.

The most common stative verbs are:

appear	doubt	imagine	love	own	remember	want
believe	forget	know	mean	possess	seem	wish
belong to	hate	like	need	prefer	understand	

BE CAREFUL!

Some verbs are stative with one meaning and not stative with another meaning.
See below:

Verb	Stative meaning/use	Non-stative meaning/use
be	used for states rather than actions *It **is** three o'clock.*	used for temporary behaviour and action at the present time *You'**re being** lazy.*
have	possess, own; experience an emotion, sensation, state, etc *I **have** pink hair at the moment.*	used for actions *I'**m having** a bath at the moment.*
feel	have an opinion, believe *I **feel** that we get too much homework.*	tough; experience an emotion, sensation, etc *I'**m feeling** a bit ill at the moment.*
think	have an opinion, believe *What **do** you **think** about our new teacher?*	consider; use your brain *What **are** you **thinking** about at the moment?*

3 Past simple and past continuous

We use past simple for:

- completed actions at a specific time in the past
  *I **bought** three CDs yesterday.*
- completed situations and states in the past
  *I **had** green hair for a while as a teenager.*
- repeated actions in the past
  *We **played** football every Saturday.*
- the main events and situations in a story
  *I **ran** out of the house, **crossed** the road and **jumped** on the bus.*

Regular verbs

Positive = subject + bare infinitive + *-ed*

*appear: I/You/He/She/We/You/They **appeared***

Negative = subject + *did not (didn't)* + bare infinitive

*I/You/He/She/We/You/They **didn't appear***

Question = *Did* + subject + bare infinitive

***Did** I/you/he/she/we/you/they **appear**?*

Irregular verbs

For a list of irregular verbs, see page 173.

The negative and question forms for irregular verbs are the same as for regular verbs.

- Positive: *Inga **went** to London.*
- Negative: *Inga **didn't go** to London.*
- Question: ***Did** Inga **go** to London?*

The only exception is the verb *be*:

- Positive: *You **were** in London. / Inga **was** in London.*
- Negative: *You **were not (weren't)** in London. / Inga **was not (wasn't)** in London.*
- Question: ***Were** you in London? / **Was** Inga in London?*

Emphatic past simple

We can use the emphatic past simple to emphasise an action or situation in the past, particularly to emphasise that it actually happened, or that it's different to what someone else thinks.

emphatic past simple = subject + *did* + bare infinitive

- Past simple: *I know you don't believe me but I **saw** a ghost.*
- Emphatic past simple: *I know you don't believe me but I **did see** a ghost.*

NOTE We CANNOT use the emphatic past simple with the verb *be*.

We use past continuous for:

- an action or situation in the past which was already happening when another action situation happened (usually used with past simple)
  *I **was walking** down the street when I **had** a great idea.*

past continuous ⟷ (I **was walking** down the street)
past simple ↓ (I **had** a great idea)

- an action or situation in the past which is interrupted or stopped by another action or situation (usually used with past simple)
  *I **was riding** my bike when I **had** an accident.*

past continuous ← (I **was riding** my bike)
past simple ↓ (I **had** an accident)

- background information and description (ie not main events) in a story
  *We got to the beach at half past two. Hundreds of people **were sunbathing** on the golden sand. (ie when we got there)*
- two unfinished situations or events in progress at the same time
  *I **was doing** my homework while Dan **was playing** his computer game.*

past continuous ⟷ (I **was doing** my homework)
past continuous ⟷ (Dan **was playing**)

! BE CAREFUL!

We do NOT use past continuous for regular or repeated actions in the past. So, we do NOT say:

✔ *I **played** football every Saturday.*
✘ ~~*I was playing football every Saturday.*~~

NOTE See *Grammar database 4* for more information on this.

Past continuous

Positive	Negative	Question
I **was eating**.	I **was not eating**. (**wasn't**)	**Was** I **eating**?
You **were eating**.	You **were not eating**. (**weren't**)	**Were** you **eating**?
He **was eating**.	He **was not eating**. (**wasn't**)	**Was** he **eating**?
She **was eating**.	She **was not eating**. (**wasn't**)	**Was** she **eating**?
It **was eating**.	It **was not eating**. (**wasn't**)	**Was** it **eating**?
We **were eating**.	We **were not eating**. (**weren't**)	**Were** we **eating**?
You **were eating**.	You **were not eating**. (**weren't**)	**Were** you **eating**?
They **were eating**.	They **were not eating**. (**weren't**)	**Were** they **eating**?

4 *used to* and *would*

- We saw in *Grammar database 3* that we can use past simple (and NOT past continuous) for repeated actions in the past.

  *I **played** basketball every Saturday when I was a teenager.*

- We can also use *used to* + bare infinitive or *would* + bare infinitive.

  *I **used to play** basketball every Saturday when I was a teenager.*
  *I **would play** basketball every Saturday when I was a teenager.*

- These forms are also possible, but they are less common:

  *I **didn't used to like** chocolate, but I do now.*
  *I **didn't use to like** chocolate, but I do now.*
  *I **used not to like** chocolate, but I do now.*

! BE CAREFUL!
For continuing states and situations (rather than actions), we CAN use past simple or *used to*, but we CANNOT use *would*.

✔ *I **loved** toy shops when I was a kid.*
✔ *I **used to love** toy shops when I was a kid.*
✘ ~~*I **would love** toy shops when I was a kid.*~~

- There are several ways of expressing the negative with *used to*. The most common is with *never*.
  *I **never used to like** chocolate, but I do now.*

! BE CAREFUL!
There are two main ways of asking questions with *used to*:

***Did** you **used to live** in Germany?* (more common)*
***Did** you **use to live** in Germany?* (less common)

***NOTE** Some people think this form is grammatically incorrect.

5 Countable and uncountable nouns

- Countable nouns are nouns we can count. They have a singular and a plural form.

  *one **cat**, two **cats***
  *a **person**, five **people***
  *One **sheep is** in the field. Two **sheep are** in the field.*

- Uncountable nouns are nouns we cannot count. They only have one form.

  *some **music**, a lot of **information***

  We CANNOT say *musics* or *informations*.

- Uncountable nouns are usually followed by a singular verb.

  *That information **is** really important.*

! BE CAREFUL!
Some nouns are countable with one meaning and uncountable with another meaning.

Countable: *The **chickens** were eating. (the birds)*
Uncountable: *That **chicken** was delicious. (the meat)*

- Words and phrases commonly used with countable and uncountable nouns:

Countable nouns	Uncountable nouns
a, an, one, two, three, etc	a piece of
a number of	an amount of
a few	a little
few	little
how many	how much
a lot of	a lot of
lots of	lots of
many	much
some	some
the	the

! BE CAREFUL!

- *Many* and *much* are usually only used in negative sentences and questions.
- In positive sentences it is much more common to use *a lot of* or *lots of* (because *many* and *much* are very formal in positive sentences).
- It is also very common to use *a lot of* and *lots of* in negatives and questions.
- *Few* usually means 'not many' whereas *a few* usually means 'some'.

  ***Few** people believe in ghosts these days.*
  (= not many)
  *I know **a few** people who believe in ghosts.* (= some)

NOTE *only a few* means 'not many'

! BE CAREFUL!

- With uncountable nouns, *little* usually means 'not much' whereas *a little* usually means 'some'.

  *There's very **little** milk left.* (= not very much)
  *There's **a little** milk left.* (some)

NOTE *only a little* means 'not much'

6 Articles

There are three articles in English: *a*, *an* and *the*. How we use them depends on whether a noun is singular or plural, countable or uncountable.

	a/an	*the*	no article
Singular countable nouns	one non-specific thing *That's **a** book.* (it doesn't matter *which* book it is)	• one specific thing *This is **the** book which I told you about.* (a specific book) • generally ***The** car is a great invention.* (= cars generally)	✗
Plural countable nouns	✗	several specific things *These are **the** books which Karen gave me.* (specific books)	generally ***Cars** are a great invention.* (= cars generally)
Uncountable specific nouns	✗	generally *That was **the** furniture Paul gave me.* (specific furniture)	***Furniture** is expensive.* (= furniture generally)

! BE CAREFUL!

Entertainment, media and sport

- *the television* = the piece of equipment, *Turn on **the** TV.*
- *watch television, on television*
  but: *listen to **the** radio, on **the** radio*
- *go to **the** cinema/**the** theatre*
  no article for games and sports, eg *I love tennis.*

Time

- for years, usually no article, eg in *2002* but: ***in the** 1990s, **in the** 20th century*, etc
- for seasons, with *in* and *during*, the meaning is usually the same either with or without article, eg *In winter* or *In the winter*
- for months, no article, eg *in January*
- for days, no article, eg *on Monday*
- *in **the** morning/**the** afternoon/**the** evening but: at night*

Geographical areas

- use *the* with: seas, mountain groups, rivers, island groups, regions, eg ***the** Mediterranean, **the** Alps, **the** Thames, **the** Bahamas, **the** Arctic*
- don't use *the* with: planets, continents, countries, towns/cities, streets, lakes, most mountains, individual islands, eg *Mars, Europe, Germany, London, Carnaby Street, Lake Superior, (Mount) Everest, Crete* but: ***the** Earth, **the** world, **the** Moon, **the** Sun, **the** USA*

Jobs

- usually with *a* or *an*,
  ***She** is **an** engineer.*
  but: use *the* with positions of authority, ***the** Mayor*
- *go to work, be at work*

Organisations

- usually use *the*, eg ***the** army, **the** navy, **the** police*, etc

Public buildings

- usually use *the*, eg ***the** bank, **the** post office*, etc
  but: *go to prison/hospital, be in prison/hospital*
- note: *He's gone to* the *prison*/the *hospital* is possible when the person is only visiting

Nationalities

- no article for particular people, eg *She's Nigerian.*
  but: use *the* when talking about nationalities in general, eg ***The** French drink a lot of wine.*

Travel

- *go home*
- ***on the** bus, **in the** car*, etc
  but: *go by car/bus/bike/plane,* etc

Education

- *go to school/university, be at school/university,* etc
  but: *He's gone to **the** school* is possible when the person is only visiting
- for subjects, usually no article, eg *I love chemistry.*

a or *an*?

- We put *an* before singular countable nouns with a vowel sound. It does NOT depend on spelling.
  ***an** umbrella, **a** university, **an** hour, **a** holiday*, etc.

7 Present perfect simple and present perfect continuous

We use present perfect simple for:

- actions and situations that happened at an unspecified time before the moment of speaking

  *I **have seen** that film loads of times.* (before now)
  *I've never **heard** of that pop group before.*
  *She's just **turned off** the TV.* (not long before now)

- actions and situations that started in the past and still happen, or are still true, at the moment of speaking

  *She **has written** short stories since she was a child.*
  (She still writes short stories.)
  *I **have believed** in ghosts ever since that night.*
  (I still believe in ghosts.)

Present perfect simple (positive):

I/You/We/They + *have* + past participle
He/She/It + *has* + past participle

Present perfect simple (negative):

I/You/We/They + *haven't/have not* + past participle
He/She/It + *hasn't/has not* + past participle

Present perfect simple (question):

Have + I/you/we/they + past participle …?
Has + he/she/it + past participle …?

Time expressions often used with present perfect simple

for (+ period of time)	*I have lived in Austria **for** three years.*
since (+ time when it started)	*I have lived in Austria **since** 2003.*
just	*He has **just** woken up.*
already	*I've got that CD **already**.* *I have **already** got that CD.*
yet (with negatives and questions)	*I haven't seen that film **yet**.* *Have you seen the new Brad Pitt film **yet**?*
still (with negatives)	*I **still** haven't found my sunglasses.*
recently/lately	*I've bought a lot of magazines **recently**.*
so far	*I've read 100 pages of this book **so far**.*
before	*Have you eaten Chinese food **before**?*
ever/never	*Have you **ever** been to Germany?* *I've **never** been to China.*

! BE CAREFUL!

We often use present perfect simple with the superlative and with ordinal numbers (first, second, third, etc).

*It's **the best** film **I've ever seen**.*
*It's the **first** time **I've been** to South America.*
*Carl **has been** to Mexico.*
(= Carl is not in Mexico now.)
*Carl **has gone** to Mexico.*
(= Carl is in Mexico or on his way to Mexico now.)

We use present perfect continuous for:

- actions and situations that started in the past and still continue at the moment of speaking

  *She **has been working** as a journalist for three years.*
- temporary actions and situations in the recent past

  ***I've** just **been reading** an interesting article about celebrities.*

Present perfect continuous (positive):

I/You/We/They + *have* + *been* + *-ing* form
He/She/It + *has* + *been* + *-ing* form

Present perfect continuous (negative):

I/You/We/They + *haven't/have not* + *been* + *-ing* form
He/She/It + *hasn't/has not* + *been* + *-ing* form

Present perfect continuous (question form):

Have + I/you/we/they + *been* + *-ing* form …?
Has + he/she/it + *been* + *-ing* form …?

Time expressions often used with present perfect continuous

for (+ period of time)	*I have been living in Belgium **for** three years.*
since (+ time when it started)	*I have been living in Belgium **since** 2003.*
just	*He has **just** been playing football.*
recently/lately	*I've been seeing a lot of Karen **recently**.*
all day, all morning, etc	*I've been doing my homework **all evening**. I need a break now.*

! BE CAREFUL!

Sometimes, there is very little difference in meaning between present perfect simple and present perfect continuous.

*I **have lived** here for two years now.*
(= I moved here two years ago.)
***I have been living** here for two years now.*
(= I moved here two years ago.)

Sometimes, there is a big difference in meaning.

***I've lived** in Paris, London and Rome.*
(= I don't live in Paris now.)
***I've been living** in Paris for two years now.*
(= I live in Paris.)

8 Comparatives and superlatives

We use comparative adjectives and adverbs to compare things or people that are different and separate from each other.

*Justine is **taller than** Melissa and Eliot.*
*Adam reads **more slowly than** his brother.*

We use superlative adjectives and adverbs to compare one member of a group with the whole group.

*Justine is **the tallest** person in the family.*
*Of all the students in the class, Pete did **the best** in the test.*

NOTE Superlative adverbs are not used very often in English.

BE CAREFUL!

- To compare two or more things that are the same, we use *as* + adjective/adverb + *as*.

  *Dave is **as clever as** Barbara.*
  *Dave ran **as quickly as** Barbara and Alan.*

- We can also use the negative form of this.

  eg *Tim **isn't as tall as** Jan.*
  (= Tim is shorter than Jan.)

Adjectives

Type of adjective	Adjective	Comparative	Superlative
Regular adjectives with one syllable	*old*	+ *-er* *older*	+ *-est* *oldest*
Regular adjectives with one syllable (ending in vowel + consonant)	*big*	double final letter + *-er* *bigger*	double final letter + *-est* *biggest*
Regular adjectives with two syllables ending *-y*	*happy*	replace *-y* with *-ier* *happier*	replace *-y* with *-iest* *happiest*
Other regular adjectives with two or more syllables	*comfortable*	*more/less* + adjective *more comfortable*	*most/least* + adjective *most comfortable*
Irregular adjective, quantifiers	*good* *bad* *far* *little* *much* *many*	*better* *worse* *further* *less* *more* *more*	*best* *worst* *furthest* *least* *most* *most*

Adverbs

Type of adverb	Adverb	Comparative	Superlative
Regular adverbs	*slowly*	*more/less* + adverb *more slowly*	*most/least* + adverb *most slowly*
Irregular adverbs	*badly* *early* *far* *fast (drive fast)* *hard (work hard)* *late* *often* *well (do well)*	*worse* *earlier* *further* *faster* *harder* *later* *more often* *better*	*worst* *earliest* *further* *fastest* *hardest* *latest* *most often* *best*

BE CAREFUL!

- usually

  comparative adjective/adverb + *than*
  (*bigger **than**, more quickly **than***, etc)

  ***the* + superlative adjective/adverb**
  (***the** best, **the** most dangerously*, etc)

- we often use *even* with comparatives:

  *Your computer is cool, but mine is **even** cooler!*

9 *will* and *be going to*

We use both *will* and *be going to* to talk about the future. Sometimes, there is very little difference in meaning. It is often just a matter of formality. *Will* is generally more formal than *be going to*.

We can use either *will* or *be going to* for:

- facts about the future

  There ***will*** *be an eclipse of the sun tomorrow.* (formal)
  *There****'s going to*** *be an eclipse tomorrow.* (informal)

- predictions (opinions about the future) not based on present evidence

  One day, people ***will*** *have holidays on Mars.* (formal)
  One day, people ***are going to*** *have holidays on Mars.* (informal)

- decisions made at the moment of speaking

  I know! ***I'll*** *get Dad a DVD for Christmas.*
  I know! ***I'm going to*** *get Dad a DVD for Christmas.*

NOTE *Will* emphasises the **decision**, whereas *be going to* emphasises the **intention**. The meaning, however, is basically the same in both sentences.

We can use *will* for:

- most first conditional sentences

  *If we leave now, we****'ll*** *be there by six o'clock.*

- offers, suggestions and requests

  I'll *help you.* ***Will*** *you help me?*

! BE CAREFUL!
With offers and suggestions in the question form, we do not use *will* with *I* and *we*. We use *shall*:

✔ ***Shall*** *I help you with the washing-up?*
✘ ~~***Will*** *I help you with the washing-up?*~~

We can use *be going to* for:

- plans and intentions (which you already have when you speak)

  I'm going to *be an astronaut when I grow up.*

- predictions based on present evidence

  *Look out! You****'re going to*** *fall!*

Will

Positive	Negative	Question
I/You/He/She/It/We/ You/They will study	I/You/He/She/It/We/You/ They **won't/will not** study	**Will** I/you/he/she/it/we/ you/they study?

Be going to

Positive	Negative	Question
I **am going to** study (I**'m**)	I **am not going to** study (I**'m**)	**Am** I **going to** study?
You **are going to** study (You**'re**)	You **are not going to** study (You**'re not**, You **aren't**)	**Are** you **going to** study?
He **is going to** study (He**'s**)	He **is not going to** study (He**'s not**, He **isn't**)	**Is** he **going to** study?
She **is going to** study (She**'s**)	She **is not going to** study (She**'s not**, She **isn't**)	**Is** she **going to** study?
It **is going to** study (It**'s**)	It **is not going to** study (It**'s not**, It **isn't**)	**Is** it **going to** study?
We **are going to** study (We**'re**)	We **are not going to** study (We**'re not**, We **aren't**)	**Are** we **going to** study?
You **are going to** study (You**'re**)	You **are not going to** study (You**'re not**, You **aren't**)	**Are** you **going to** study?
They **are going to** study (They**'re**)	They **are not going to** study (They**'re not**, They **aren't**)	**Are** they **going to** study?

10 Present simple and present continuous to talk about the future

We can also use present simple or present continuous to talk about the future.
We can use present simple:

- for timetables, arrangements and fixed events, which the speaker cannot change

  *The flight **leaves** at 3pm tomorrow.*

- after *if* in first conditional and zero conditional sentences (see *Grammar database 15*)

  ***If it rains** tomorrow morning, we'll cancel the match.*

- after certain time expressions, such as *when* and *while* (see *Grammar database 16*)

  *I'll see you **when I get** home next week.*

We can use present continuous for:

- arrangements made before the moment of speaking

  *We**'re leaving** at 3pm next Thursday.*

! BE CAREFUL!

✘ ~~I'm working as a doctor when I'm older.~~
It is NOT an arrangement.

11 Modals 1 (ability, obligation, advice, permission)

Modals	
can	(can't/cannot)
could	(couldn't/could not)
may	(may not)
might	(mightn't/might not)
will	(won't/will not)
would	(wouldn't/would not)
shall	(shan't/shall not)
should	(shouldn't/should not)
must	(mustn't/must not)

! BE CAREFUL!

Modals have only one form. They do NOT take an '-s' in the third person singular.
✘ ~~He **coulds** swim.~~

Semi models

have to

It has a similar meaning to *must*, but it does change its form depending on person and tense.

have/has (got) to

(*don't/doesn't have to/do/does not have to, haven't/ hasn't got to/have/has not got to + didn't have to,* etc)

ought to (oughtn't to/ought not to)

It has a similar meaning to *should*. It doesn't change its form depending on person and tense.

! BE CAREFUL!

Modals are never followed by the full infinitive (with *to*). Use the bare infinitive.
✔ *I **can't go** to the party.*
✘ ~~*I **can't to go** to the party.*~~

Ability

can

now: *I **can** help you now, if you like.*
generally: *Paul **can** play the guitar really well.*

! BE CAREFUL!

For future ability we usually use *will be able to*.
*She**'ll be able to** swim after a few more lessons.*

But we use *can* when we make decisions now about future ability.

*I **can** help you tomorrow, if you like.*

Can CANNOT be used as an infinitive.
Use *to be able to*:

✔ *I'd love **to be able to swim**.*
✘ ~~*I'd love **to can swim**.*~~

could

past: *He **could** swim when he was three years old.*

hypothetical (now/future/generally):
*I wish I **could** swim.*

! BE CAREFUL!

To talk about the hypothetical past with *could*, we have to use the modal perfect (*could* + *have* + past participle). See *Grammar database 13* for further information.

Obligation

must

(personal obligation)

now: *I **must** call Pete now.*
future: *I **must** call Pete tonight.*
generally: *I **must** try harder at school.*

have to (external obligation)

now: *He **has to** go now.*

future: *I **have to** go in five minutes,* or *I'**ll have to** go in five minutes.*

generally: *She **has to** go to bed at 10pm on school nights.*

BE CAREFUL!

When talking about the past for personal or external obligation, use *had to*.

*I **had to** call the doctor last night.*
*You **mustn't** do Exercise C.* (= Don't do Exercise C.)
*You **don't have to** do Exercise C.*
(= You can if you want to but it isn't necessary.)

It is very unusual to use *must* for questions.
Use *have to*.

*Do we **have to** have a test next Tuesday?*

Must CANNOT be used as an infinitive. Use *have to*.

✔ *I'd hate **to have to** move house.*
✘ ~~*I'd hate **to must** move house.*~~

Advice

We can use *should* and *ought to* to ask for and give advice. There is very little difference in meaning between *should* and *ought to*. However, *should* is more common in spoken and written English (both formal and informal) than *ought to*.

now: *You **should/ought to** go to bed if you're tired.*

future: *You **should/ought to** have a party next week.*

generally: *You **should/ought to** exercise more.*

BE CAREFUL!

To talk about the past with *ought to* or *should*, we have to use the modal perfect (*ought to/should* + *have* + past participle). See *Grammar database 13*.

Permission

We can use *can*, *could* and *may* to ask for and give permission. They mean the same thing, but *could* is more polite than *can*, and *may* is more polite than *could*.

now: ***Can/Could/May** I have some more ice cream?*

future: ***Can/Could/May** I go to a party on Tuesday night?*

generally: ***Can/Could/May** I invite my friends round whenever I like?*

BE CAREFUL!

To talk about past permission in reported speech*, use *could*.

*You said I **could** go to a party last week so why can't I this week?*

* see *Grammar database 24*.

To talk about past permission (but not in reported speech), we don't use a modal.

✔ *I **was allowed to go** to the party last week.*
✔ *They/You **let** me **go** to the party last week.*
✘ ~~*I **could go** to the party last week.*~~

12 Modals 2 (possibility, probability, certainty)

Possibility

We can use *may*, *might* and *could* to say that something is possible. They have a similar meaning, but sometimes we use *might* to show something is less likely to happen.

*That **may/might/could** be the postman.* (now)

BE CAREFUL!

For non-stative verbs, we often use the continuous infinitive after *may*, *might* or *could* when talking about actions happening now.

*Anne **may/might/could be driving** home from work now.*

now: *That **may/might/could** be the postman.*

future: *I think it **may/might/could** snow later today.*

generally: *There **may/might/could** be penguins in Antarctica, but I'm not sure.*

BE CAREFUL!

To talk about past possibility with *may*, *might* or *could*, we have to use the modal perfect: *may/might/could* + *have* + past participle.
See *Grammar database 13*.

Probability

We can use *should* and *ought to* to say that something is quite likely. There is little difference in meaning between *should* and *ought to*. However, *should* is more common in spoken and written English (both formal and informal) than *ought to*.

now: *Anne* ***should/ought to*** *be on the way home now.*

BE CAREFUL!

For non-stative verbs, we often use the continuous infinitive after *should* or *ought to* when talking about actions happening now.

Anne should/ought to be *driving home from work now.*

future: *I* ***should/ought to*** *finish the project tomorrow, if all goes well.*

generally: *Most people* ***should/ought to*** *be able to understand this.*

BE CAREFUL!

For non-stative verbs, we often use the continuous infinitive after *should or ought to* when talking about actions happening now. To talk about past probability with *ought to* or *should*, we have to use the modal perfect: *ought to/should* + *have* + past participle. See *Grammar database 13.*

Certainty

must

now: *You* ***must*** *be tired.*
(= I'm sure you're tired.)

BE CAREFUL!

For non-stative verbs, we often use the continuous infinitive after *must* when talking about actions happening now.

Bill ***must be*** *walking the dog.*
(= I'm sure he's walking the dog.)

future: *The film* ***must*** *be on tomorrow.*
(= I'm sure it's on tomorrow.)

generally: *You* ***must*** *get lonely living on your own.*
(= I'm sure you get lonely.)

can't

now: *He* ***can't*** *be tired.*
(= I'm sure he's not tired.)

BE CAREFUL!

For non-stative verbs, we often use the continuous infinitive after *can't* when talking about actions happening now.

Bill ***can't be*** *walking the dog.*
(= I'm sure he's not walking the dog.)

future: *The film* ***can't*** *be on tomorrow.*
(= I'm sure it's not on tomorrow.)

generally: *She* ***can't*** *be American.*
(= I'm sure she's not American.)

BE CAREFUL!

To talk about past certainty with *must* or *can't*, we have to use the modal perfect: *must/can't* + *have* + past participle. See *Grammar database 13.*

13 Modal perfect

We can use the modal perfect to talk about the past.
modal perfect = modal + *have* + past participle

You ***should have seen*** *what Emma wore to the party.*

Possibility	*Simon* ***may/might/could*** *have been at the party. I can't really remember.* (= It's possible he was at the party.)
Certainty	*Francis* ***must*** *have been 11 when he moved to France.* (= I'm sure he was 11.) *Francis* ***can't/couldn't*** *have been 10 when he moved to France.* (= I'm sure he wasn't 10.)
Hypothetical situations	*I* ***could/would*** *have passed the exam if I'd studied harder.* (= I didn't pass because I didn't study hard enough.) note: here *could* = *would have been able to*
Opinion	*You* ***ought to/should*** *have called me.* (= You didn't call me but I wish you had called me.) *He* ***oughtn't to/shouldn't*** *have spoken to her like that.* (= He did speak to her like that but I think what he did was wrong.)

NOTE modal perfect continuous = modal + *have* + *been* + *-ing* form
We ***must have been dancing*** *for hours.*

We use the modal perfect continuous:

- for actions in progress or interrupted when another action happens
  *He **can't have been driving** carefully when he crashed the car.*
- to emphasise that an action continued for a long time
  *Jan **must have been talking** on the phone for at least three hours!*

14 *-ing* form or full infinitive?

Verbs and verb phrases followed by the *-ing* form

admit	finish
appreciate	give up
avoid	imagine
be capable of	involve
be good/bad, etc at	look forward to
be interested in	mention
can't help	mind
can't stand	miss
consider	practise
delay	succeed in
deny	suggest
dislike	talk about
enjoy	think of
feel like	

Verbs and verb phrases followed by the full infinitive

afford	intend
agree	learn
appear	manage
arrange	offer
ask	plan
attempt	prepare
be pleased/able/surprised, etc	pretend
choose	promise
decide	refuse
expect	seem
fail	want
happen	wish
help	would like
hope	

Verbs and verb phrases followed by both the *-ing* form and the full infinitive with little or no difference in meaning

begin continue love hate prefer* start

(*see *Grammar database* 29)

Verbs and verb phrases followed by both the *-ing* form and the full infinitive with a difference in meaning

	+ *-ing* form	+ full infinitive
remember	remember a previous experience *Do you **remember going** to that great restaurant in Paris last summer?*	carry out an intention *I must **remember to go** to the post office on my way home.*
forget	forget a previous experience *I'll never **forget going** to that great restaurant in Paris last summer.*	not carry out an intention *I **forgot to go** to the post office on my way home.*
stop	stop an action or situation ***Stop talking** and listen to me!*	stop something in order to do something else *We **stopped to buy** some sweets on the way home.*
go on	continue *Are you going to **go on collecting** pencils all you life?*	start something new *I started by collecting pencils, but then I **went on to collect** ink pens and biros.*
regret	be sorry for what has happened *I **regret giving up** stamp collecting. It was a great hobby.*	be sorry for what you are about to say *I **regret to inform** you that your application was not successful.*
like	enjoy *Do you **like collecting** postcards?*	choose to/be in the habit of/think it right to do *I **like to have** a healthy diet.*
try	do something to see what will happen ***Try asking** Bob. He should know what to do.*	make an effort/see if you can do something difficult *I **tried to jump** up and touch the ceiling but it was too high.*

15 Zero, first and second conditionals

There are four main types of conditional sentences. These are often called the zero conditional, the first conditional, the second conditional and the third conditional. See *Grammar database 17* for information about the third conditional.

Zero conditional

Use: to talk about general truths

Structure: *If* + present simple, present simple

*If you **have** a brother or sister, you **are not** an only child.*

NOTE We can also swap the two halves of the sentence round.
***You are not** an only child **if** you **have** a brother or sister.*

First conditional

Use: to talk about possible or likely situations now, in the future, or generally

Structure: *If* + present simple, *will/won't* + bare infinitive

***If** it **rains** tomorrow, we'**ll stay** at home.*
***If** it **rains** tomorrow, we **won't go** to the beach.*

NOTE We can also swap the two halves of the sentence round.
*We **won't go** to the beach **if** it **rains** tomorrow.*

! BE CAREFUL!
✗ ~~If it will rain tomorrow~~ …

NOTE It is possible to use other modals instead of *will*, depending on meaning.

*If you finish the test early, you **can** go home.*
*If you work hard, you **should** pass the exam.*
*If I'm tired, I **may/might** decide not to go to the party.*

We can also use the imperative for commands, instructions and advice.
*If you have any problems, **tell** me.*

Second conditional

Use: to talk about impossible, unlikely or hypothetical situations now, in the future or generally

Structure: *If* + past simple, *would/wouldn't* + bare infinitive

***If** I **had** lots of money, I **would buy** a new CD player.*
***If** I **won** the lottery, I **wouldn't quit** my job.*

NOTE
- We can also swap the two halves of the sentence round.
  *I **would buy** a new CD player if I **had** lots of money.*
- There are two forms of the verb *to be* with the second conditional.

1 *I/he/she **was** …*
(informal, often used in speech)
*If I **was** rich, I'd buy a big house.*

2 *If I/he/she **were** …*
(formal, often used in writing)
*If I **were** rich, I would buy a big house.*

- It is possible to use other modals instead of *would*, depending on meaning.
  *If I lived on my own, I **could** do exactly what I wanted!* (= would be able to)
  *If I lived on my own, I **might** decide to get a cat.*

16 Time clauses

We saw in *Grammar database 15* that the *if* clause of the first conditional is *If* + present simple. We do not use *will*, even when we are talking about the future.

*If it **rains** tomorrow, …*

The same thing is true with these time words and phrases. We use the present simple and NOT *will* to talk about the future.

when	*I'll call you **when I get** home.*
as soon as	*I'll call you **as soon as I get** home.*
before	*I'll call you **before I leave**.*
after	*I'll call you **after I speak** to Susan.*
until/till	*I'll stay here **until** Dave **arrives**.*
while	*I'll stay here **while** you **do** the shopping.*

NOTE It is also sometimes possible to use the present continuous and present perfect with these time phrases.

*I'll call you a**fter I've spoken** to Susan.*
*I'll think of you **while I'm swimming** in the Aegean.*

17 Third conditional

Use: to talk about hypothetical situations in the past

Structure: *If* + past perfect, *would/wouldn't* + *have* + past participle

***If** you **had studied**, you **would have passed** the test.*

(= You didn't study. You didn't pass the test.)

- It is possible to use other modals instead of would, depending on meaning:

  *If you had studied, you **might** have passed the test.*
  *If you had studied, you **could** have passed the test.*

  See *Grammar database 23* for more information on the past perfect.

NOTE We can also swap the two halves of the sentence round.
*You **would have passed** the test **if** you **had** studied.*

! BE CAREFUL!

The third conditional is only used for hypothetical situations in the past (ie to talk about situations that didn't actually happen).

18 Relative clauses

There are two types of relative clauses: defining and non-defining. With both types, we use different relative pronouns depending on what we are referring to.

- *who* for people

  *The woman **who** won the prize was called Mrs Taylor.*

- *which* for things

  *The prize **which** she won was very valuable.*

- *when* for times

  *That was the day **when** I decided to become a comedian.*

- *where* for places

  *London is the city **where** he grew up.*

- *why* for reasons

  *That's the reason **why** the sitcom is so popular.*

- *whose* – the possessive of *who*

  *She's the girl **whose** father is a famous comedian.*

! BE CAREFUL!

We can also use *in which*, *to which*, *at which*, etc instead of *where* and *when*.

*London is the city **in which** he grew up.*
or *London is the city **which** he grew up **in**.*

The choice of *in*, *at* or *to*, etc depends on the preposition the verb or noun usually takes. So, you grow up in a place – we can use *in which*; you go to a place – we can use *to which*; you arrive at a building – we can use *at which*, etc.

Defining relative clauses

Defining relative clauses give us essential information.We cannot remove the relative clause and still understand the sentence. For example, imagine there are two boxes of different colour. The grey box is empty.The blue box is full.

We can say: *The box **which is blue** is full.*
But if we just say '*The box is full.*' then the sentence makes no sense because there are two boxes and it's not clear which one we are talking about.
The colour of the box is not extra information.
It is essential information.
With defining relative clauses, we:

- CANNOT use commas

  ✔ *The box **which is blue** is full.*
  ✘ ~~*The box, **which is blue**, is full.*~~

- CAN replace *who*, *which*, *when* and *why* with *that*

  ✔ *The box **that is blue** is full.*

NOTE When the subject of the defining relative clause is different to the subject of the rest of the sentence, we can sometimes leave out the relative pronoun completely.

✔ *The prize* ***which she won*** *was very valuable.*
✔ *The prize* ***that she won*** *was very valuable.*
✔ *The prize* ***she won*** *was very valuable.*

Non-defining relative clauses

Non-defining relative clauses give us extra information. We can remove the relative clause and still understand the sentence. For example, imagine there is a blue box on its own. It is full.

We can say: *The box,* ***which is blue****, is full.*
If we just say '*The box is full.*' the sentence still makes sense. The fact that it is blue is just extra information.

With non-defining relative clauses, we:

- MUST use commas
  ✔ *The box,* ***which is blue****, is full.*
  ✘ ~~*The box* ***which is blue*** *is full.*~~
- CANNOT replace the relative pronoun with *that*
  ✔ *The box,* ***which is blue****, is full.*
  ✘ ~~*The box,* ***that is blue****, is full.*~~
- CANNOT ever leave out the relative pronoun
  ✔ *The box,* ***which/that*** *is blue, is full.*
  ✘ ~~*The box,* ***is blue****, is full.*~~

19 Revision of conditionals and *unless*

In *Grammar database 15*, we looked at zero, first and second conditionals. In *Grammar database 17*, we looked at the third conditional. Another way of thinking about conditionals is to see each conditional sentence in two parts: the condition and the result.

If we ***score*** *another goal, we****'ll win*** *the match.*
CONDITION RESULT

If they ***had*** *more money, they* ***would buy*** *some better players.*
CONDITION RESULT

If we ***hadn't gone*** *to the party, we* ***would have watched*** *the match on TV.*
CONDITION RESULT

Conditions

For the conditions, you have to learn which tense to use, because the tenses are used in a strange way.

	Now/Future/Generally	Past
real/likely/possible situations	PRESENT SIMPLE *If we* ***score*** *another goal ...* (first conditional)	✘
hypothetical/unlikely/ impossible situations	PAST SIMPLE *If we* ***scored*** *another goal ...* *If we* ***had scored*** (second conditional)	PAST PERFECT *If we* ***had scored*** *another goal ...* (third conditional)

Results

For the results, the grammatical rules are the same as with non-conditional sentences:

- **modals for real situations:**
  will, can, may, might, should
- **modals for hypothetical situations:**
  would, could, might, should
  now/future/generally:
  modal + bare infinitive (eg *will go*)
- **past:** modal + present perfect bare infinitive (eg *would have gone*)
- **commands, instructions and advice:** imperative (eg *... go to bed.*)
- **questions:** question form (eg *... can we have a party?*)
- **general truths:** present simple (eg *... water boils at 100°C*)

unless

We can also sometimes use *unless* in conditional sentences. *Unless* can replace *if not* and means 'except if'.

***If we don't score** another goal, we'll lose.* or
***Unless we score** another goal, we'll lose.*

*I couldn't watch the match **if I didn't have** a TV.*
*I couldn't watch the match **unless I had** a TV.*

*She wouldn't have won **if she hadn't been** such a good player.*
*She wouldn't have won **unless she'd been** such a good player.*

! BE CAREFUL!

We CANNOT use *unless* to replace *if not* when *if not* doesn't mean 'except if'. So, we can say:

✔ ***If** I **wasn't** ill, I'd play tomorrow.*

But *if not* here doesn't mean 'except if' because you are actually ill so we CANNOT say:

✘ ~~***Unless** I was ill, I'd play tomorrow.*~~

20 *so, such, too, enough*

We use *so*, *such*, *too* and *enough* to talk about amounts.

so

- *so* + adjective/adverb + *that* clause

  *She's **so good (that)** she could be a professional.*
  *She plays **so well (that)** she could be a professional.*
- *so* + *many/much* + noun + *that* clause

  *There were **so many footballs (that)** I didn't know which one to choose.*
  *There was **so much noise (that)** I couldn't hear.*

NOTE We can also use *so* without a *that* clause. This means the same as *very* or *really*, but it's more emphatic.
*He's **so** rich! = He's **very** rich! or He's **really** rich!*

such

- *such* + *a/an* + adjective + singular noun + *that* clause

  *She's **such a** good player **(that)** she could be a professional.*
- *such* + adjective + plural noun + *that* clause

  *They are both **such** good players **(that)** they could be professionals.*

NOTE

- We can also use *such* without a *that* clause. This means the same as 'very' or 'really', but it's more emphatic.

  *He's **such** a good player!*
  = He's a very/really good player.
  *They're **such** good players!*
  = They're very/really good players.
- We can put *such* before *a lot of* to emphasise the amount.

  *He's got **such a lot of** tennis rackets.*
  (= so many)
  *They made **such a lot of** noise.* (= so much)

too

- We usually use *too* to criticise, or to say that something is negative or bad.

  *He drives **too** fast.*
  = He drives so fast (that) it's bad.
- *too* + adjective/adverb

  *He's **too slow**.*
  *He runs **too slowly**.*
- *too* + adjective/adverb + full infinitive

  *He's **too slow to be** in the athletics team.*
  *He runs **too slowly to be** in the athletics team.*
- *too* + adjective/adverb + *for*

  *He's **too slow for** this athletics team.*
  *He runs **too slowly for** this athletics team.*

NOTE

- We can also combine *for* and the full infinitive in one sentence.

  *It was too cold **for me to go** swimming.*
- We can also say *too many* or *too much*. This means 'so many/much that it's bad'.

  *There are **too many** slow runners in our athletics team.*
  *Our teacher gives us **too much** homework.*

! BE CAREFUL!

Too is never followed by a *that* clause.

enough

- *enough* means 'the right amount/number of'
- *not enough* means 'less than the right amount/number of'
- *(not) enough* + noun + full infinitive

  I've got ***enough money to buy*** *the ticket.*
  *I have****n't*** *got* ***enough money to buy*** *the ticket.*
- *(not) enough* + noun + *for*

  I've got ***enough money for*** *the ticket.*
  *I have****n't*** *got* ***enough money for*** *the ticket.*
- *(not +)* adjective/adverb + *enough* + full infinitive

  I'm ***good enough to be*** *in the team.*
  I'm ***not good enough to be*** *in the team.*
  She ran ***fast enough to win*** *the race.*
  *She did****n't*** *run* ***fast enough to win*** *the race.*
- *(not +)* adjective/adverb + *enough* + *for*

  I'm ***good enough for*** *the team.*
  I'm ***not good enough for*** *the team.*
  She trained ***hard enough for*** *the race.*
  *She did****n't*** *train* ***hard enough for*** *the race.*

NOTE We can also combine *for* and the full infinitive in one sentence.

It ***wasn't warm enough for*** *me* ***to go*** *swimming.*
= It was ***too cold for*** *me* ***to go*** *swimming.*
He's ***not tall enough to be*** *a basketball player.*
= He's ***too short to be*** *a basketball player.*

! BE CAREFUL!

Enough is never followed by a *that* clause.

21 The passive

Look at this sentence:

Sandy broke the window *yesterday.*

↓ ↓ ↓

subject verb object

A sentence like this with *subject + verb + object* is called an active sentence or a sentence in the active voice. But we can turn it round, so *the window* comes at the beginning of the sentence. To do this, we have to make it a passive sentence or put it into the passive voice.

Turning an active sentence into a passive

There are five main steps:

1 take the object of the first sentence and make it the subject of our new sentence:

The window …

2 add the verb *to be* in the same tense as in the active sentence (*broke* = past simple):

The window was …

3 add the past participle of the verb in the active sentence (*broke* → *broken*):

The window was broken …

4 add *by* + the subject of the first sentence (*Sandy*):

The window was broken by Sandy …

5 finish off the sentence in the appropriate way:

The window was broken by Sandy yesterday.

The passive is: noun/pronoun + *be* + past participle (+ *by/with/of* + noun).

NOTE

- We often don't use *by* + the subject of the first sentence if:
  - we don't know who did/does it

    Active: *Someone has stolen my watch!*
    Passive: *My watch has been stolen!*
  - it's obvious who did/does it

    Active: *The police arrested her last week.*
    Passive: *She was arrested last week.*
  - it's not important who did/does it

    Active: *They are going to knock down the building.*
    Passive: *The building's going to be knocked down.*
- We usually use *with* when we talk about the things we use to do the action (such as tools and equipment).

  The wall was painted ***with*** *a special paint.*
- When we talk about materials, we usually use *of*.

  That table is made ***of*** *wood.*

Passive forms

Tense	Active	Passive
Present simple	*Volunteers **clean** the beach.*	*The beach **is cleaned** by volunteers.*
Present continuous	*Volunteers **are cleaning** the beach.*	*The beach **is being cleaned** by volunteers.*
Present perfect simple	*Volunteers **have cleaned** the beach.*	*The beach **has been cleaned** by volunteers.*
Past simple	*Volunteers **cleaned** the beach.*	*The beach **was cleaned** by volunteers.*
Past continuous	*Volunteers **were cleaning** the beach.*	*The beach **was being cleaned** by volunteers.*
Past perfect simple	*Volunteers **had cleaned** the beach.*	*The beach **had been cleaned** by volunteers.*
Future simple	*Volunteers **will clean** the beach.*	*The beach **will be cleaned** by volunteers.*
be going to	*Volunteers **are going to clean** the beach.*	*The beach **is going to be cleaned** by volunteers.*
Bare infinitive	*Volunteers **must clean** the beach.*	*The beach **must be cleaned** by volunteers.*

22 The causative

Look at this sentence:

Someone paints Carl's house every two years.

This sentence is in the active. Carl doesn't do the painting himself. He pays/gets/asks someone else to do it for him.

As we saw in *Grammar database 21*, we can make that sentence passive:

Carl's house is painted every two years.

Or we can put it into the causative form. We do that to emphasise that someone else does something for us.

Carl gets/has his house painted every two years.

Turning a subject-verb-object sentence

There are five main steps:

1 take the person who owns or has the object of the first sentence and make it the subject of our new sentence. Here, Carl owns the house:

Carl …

2 add the verb *to have* or the verb *to get* (*get* is less formal than *have*) in the same tense as the verb in the active sentence (*paints* = present simple)

Carl has … or ***Carl gets …***

3 add the object of the first sentence plus an appropriate pronoun or article.

Carl has his house … or ***Carl gets his house …***

4 add the past participle of the verb in the first sentence (*paints* → *painted*).

Carl has his house painted … or ***Carl gets his house painted …***

5 finish off the sentence in an appropriate way.

Carl has his house painted every two years. or
Carl gets his house painted every two years.

So, the causative is: noun + *have/get* + noun + past participle (+ *by/with* + noun)

NOTE

- If we want to state exactly who does the action, we can use *by* (like with the passive).

  *Carl has his house painted **by a professional painter** every two years.*

- If we want to mention the tools and equipment or the things they use, we can use *with* (like with the passive).

  *Carl has his house painted **with a special paint** every two years.*

Causative forms

Tense	subject + verb + object sentence	The causative
Present simple	*A professional painter **paints** Carl's house.*	*Carl **has/gets** his house **painted** by a professional painter.*
Present continuous	*A professional painter **is painting** Carl's house.*	*Carl is **having/getting** his house **painted** by a professional painter.*
Present perfect simple	*A professional painter **has painted** Carl's house.*	*Carl **has had/got** his house **painted** by a professional painter.*
Past simple	*A professional painter **painted** Carl's house.*	*Carl **had/got** his house **painted** by a professional painter.*
Past continuous	*A professional painter **was painting** Carl's house.*	*Carl **was having/getting** his house **painted** by a professional painter.*
Past perfect simple	*A professional painter **had painted** Carl's house.*	*Carl **had had/got** his house **painted** by a professional painter.*
Future simple	*A professional painter **will paint** Carl's house.*	*Carl **will have/get** his house **painted** by a professional painter.*
be going to	*A professional painter **is going to paint** Carl's house.*	*Carl **is going to have/get** his house **painted** by a professional painter.*
Bare infinitive	*A professional painter **must paint** Carl's house.*	*Carl **must have/get** his house **painted** by a professional painter.*

23 Past perfect simple and past perfect continuous

Past perfect simple

Positive	Negative	Question
I **had eaten**. (I**'d**)	I **had not eaten**. (I **hadn't**)	**Had** I **eaten**?
You **had eaten**. (You**'d**)	You **had not eaten**. (You **hadn't**)	**Had** you **eaten**?
He **had eaten**. (He**'d**)	He **had not eaten**. (He **hadn't**)	**Had** he **eaten**?
She **had eaten**. (She**'d**)	She **had not eaten**. (She **hadn't**)	**Had** she **eaten**?
It **had eaten**. (It**'d***)	It **had not eaten**. (It **hadn't**)	**Had** it **eaten**?
We **had eaten**. (We**'d**)	We **had not eaten**. (We **hadn't**)	**Had** we **eaten**?
You **had eaten**. (You**'d**)	You **had not eaten**. (You **hadn't**)	**Had** you **eaten**?
They **had eaten**. (They**'d**)	They **had not eaten**. (They **hadn't**)	**Had** they **eaten**?

*very unusual in written English

We usually use past perfect simple to show that something in the past happened before something else in the past.

*The week before I wrote to the company, I **had called** them.*

I called them. I wrote to them. Now

We also use the past perfect simple in:

- reported speech (see *Grammar database 24*)
  *Phil said he **had sent** me an email.*
- third conditional sentences (see *Grammar database 17* and *19*)
  *If you**'d come** to the party, you would have met Francis.*
- wishes about the past (see *Grammar database 28*)
  *I wish I **hadn't lied** to Gareth.*

NOTE

The past perfect simple is often used with these words and phrases:

before	*They'd arrived **before** we started.*
after	*We started **after** they'd arrived.*
for	*I'd worked there **for** three years before I quit.*
since	*I'd worked there **since** the previous summer.*
when	*We'd started **when** they arrived.*
just	*We'd **just** started when they arrived.*
already	*We'd **already** started when they arrived.*
It was the first/ best, etc + noun	***It was the first time** I'd been to Gibraltar.* ***It was the best film** I'd ever seen.*

Past perfect continuous

Positive	Negative	Question
I **had been waiting**. (I**'d**)	I **had not been waiting**. (I **hadn't**)	**Had** I **been waiting**?
You **had been waiting**. (You**'d**)	You **had not been waiting**. (You **hadn't**)	**Had** you **been waiting**?
He **had been waiting**. (He**'d**)	He **had not been waiting**. (He **hadn't**)	**Had** he **been waiting**?
She **had been waiting**. (She**'d**)	She **had not been waiting**. (She **hadn't**)	**Had** she **been waiting**?
It **had been waiting**. (It**'d***)	It **had not been waiting**. (It **hadn't**)	**Had** it **been waiting**?
We **had been waiting**. (We**'d**)	We **had not been waiting**. (We **hadn't**)	**Had** we **been waiting**?
You **had been waiting**. (You**'d**)	You **had not been waiting**. (You **hadn't**)	**Had** you **been waiting**?
They **had been waiting**. (They**'d**)	They **had not been waiting**. (They **hadn't**)	**Had** they **been waiting**?

*very unusual in written English

We usually use the past perfect continuous to show that a situation continued in the past until another situation in the past happened.

*I'**d been working** all morning so I decided to have a break.*

I was working all morning.

← ↓ ↓

I decided to have a break. **Now**

We also use the past perfect continuous in reported speech (see *Grammar database 24*).

*Phil said he **had been waiting** for me for three hours.*

NOTE

The past perfect continuous is often used with these words and phrases:

all morning/day, etc	*We'd been working **all morning**.*
just	*We'd **just** been talking about him when he walked in.*
for	*We'd been calling him **for** hours before he finally called us.*
since	*We'd been planning to visit Jamaica **since** the previous summer.*

We can often use the past simple or past continuous instead of the past perfect (simple or continuous), particularly with *after* or *before*.

*I ate lunch **after** my mum **left**. = I ate lunch **after** my mum **had left**.*

24 Reported speech

We use reported speech when we want to say what someone else said.

Jan said that she was going to bring a pizza.

There are some things you have to remember when reporting what someone else said.

Tense changes 1

If the reporting verb is in the past (eg *said*), we usually have to change the tense of what the person actually said.

Direct speech	Reported speech	Examples
Present simple	Past simple	*'I **am** 16,' said Angela. →* *Angela said (that) she **was** 16.*
Present continuous	Past continuous	*'I **am learning** English,' said Ben. →* *Ben said (that) he **was learning** English.*
Present perfect simple	Past perfect simple	*'I **have had** a bath,' said Simon. →* *Simon said (that) he **had had** a bath.*
Present perfect continuous	Past perfect continuous	*'I**'ve been working** all morning,' said Anne. →* *Anne said (that) she **had been working** all morning.*
Past simple	Past perfect simple	*'I **sent** Dave a text message,' said Liam. →* *Liam said (that) he **had sent** Dave a text message.*
Past continuous	Past perfect continuous	*'We **were playing** basketball,' said Joanne. →* *Joanne said (that) they **had been playing** basketball.*
am/is/are going to	*was/were going to*	*'We**'re going to play** basketball,' said Joanne. →* *Joanne said that they **were going to play** basketball.*

NOTE

- Past perfect simple and continuous do not change tense.
  *'I **'d been waiting** for an hour,' said Fiona.*
  *Fiona said (that) she **had been waiting** for an hour.*
- We often don't make any changes to the verb tense when we are reporting a scientific fact or when something is still true.
  *'Water **boils** at 100° C,' said the scientist. →*
  *The scientist said that water **boils** at 100°C.*

Tense changes 2

If the reporting verb is in the past (eg *said*), we also have to change some modals.

Direct speech	Reported speech	Examples
will	*would*	*'I'**ll** help you,' said Sean. →* *Sean said (that) he **would** help me.*
can	*could*	*'I **can** help you,' said Sean. →* *Sean said (that) he **could** help Alison.*
must/have to	*had to*	*'I **must** help Alison,' said Sean. →* *Sean said (that) he **had to** help me.*
may	*might*	*'I **may** be there,' said Sean. →* *Sean said (that) he **might** be there.*

Other word changes

- We also usually have to change some pronouns and other similar words.
  *'I'll do **my** homework later,' said Carol. Carol said she would do **her** homework later.*

Direct speech	Indirect speech	Examples
this/that + noun	*the* or *that*	*'I love **this** pizza', said Hazel. →* *Hazel said (that) she loved **the/that** pizza.*
this/that + verb	*it*	*'**That** is the coolest watch I've ever seen,' said Steve. →* *Steve said (that) **it** was the coolest watch he'd ever seen.*
these/those + noun	*the* or *those*	*'I'm going to buy **these** trainers,' said Paul. →* *Paul said (that) he was going to buy **the/those** trainers.*
these/those + verb	*they*	*'**Those** are the coolest trainers I've ever seen,' said Steve. →* *Steve said (that) **they** were the coolest trainers he'd ever seen.*
verb + *these/those* (without an object)	*them*	*'I'm going to buy **these**,' said Paul. →* *Paul said (that) he was going to buy **them**.*

- Words connected to time and place also often change.

Direct speech	Reported speech	Examples
here	*there*	*'I love it **here**,' said Megan. →* *Megan said (that) she loved it **there**.*
now/at the moment	*then* or *at that moment*	*'I'm doing it **now**,' said Fred. →* *Fred said (that) he was doing it **at that moment**.*
today	*that day*	*'I'll do it **today**,' said Fred. →* *Fred said (that) he would do it **that day**.*
tomorrow	*the following day* or *the next day*	*'I'll do it **tomorrow**,' said Fred. →* *Fred said (that) he would do it **the following day**.*
tonight	*that night*	*'I'll do it **tonight**,' said Fred. →* *Fred said (that) he would do it **that night**.*
next week/month/year	*the following week/month/year*	*'I'll do it **next week**,'* said Fred. → *Fred said (that) he would do it **the following week**.*
yesterday	*the day before* or *the previous day*	*'I did it **yesterday**,' said Fred. →* *Fred said (that) he had done it **the day before**.*
last week/month/year	*the previous week/month/year*	*'I did it **last year**,' said Fred. →* *Fred said (that) he had done it **the previous year**.*
ago	*before*	*'I did it two hours **ago**,' said Fred. →* *Fred said (that) he had done it two hours **before**.*

! BE CAREFUL!

We don't always have to use the verb *say* with reported speech. We can also use other verbs such as *tell, suggest, promise,* etc. *Say* and *tell* take different grammatical structures. Compare:

say	*tell*
*He **said** (that) it had been cold.* ***He said to us** (that) it had been cold.*	***He told us** (that) it had been cold.*
*She **said that I had to** go away.*	*She **told me** to go away.*
*I didn't **say anything to Paul**.*	*I didn't **tell Paul anything**.*
	+ *tell* (someone) *a joke/a story/a secret/the time*

25 Reported questions

In *Grammar database 24* we looked at reported speech. We saw that you often have to change tenses, modals and other words when you go from direct to reported speech. We use the same rules when we report questions that people have asked.

have, do or *be* and modal questions

If a direct question begins with the verbs *have, do* or *be* (usually as auxiliary verbs), or a modal (*will, can*, etc), we use *if* or *whether* in the reported question. This is the kind of direct question which requires the answer *yes* or *no*.

*'**Do** you want some more tea?' asked Mr Peters. →*
*Mr Peters asked **if/whether** I wanted some more tea.*

*'**Have** you seen the new Bruce Willis movie?' asked Rolf. →*
*Rolf asked **if/whether** I had seen the new Bruce Willis movie.*

*'**Are** you going to the match tomorrow, Megan?' asked Sally. →*
*Sally asked Megan **if/whether** she was going to the match the next day.*

*'**Will** you help me next week, George?' asked Alan. →*
*Alan asked George **if/whether** he would help him the following week.*

Look at the examples on the previous page. You'll see that the tenses, modals and time phrases, etc have changed in the same way as with reported speech. For example, in the first sentence *Do you want* is present simple. It becomes past simple (*wanted*) in reported speech. In the last example, *will* becomes *would*.

In direct questions we use the question form (*Do you want …?, Have you seen …?, Are you going …?, Will you help …?*). In reported questions we do not use the question form (*asked if I wanted, asked if I had seen, asked if she was going, asked if he would help*).

Wh- questions

With questions beginning with *what, who, which, when, where, why* and *how* we do NOT use *if* or *whether*. We use the same question word as we used in the direct question, but we do NOT use the question form and we do change tenses, modals, etc.

'***What do you want** for breakfast?*' → *My mum asked me **what I wanted** for breakfast.*

'***Where can we play** football?' asked Dave.* → *Dave asked us **where we could play** football.*

! BE CAREFUL!

We do NOT use question marks (?) with reported questions.

✔ *Dave asked us where we could play football.*
✘ *~~Dave asked us where we could play football~~?*

26 Indirect questions

Indirect questions are similar in some ways to reported questions, but they're not exactly the same. Look at this direct question:

Where's the bank? (grammatically correct but not very polite)

We often use indirect questions to be polite.

Can you tell me where the bank is? (polite)
I wonder if you could tell me where the bank is. (very polite)

There are some important things to remember:

1 Question marks

Some indirect questions need question marks, and some don't. It depends on the phrase at the beginning:

With a question mark	Without a question mark
Can/Could you tell me …?	I wonder if you can/ could tell me …
Can/Could you let me know …?	I wonder if you could let me know …
Do you know …?	I wonder if you know …
Do you think you can/could tell me …?	I would like to know …
Would you mind telling me …?	
Can/Could I ask …?	

2 Word order

Like with reported questions, we do NOT use the question form in indirect questions.

direct question: *What time **is it?***

indirect question: ✔ *Do you know what time **it is**?*
✘ *~~Do you know what time **is it?**~~*

3 *have, do* or *be* and modal questions

Like with reported questions, direct questions that start with the verbs *have, do* or *be* or a modal use *if* or *whether* in indirect questions.

direct question: ***Will** you be there tomorrow?*

indirect question: *I'd like to know **if/whether** you'll be there tomorrow.*

4 *Wh-* questions

Like with reported questions, direct questions that start with a *wh-* question (*when, where,* etc) use the same word in the indirect question.

direct question: ***What** time is it?*

indirect question: *Do you know **what** time it is?*

5 Tense changes, etc

With reported speech and reported questions, we often have to change tenses, modals and time phrases, etc. We do NOT do that with indirect questions.

direct question: ***Are** you going to come on Friday?*

indirect question: ✔ *Do you know if you **are** going to come on Friday?*
✘ *~~Do you know if you **were** going to come on Friday?~~*

27 Future perfect simple and future continuous

Future perfect simple

The future perfect simple is: *will* + *have* + past participle

We use the future perfect simple to show that a situation will finish at or before a certain time in the future.

*I **will have packed** all the suitcases by six o'clock.*

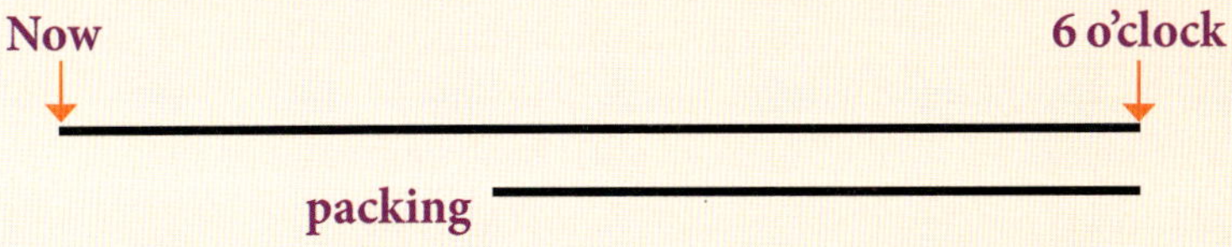

Future continuous

The future continuous is: *will* + *be* + *-ing* form

We often use the future continuous to show that an action is in progress (ie still continuing) at a certain time in the future

*I **will** still **be packing** at five o'clock.*

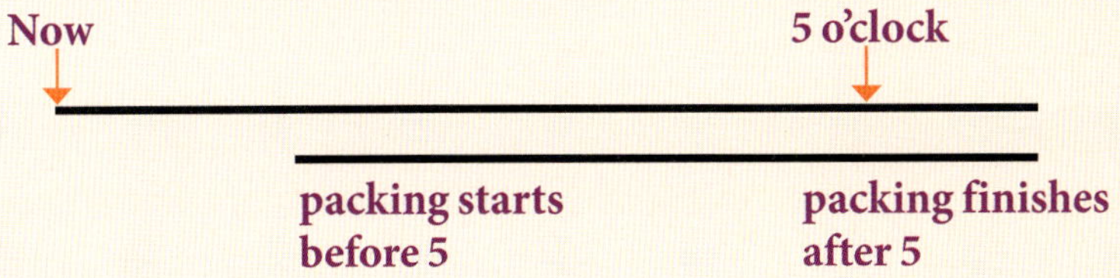

NOTE

We can also use the future continuous to express repeated actions and habits in the future:

✔ *I think humans **will travel** to Mars frequently in 1000 years.*
✔ *I think humans **will be travelling** to Mars frequently in 1000 years.*

Time words and phrases

We often use *by* with the future perfect simple and *at* with the future continuous, but it is also possible sometimes to use other time words and phrases.

before	*I'll be swimming in the Mediterranean **before** next Tuesday.* *I'll definitely have arrived **before** 8pm.*
in	*We'll be swimming in the Med **in** a couple of days.* *I think we'll have heard from him **in** a couple of days.*
next	*We'll be swimming in the Med **next** week.* *She'll have lived there for three years **next** January.*
this time	***This time** tomorrow, we'll be swimming in the Med.* ***This time** tomorrow, I'll have packed all the suitcases.*
by the time	***By the time** he arrives, we'll have finished dinner.* ***By the time** he arrives, we'll be flying to America.*

28 *wish* and *if only*

We can use *wish* and *if only* to talk about hypothetical situations in the past, present, future or generally. *Wish* and *if only* have very similar meanings, but *if only* is more emphatic than *wish*. Like with conditionals, you have to learn which tenses we use with *wish* and *if only*, because they're different to normal English.

We can use …	For …	Examples
wish/if only + simple	hypothetical situations now, in the future or generally	*I wish/If only I had enough money* (= I don't have enough money but I would like to have enough.)
wish/if only + continuous	hypothetical situations now, in the future or generally	*I wish/If only they weren't staying so far away.* (= They are staying far away but I'd like them to stay closer.)
wish/if only + *could* + bare infinitive	hypothetical ability or permission now, in the future or generally	*I wish/If only you could come with us.* (= You can't come with us but I'd like you to.)
wish/if only + *would* + bare infinitive	expressing criticism or complaint about situations now, in the future or generally	*I wish/If only you'd be quiet!* (= You aren't quiet but I want you to be.)
wish/if only + past perfect simple	hypothetical situations in the past (regrets)	*I wish/If only I hadn't told Bill I hated him.* (= I told Bill I hated him and now I regret it.)

! BE CAREFUL!

We only use *wish* and *if only* for hypothetical situations. Don't use them if the situation isn't hypothetical, and don't use *hope* if the situation is hypothetical.

*I **wish you could** come.*
(= I'd like you to come but I know you can't.)
*I **hope you can** come.*
(= I'd like you to come and maybe you'll be able to.)

29 *prefer, would rather, had better*

prefer and *would rather*

We use *prefer* and *would rather* to express preference.

*I'd **prefer** to stay in tonight.*
*I'd **rather** stay in tonight.*

prefer

We often use these patterns to express our general likes and dislikes:

prefer + noun

*I **prefer** coffee **to** tea.*
*I **prefer** coffee **rather than** tea.*

prefer + *-ing* form

*I **prefer** drink**ing** coffee **to** (drink**ing**) tea.*
*I **prefer** drink**ing** coffee **rather than** (drink**ing**) tea.*

prefer + full infinitive

*I **prefer to drink** coffee **rather than** (drink) tea.*

prefer not + full infinitive

*I **prefer not to drink** coffee before bed.*

NOTE We usually say *I prefer not to …* rather than *I don't prefer …*

When we want to express preference regarding a specific decision or a hypothetical situation, we often use *would prefer* with these patterns:

would prefer + noun

*I **would prefer** a cruise **to** a camping holiday.*
*I **would prefer** a cruise **rather than** a camping holiday.*

would prefer + full infinitive

*I **would prefer to go** on a cruise **rather than** (go on) a camping holiday.*
*I **would prefer to stay** at home tonight **rather than** go out.*

! BE CAREFUL!

If you are using *prefer* + full infinitive, you CANNOT put *to* in between the two things you are comparing.

✔ *I would prefer to be happy **rather than** rich.*
✘ ~~*I would prefer to be happy **to** rich.*~~

would rather

We can use *would rather* for general likes and dislikes or specific decisions.

*Generally, I **would rather** have coffee **than** (have) tea.*
***I'd rather not** go out tonight as I'm tired.*

BE CAREFUL!

- When we are talking about ourselves, we use *would rather* + bare infinitive (as in *I'**d rather** have coffee than tea.*).
- We can also use *would rather* to talk about other people's actions. It has a similar meaning to 'I (don't) want you/him, etc to …' and it is usually followed by the past simple.

  *I'**d rather** you **told** me the truth.* (now, in the future or generally – NOT in the past)

  *I'**d rather** he **didn't call** me Pat.* (now, in the future or generally – NOT in the past)

had better

Had better has a very similar meaning to *should* and *ought to*. It means 'I really want you/him, etc to …' or 'I really think it's a good idea for you/him, etc to …'

*You'**d better** listen to me carefully!*
*He'**d better** be home by six o'clock.*
*We'**d better** eat less fatty food from now on.*

BE CAREFUL!

Had better not means 'I really don't want you/him, etc to …' or 'I really think it's a bad idea for you/him, etc to …'

*You'**d better not** lie to me.*
*He'**d better not** fail the exam.*
*We'**d better not** eat so much fatty food from now on.*

30 Direct and indirect objects

Look at these sentences:

I gave the book to Phil. or *I gave Phil a book.*
I bought a book for Phil. or *I bought Phil a book.*

We can do this with many verbs without changing the meaning.

Sometimes, changing the position of the two objects after the verb changes the emphasis of the sentence. Compare:

*I gave Phil **a book** (rather than a CD).*
the book is emphasised

*I gave a book **to Phil** (and a CD to Megan).*
Phil is emphasised

With some verbs that take two objects, such as *explain* and *suggest*, you cannot change position of the objects.

✔ *He explained the answer to us.*
✘ ~~*He explained us the answer.*~~

31 Question tags

We can use question tags to:

- ask someone to agree with us

  *It's a lovely day, **isn't it?***
- check that something is true

  *You didn't buy those really expensive shoes, **did you?***

BE CAREFUL!

When we are asking someone to agree with us, our voice goes down at the end of the sentence. When we are checking that something is true, our voice goes up at the end.

- With most question tags, if the verb is negative we use a positive question tag. If the verb is positive we use a negative question tag.

be + *have* (as auxiliary verb) + modals

In sentences where the verb is *be* (either as a main verb or as an auxiliary verb), *have* (only as an auxiliary verb) or a modal, we make question tags using the same verb or modal in the same person and tense.

*You'**re** 16 years old, **aren't** you?*
*She **hasn't** been to France, **has** she?*
*Tracy **can** come with us, **can't** she?*
*They **won't** be there, **will** they?*

Other verbs

With all other verb forms, we use the verb *do* in the question tag in the same person and tense as the first verb.

You ***buy*** *lots of shoes,* ***don't*** *you?*
She ***had*** *a good idea,* ***didn't*** *she?*

! BE CAREFUL!

- If the verb *have* is being used as an auxiliary verb, we use *have* in the question tag.

  If the verb *have* is a main verb and there's no other auxiliary verb, we use *do* in the question tag.

  eg *You've got a pen,* ***haven't*** *you?*
  I ***had*** *a pen somewhere,* ***didn't*** *I?*

Verb form	Question tag
Let's ***Let's*** *go shopping tomorrow,* ***shall we?***	**shall we?**
I'm (NOT followed by not) ***I'm*** *coming shopping too,* ***aren't I?*** *(I'm* ***not*** *going shopping,* ***am I?****)*	**aren't I?**
Don't (negative imperative) ***Don't*** *be late,* ***will you?***	**will you?**

- In sentences with a negative word like *never, no, nobody*, etc, we use a positive question tag.

  You're ***never*** *on time,* ***are*** *you?*
  Nobody *ever helps me,* ***do*** *they?*

- If the subject of the main verb is *someone*, *nobody*, etc, we use *they* in the question tag.

  Someone *will want to buy it, won't* ***they?***

32 *although, even though, despite, in spite of*

Look at this sentence:

The supermarket is cheaper ***but*** *it's further away.*
We can use *but* to contrast two ideas. However, *but* is not very formal. If we want to be more formal, particularly when writing, we can use *although, even though, despite* or *in spite of.*

although/even though

Although and *even though* basically mean the same thing but *even though* is more emphatic than *although.*They both follow the same grammatical structure.

even though/although **+ subject + verb, subject + verb**

Although *the supermarket is cheaper, it's further away.*
Even though *the supermarket is cheaper, it's further away.*

> **NOTE** We can also put *although* and *even though* in the middle of the sentence.
> *The supermarket's further away,* ***although*** *it is cheaper.*
> *The supermarket's further away,* ***even though*** *it is cheaper.*

in spite of/despite

In spite of and *despite* mean exactly the same thing. They also take the same grammatical structures.

in spite of/despite + *-ing* form, subject + verb

Despite being *cheaper, the supermarket is further away.*
In spite of being *cheaper, the supermarket is further away.*

in spite of/despite **+ *the fact (that)* + subject + verb, subject + verb**

Despite the fact (that) *it's cheaper, the supermarket is further away.*
In spite of the fact (that) *it's cheaper, the supermarket is further away.*

in spite of/despite **+ noun, subject + verb**

Despite its cheapness*, the supermarket is further away.*
In spite of its cheapness*, the supermarket is further away.*

> **NOTE** For all of these structures, we can also put *in spite of/despite* in the middle of the sentence.
> *The supermarket is further away* ***despite*** *being cheaper.*

Alphabetical index of grammar points

Webquests

Units 1–2

Find the answers online!

1 Eton College is a famous private school in the UK. Who started the school?

2 In what year?

3 In France, the main language is French. What's the main language in Spain?

4 Houdini was a famous magician. What was his first name?

5 What's the word in English for a bad or scary dream? It starts with *n*.

6 Philadelphia is a city in the US. What state is it in?

7 You read about a ship called the *USS Eldridge*. What do the letters *USS* stand for?

8 A *poltergeist* is a type of ghost. What language does the word *poltergeist* come from?

9 The word *exam* is a shortened form of a longer word. Which word?

10 People sometimes use another phrase to describe a UFO. It's two words, the first word is *flying* and the second word starts with *s*. What's the second word?

Units 3–4

Find the answers online!

1 Bank robbers robbed the Dunbar Armored facility in the USA in 1997. How much money did they escape with?

2 One of the most famous singers today is Lady Gaga. What year was she born?

3 From 1788 to 1868, Britain sent criminals to live in which country?

4 Hollywood is famous for films. In which city would you find Hollywood?

5 During a trial with a jury, how many people are there on the jury in the UK?

6 Rihanna is a famous singer. What is her full name?

7 The *Mona Lisa*, the famous painting, was once stolen. In which year?

8 Johnny Depp is a famous actor. What's his middle name?

9 Which of the following might a police officer carry: handcarts, handbells or handcuffs?

10 Justin Bieber is a well-known singer from Canada. What was his first album called?

Units 5–6

Find the answers online!

1 Neil Armstrong was the first person to stand on the Moon. Who was the second person?

____

2 How many moons does Mars have?

____

3 Today, there are hundreds of satellites above the Earth. What was the name of the very first satellite that humans put into space?

____

4 In which year did this satellite first go into space?

____

5 The planet Mars is named after a Roman god. Mars was the Roman god of what?

____

6 The first human to travel into space left the Earth in 1961. What was his name?

____

7 Astronomers use telescopes to see things that are a very long way away. What do scientists use to see things that are extremely small?

____

8 NASA is the US government's space agency. What do the letters *NASA* stand for?

____

9 Who directed the film *Mars Attacks!*?

____

10 In the film, who plays the President of the USA?

____

Units 7–8

Find the answers online!

1 Who wrote the opera *Madame Butterfly*?

____

2 Edinburgh and Glasgow are cities in which country?

____

3 In which city would you find the Louvre museum?

____

4 Carolyn Hax is a well-known agony aunt in which country?

____

5 Which language does the word *karaoke* come from?

____

6 The singer Dolly Parton played an agony aunt in which film in 1992?

____

7 Broadway Avenue in New York is particularly associated with which form of entertainment: cinemas, theatres or concerts?

____

8 Shakespeare is the most famous English playwright. Where was he born?

____

9 In which city would you find the Uffizi Gallery?

____

10 Is a *multiplex* a kind of theatre, a kind of museum or a kind of cinema?

____

Units 9–10

Find the answers online!

1 In the sport badminton, you hit something over a net with a racket but it's not a ball. What is it?

____

2 In ice hockey, you hit something with your stick but it's not a ball. What is it?

____

3 How many players make up an ice hockey team?

____

4 Snooker is a game similar to pool and billiards, in which you hit balls on a table. If you successfully pot the black ball (ie knock it into a pocket), how many points do you get?

____

5 What's the name of the stick you use to hit the white ball in snooker?

____

6 In tennis, if the score is *40-all*, both players have scored three points. If the score is *40-love*, one player has three points. How many points does the other player have?

____

7 The word *sitcom* comes from two words. The second one is *comedy*. What's the first?

____

8 Which famous comic actor made the films *The Tramp*, *The Gold Rush*, *Modern Times* and *The Great Dictator*?

____

9 Which British comic actor has played the characters Mr Bean, Edmund Blackadder and Johnny English?

____

10 Jacques Tati was a famous comic actor. What nationality was he?

____

Units 11–12

Find the answers online!

1 The Worldwide Fund for Nature tries to protect the environment around the world. What was its old name?

____

2 A text message is also called an SMS. What do the letters *SMS* stand for?

____

3 What animal appears on the symbol for the Rainforest Alliance?

____

4 When was the first text message sent to a mobile phone?

____

5 Which of these is an environmental organisation: Worldpeace, Lifepeace or Greenpeace?

____

6 Which language do people in Holland speak?

____

7 What do we call a place that tries to get energy from the wind: a wind factory, a wind net or a wind farm?

____

8 What is the French phrase *bien sûr* in English?

____

9 Where would you find most people who speak Mandarin?

____

10 Which ancient city do you most associate with Latin?

____

Units 13–14

Find the answers online!

1 If you have a job interview at a large company, you might meet the HR Manager. What do the letters *HR* stand for?

____

2 On ships, they often use different words for things. For example, the kitchen is called the galley. What do the words *port* and *starboard* mean on a ship or boat?

____

3 A lorry or truck driver probably has an HGV licence. What do the letters *HGV* stand for?

____

4 *Ventura* is a very big cruise ship. Which company owns and runs *Ventura*?

____

5 One of these phrases means 'lose your job because you did something wrong': *get the bag* / *get the case* / *get the sack*. Which one?

____

6 What's the largest passenger plane in the world?

____

7 What's another word for an advert on TV? Clue: it starts with the letter *c*.

____

8 The London Eye is a major tourist attraction in London. How many metres high is it?

____

9 If you want to go to some countries, it's not enough to have a passport. You also need another document. What's it called? Clue: it starts with the letter *v*.

____

10 What's another word for a helicopter? Clue: it starts with *ch*.

____

Units 15–16

Find the answers online!

1 Where was James Dyson born?

____

2 Which of these is a famous New York department store: *Harrods* or *Bloomingdale's*?

____

3 Where do you normally go to get a BA qualification?

____

4 When did the first cash machine start operating in the UK?

____

5 One popular exam in English is the Cambridge PET. What do the letters *PET* stand for?

____

6 Which of these is a bank holiday in the UK: Shrove Tuesday, Bonfire Night or New Year's Day?

____

7 General knowledge questions are sometimes about history. Here's one: in which year did Elizabeth II become Queen of England?

____

8 One of the biggest online shops is *Amazon*. When did *Amazon* first go online?

____

9 General knowledge questions are sometimes about geography. Here's one: what is the capital of Australia?

____

10 One punctuation mark is the ampersand. What does it look like and what does it mean?

____

Macmillan Education
4 Crinan Street
London N1 9XW
A division of Springer Nature Limited
Companies and representatives throughout the world

ISBN 978-0-230-43351-9

This edition 2013
First published 2004

Designed by Peter Burgess
Illustrated by Maro Alexandrou, Yannis Bardakos, Mark Brierly, Fran Brylewska, Nigel Dobbyn, Panos Kapsaskis, Christos Skaltas, Daniela Stamatiadi, Eleni Tsambra.
Cover design by Peter Burgess
Picture research by Susannah Jayes

Malcolm and Steve would like to thank the staff at Macmillan for all their hard work bringing this project to fruition, and all the many people around the world – too many to mention – who continue to support and provide feedback on the *Laser* series.

The authors and publishers would like to thank the following for permission to reproduce their photographs:

Alamy/67 photo p29(B), Alamy/AKP Photos p72, Alamy/Aurora Photos p84(cl), Alamy/Bill Bachmann p80(bl), Alamy/Beyond Fotomedia GmbH p127(6b), Alamy/Ken Biggs p29(A), Alamy/British Retail Photography p29(D), Alamy/Richard Green/Commercial p44(bm), Alamy/Ashley Cooper p102(bl), Alamy/Corbis Premium RF p12, Alamy/Corbis Super RF p56(4), Alamy/Cultura Creative p80(cmr), Alamy/Ian Dagnall p106, Alamy/Don Despain p124(cl), Alamy/geogphotosfilm p102(br), Alamy/Glow Images p14, Alamy/Jeff Greenberg p56(tr), Alamy/Drew Hadley p128(cr), Alamy/Robert Harding Picture Library Ltd p108, Alamy/David Hoffman p100(br), Alamy/D.Hurst p138(cmr), Alamy/Justin Kase zsxz p29(E), Alamy/Paul Matzner p95, Alamy/MBI p56(3), Alamy/Moodboard p116(cl), Alamy/nobleIMAGES p102(bc), Alamy/David Pearson p92, Alamy/Ben Molyneux People p42, Alamy/Andres Rodriguez p138(bcr), Alamy/travelpixs p85(cl), Alamy/UpperCut Images p147, Alamy/Steve Vidler p124(br), Alamy/russ witherington p119; **Apple Inc.** p138(bmr); **Bananastock** pp29(C), 89(2, 3, 4), 91(c), 127(4b); Corbis pp18(C), 116(cr), Corbis/Hero Atlantide p18(D), Corbis/Ben Blankenburg p56(2), Corbis/Jose Luis Pelaez Inc/Blend Images p58, Corbis/David Katzenstein/Citizen Stock p87(bc, bl), Corbis/ER Productions p56(5), Corbis/Elmer Frederick Fischer p88(5), Corbis/Floresco Productions p81(bcl), Corbis/Stephen Frink p88(3), Corbis/Rick Gayle p144(tcr), Corbis/Patrik Giardino pp56(6), 144(tr), Corbis/Image Source p91(e), Corbis/Jed Share and Kaoru p144(bcr), Corbis/Sharie Kennedy/LWA p84(bl), Corbis/Serge Kozak p91(d), Corbis/James Marshall p32, Corbis/Mika p91(a), Corbis/Kevin R Morris p91(b), Corbis/Ocean p138(tcr), Corbis/Fabrice Lerouge/Onoky p87(br), Corbis/Jose Luis Pelaez Inc p56(1), Corbis/Phototravel p18(E), Corbis/PictureNet pp88(2, 6), 144(br), Corbis/Anthony Redpath p54, Corbis/Chuck Savage p18(B); **Eyewire** p139; **Getty Images** p107, Getty Images/AFP p38(tmr), Getty Images/opus/a.collectionRF p74, Getty Images/Daniel Allan p127(5a), Getty Images/Jennifer Boggs p116(tr), Getty Images/Francesco Carta fotographo p9(cl), Getty Images/China Tourism Press p127(5b), Getty Images/Jenna Citrus p81(cmll), Getty Images/Danita Delimont p130, Getty Images/Digital Vision p127(1a, 3b), Getty Images/George Doyle p127(4a), Getty Images/FilmMagic pp34(tr), 35(tl), 36(bcl), 40, Getty Images/Flying Colours Ltd p18(A), Getty Images/Gamma-Rapho p100(bl), Getty Images/Jamie Grill p81(bl), Getty Images/Kauko Helavuo pp44–45(c), 50, Getty Images/Hill Street Studios p57, Getty Images/Image Source pp24, 89(1), 127(2a), Getty Images/Ray Kachatorian p80(cr), Getty Images/Plush Studios/DH Kong p127(3a), Getty Images/Ron Levine p9(bl), Getty Images/Chris Lowe p85(bl), Getty Images/Joos Mind p117, Getty Images/Sean Murphy p127(2b, 6a), Getty Images/NBC Newswire p36(bc), Getty Images/PT Images p9(tl), Getty Images/Andersen Ross p127(1b), Getty Images/Andy Sacks p13, Getty Images/Stockbyte pp88(4), 128(tr), Getty Images/Susanne Walstrom pp8, 9(tcml, cml, bcml), Getty Images/WireImage pp35bc, 35(br), 36(br), 38(tm), 38(tr), 39; **Rex Features** p34(tc), Rex Features/Geoff Wilkinson p134; **Sony Computer Entertainment Europe Ltd** p138(tcmr); **Stockbyte** p88(1).

Printed and bound in Poland by CGS

2022 2021 2020 2019
28 27 26 25 24 23 22 21